Awakening to Wholeness

A Practical Guide to Psychological Healing,
Personal Development & Spiritual Growth

Lee Bladon

Awakening to Wholeness
© 2012 by Lee Bladon

All rights reserved. No part of this book may be reproduced or utilized in any form or by any means, electronic or mechanical, including photocopying, scanning, recording, or by any information storage and retrieval system, without permission in writing from the author, except for brief quotations embodied in literary articles and reviews.

Website: www.EsotericScience.org

ISBN Number: 9781471793080

Contents:

	Preface	Page 5
	Disclaimer	Page 7
Chapter 1	Human Consciousness	Page 9
Chapter 2	The Human Condition	Page 39
Chapter 3	Human Potential	Page 79
Chapter 4	Personal Development	Page 117
Chapter 5	Self-Help Techniques	Page 157
Chapter 6	Spiritual Development	Page 183
Chapter 7	Awakening, Realisation & Enlightenment	Page 213
	List of Diagrams	Page 239
	List of Techniques	Page 241
	Bibliography	Page 243
	Index	Page 245

Preface:

Awakening to Wholeness is the result of my endeavours to experientially investigate the dynamics of psycho-spiritual transformation and the most effective methods of psychological healing and spiritual development, and to present it all in a single, clear, concise, comprehensive, engaging, easy-to-read volume.

I am not a scholar or a sage; I am simply someone with useful knowledge and experience. I am still walking the path but I have learned a lot along the way, both intellectually and experientially. This book is a synthesis of everything I have learned and experienced over the years. It is not just a rehash of existing material that is already out there; it is a fresh presentation that adds something new. It is the result of years of study, self-inquiry, contemplation, intuition, processing and practice.

Some of the many sources I have learned from include: The Diamond Approach (A.H. Almaas), Psychosynthesis (Roberto Assagioli & John Firman), Internal Family Systems (Dick Schwartz), Hakomi (Ron Kurtz) and Heart Becoming (Thessa Sophia). To all these people I offer my sincere thanks, but my biggest thanks go to "Life" – the greatest teacher of them all. From my early childhood right up to the present day – each and every experience has contributed to my development and my understanding, and this book is the product of all that experience.

When I was researching and writing my first book, *The Science of Spirituality*, I was driven to understand the truth primarily from an intellectual perspective, but once I had achieved that I realised it wasn't quite enough. Intellectual knowledge is of the mind, so it doesn't truly satisfy the soul. In order to really <u>know</u> the truth it has to be felt – experienced within. So the direction of my quest turned inwards and I really started to uncover the truth about human existence and our evolutionary journey through life. My mind used to be the main source of my information, and my soul would confirm it; but now my soul is the main source and my mind just helps with the confirmation. True knowing is experiential, not just mental.

I have written this book to share my knowledge and experience with anyone who is interested. I hope it helps you discover your own truth and realise the truth of your being. Please don't take my word for anything in this book; you really have to discover it and experience it for yourself. I am not trying to convince anyone of anything because I have no investment in what anyone else believes. My only wish is that we all discover the truth of who we are – and we will, when the time is right.

So are you ready to join me on an amazing journey of self-discovery?

Lee Bladon

Disclaimer:

The information, practices and techniques described in this book are not intended or implied to be a substitute for professional medical or psychological advice. The information, practices and techniques described in this book are not intended for self-diagnosis or self-treatment, and should not be used to diagnose or treat mental health problems. Please consult a qualified health care professional about any medical or psychological issues. The author is not qualified to give medical or psychological advice, so please do not ask. The information, practices and techniques described in this book are for educational purposes only. If you decide to utilise any of the information, practices or techniques described in this book, you do so at your own discretion. The author is not responsible for any adverse effects or consequences resulting from the use of any of the information, practices or techniques described in this book. If any adverse effects are encountered, stop immediately and seek professional advice.

Chapter 1: **Human Consciousness**

Introduction

The world defines us by our name, gender, nationality, race, religion, height, weight, role, job, etc., but these superficial descriptions are not who we truly are. If we look a little deeper we may describe ourselves in terms of our beliefs, thoughts, mood, emotions, desires, interests, etc. But these things are transient – they change, they evolve, they come and go – they are not constant so they cannot be who we truly are.

If we look back over our entire life we notice that one thing has remained constant over the years – our sense of awareness. Our awareness is the common factor that links our earliest childhood memories to the present day. Our awareness has experienced every event in our life; in a seamless series of present moments. When we sense deeper into our field of awareness we discover that it has qualities, attributes, characteristics and a sense of identity that goes far deeper than our personality. This is the essence of who we truly are.

The Self

The Self is both a field of consciousness and a point of consciousness, which is the core of our being - see Figure 1 on page 12. The Self (monad) is the centre of our field of awareness (soul), and our field of awareness (soul) is an extension of our Self. The Self has two primary functions:

1. **Directing our life** (will): The Self interacts with the world by directing our thoughts (mind), emotions (heart) and actions (body).
2. **Experiencing our life** (awareness):
    a) **Directly**: The Self experiences life directly through its field of awareness (the soul).

b) **Indirectly**: The Self experiences life indirectly by perceiving our personality's thoughts (mind), emotions (heart) and senses (body).

The mind, heart and body (which collectively make up our personality) are not our true Self, but they are aspects of our Being. It has been said that "we are spiritual beings having a human experience". Our Self is the transpersonal/spiritual element; our mind, heart and body are the personal/human elements; and our field of pure awareness (soul) unites them all into a Human Being.

The mind, heart and body enable us to function in the world and experience the fullness of life:

1. The mind is the domain of our thoughts, concepts and beliefs.
2. The heart is the domain of our emotions and desires.
3. The body is the domain of our instincts, impulses and actions.

Like the Self, the mind, heart and body are centres of consciousness and fields of consciousness . We will focus on the centres first:

- The human brain is divided into 3 main sections: the Neo-Cortex, the Limbic System and the Basal Brain, which are associated with thoughts, emotions and actions respectively.
- The human body is also divided into 3 main sections: the Head, the Thorax (chest) and the Abdomen (belly), which are associated with thoughts, emotions and instincts respectively.
- The Eastern traditions recognise three centres of subtle energy and consciousness which are located in the head (upper tan tien), chest (middle tan tien) and belly (lower tan tien or hara).
- The Sufi tradition recognises three centres of subtle energy and consciousness which are located in the head (path), chest (oth) and belly (kath).
- Gurdjieff recognised three centres of energy and consciousness which are located in the head (thinking centre), chest (emotional centre) and belly (moving centre).
- The Enneagram recognises three centres of intelligence: the head centre, the heart centre and the body centre.

- Theosophy and esoteric science recognise three centres of energy and conscious which are located in the head (mental permanent molecule), chest (emotional permanent atom) and belly (physical permanent atom). Refer to my first book, *The Science of Spirituality*, for further details.

For simplicity I will identify these three centres by their physiological locations:

1. **The Head centre** is located in the centre of the head (between the temples). It is our primary centre of mental consciousness and our mental energy store.
2. **The Heart centre** is located in the centre of the chest (behind the centre of the breastbone). It is our primary centre of emotional consciousness and our emotional energy store. It is also known as the "high heart", the "soul seat" (Barbara Brennan) and the "assemblage point" (Carlos Castaneda).
3. **The Body/Belly centre** is located in the centre of the abdomen (just below the navel). It is our primary centre of physical consciousness and our body's vital energy store. Its physical counterpart is the abdominal brain; about 100 million neurons that can function independently of the cranial brain to control some of the body's basic functions.

The fields of consciousness surrounding these three centres pervade and surround the entire human body, but the majority of their activity is concentrated in the area surrounding each centre – refer to Figure 2 on page 12.

The Self's primary field of consciousness (the soul or the causal body) pervades the entire physical body and extends about 100cm (40") beyond, as depicted in Figure 1. The mind's field of consciousness (the mental body) is concentrated in the head but it pervades the entire physical body and extends about 60-80cm (24-30") beyond. The heart's field of consciousness (the emotional body) is concentrated in the chest but it pervades the entire physical body and extends 30-50cm (12-20") beyond. The body's field of consciousness (the energy body) is concentrated in the belly but it pervades the entire physical body and extends about 2cm (1") beyond. The mind, heart and body centres are connected together for seamless integration of consciousness, and the Self can move its awareness around them at will. Collectively these three centres of consciousness constitute the authentic personality.

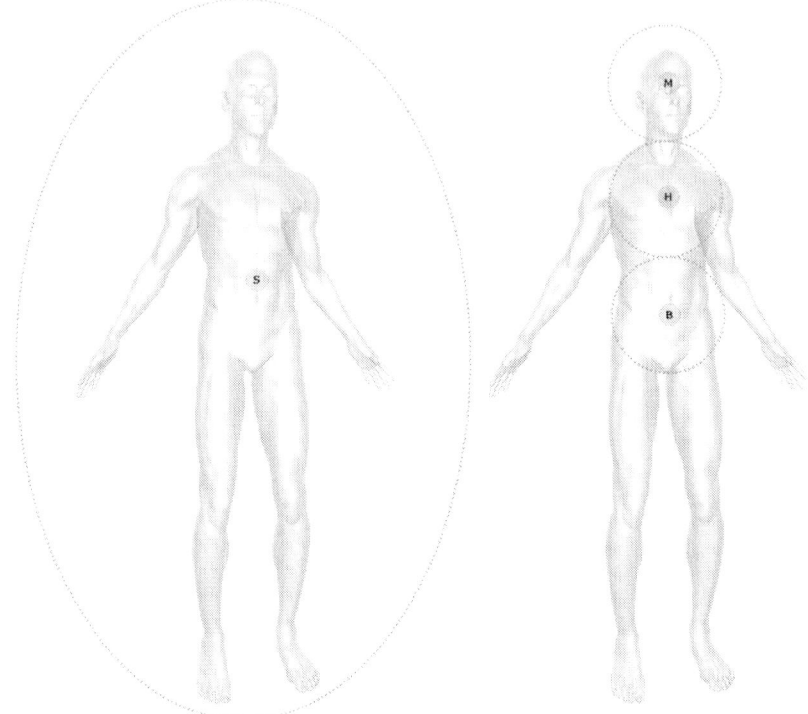

Figure 1: The Self and its Field of Awareness (Soul)
                                Figure 2: The Mind, Heart & Body Centres

Just as the Self operates through three primary centres of consciousness (mind, heart and body), each of the three centres operates through three secondary centres of consciousness. These secondary centres are known as the seven major chakras. Figure 3 depicts the relationship between the Self, the three centres and the seven chakras. The chakras help to integrate the centres of consciousness with the body's energy meridians and nervous system. Please refer to my first book, *The Science of Spirituality*, for further information. The Self integrates with the physical body through the following sequence:

1. Human Consciousness

Self > 3 Centres > 7 Chakras > Meridians > Nervous System > Body

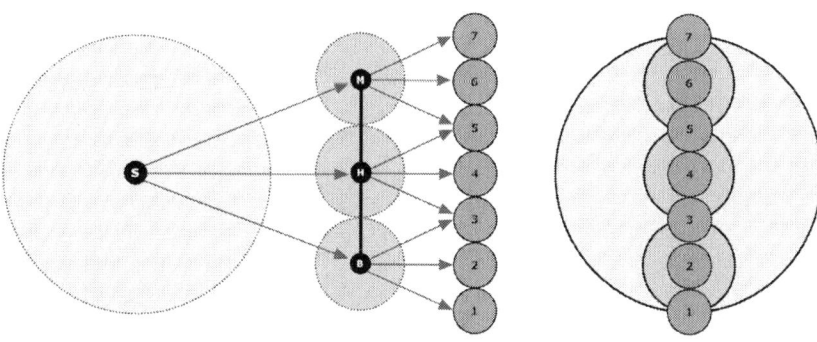

Figure 3: Self, Centres & Chakras – Expanded and super-imposed views

We are not a Self living within a body; we are a body, heart and mind living within a Self/soul. Our body, heart and mind all exist within the field of our Self (soul). Our body, heart and mind only exist for a few decades within the eternal field of our Self (soul).

Creation of the False-Self

The previous section described who we really are, but that is probably not who we think we are. The "I" that we think we are is probably not who we really are. Unless we are Self-realised or enlightened, we are "asleep" to our true nature – we have forgotten who we truly are. We live from a self-created (false) centre of consciousness which is known as the ego-self.

When we were born, our personal consciousness was undeveloped and inexperienced, and we had very little understanding of the world outside of us. As we learnt about the world we gradually constructed a mental model of how we believed things were out there. The more we learnt about the outer-world, the more complex our inner-world model became. Over time, it developed into a meticulously detailed virtual representation of reality. The virtual-reality world inside our mind was a near-perfect representation of the real world, but it was (and still is) coloured by our beliefs and distorted by our misconceptions.

Our interactions with other people helped us to fit them into our inner model, and their interactions with us helped us to develop our own concept of self and fit that into our inner model. The concept of self that we developed through our interactions with others was that we are a separate individual contained within a physical body. This was very different to our inherent sense of true-Self, which is pure, radiant, infinite and one-with-everything. So, at this early stage of life we could sense two different selves – our true-Self and our "false" mental concept of self. The two selves were so different that we didn't know which one to go with – we didn't know who we were.

Our parents related to us as if we were a separate individual in a physical body (our false-self); not as if we were an infinite radiant being (our true-Self). They interacted with our false-self and pretty much ignored our true-Self. Only our false-self got validated, so we eventually went with that one. Essentially, the false-self came into being because we were not seen for who we truly are. Our false-self became our identity and our virtual inner-world became our home.

Obviously, we can't live solely in our virtual world because we have to eat, drink and interact with the real world in order to survive. We have to maintain a connection between our virtual inner world and the real world, so we project our virtual world and virtual-self out onto the real world. This gives us the impression that we (false-self) are living in the real world. We perceive the real world with our virtual world seamlessly projected over it. This virtual world overlay is what makes an anorexic person believe they are fat, or a tone-deaf person believe they are a great singer.

When our two images of "reality" don't match up; when our real-world experience clashes with our inner-world expectations, our inner-world and our (false) sense of self are de-stabilised. This makes us anxious, so we feel compelled to reinforce our (false) sense of self and our model of reality by justifying, denying or blaming someone else. Our false-self feels safe and in control in its virtual inner world, but it has very little influence on the real outer-world, so we often get frustrated when things don't go our way.

Our virtual world provides the added benefit of distancing us from the confusing, distressing and traumatic situations of the real world. As a young child we learnt how to use our virtual world as a psychological buffer to soften the impact of real-world distress. It allowed us to block out or distort certain aspects of our reality, paint a rosier picture of our life and justify other people's negative behaviour towards us. It allowed our innocent and immature personal consciousness to cope with the sometimes harsh realities of the real world. Over time we stopped perceiving the real world directly because it felt safer to perceive life indirectly, through the intermediary of the mind. Over time we became so identified with our false-self and our virtual-world that we fell asleep to objective reality and forgot who we truly are.

Creation of the Ego (the false personality)

Soon after we identified with our false concept of self, but before we learnt to use our virtual world as a psychological buffer, something very significant occurred. Next to the creation of the false-self it was probably the most significant event of our life because it fundamentally shaped our self-image, our view of the world and our entire approach to life. This momentous event was our first psychological wound – the first time our newly-created false-self felt hurt. It had a profound effect on us because our false-self had not "solidified" yet, and the primary wound is what solidified it. The primary wound shaped the nature of our false-self by programming it with our primary belief. Our primary belief was our innocent false-self's response to our primary wound. As a direct result of the primary wound our false-self naively and incorrectly believed that it was inadequate or deficient in some way. The primary belief was "I am not good enough", or something similar, such as: I am unlovable, helpless, lost, abandoned, insecure, powerless or unworthy. From the perspective of the false-self there is an element of truth in these beliefs because compared to the true-Self the false-self is like a poor black and white photocopy of a scintillatingly beautiful living masterpiece, and deep down we know it. But from the perspective of our true-Self there is zero truth in these beliefs – we are none of these negative things – we are perfect, radiant, complete and limitless.

The primary belief that imprinted into our false-self is the seed around which our ego formed. Our entire ego and our general approach to life were heavily influenced by that one false belief. Soothing the feelings of lack associated with our primary belief became our main objective in life. Few of us are aware of this underlying objective that profoundly shapes our approach to life, because it dwells deep within us, at the very core of our being. Most of us avoid going into the depths of our being because we don't want to stir up our repressed hurts, fears and inadequacies. We generally like to keep our awareness at the periphery of our being, just as we generally like to keep our conversations and relationships on a superficial level where little harm can be done.

So what exactly is the ego? The ego is the false-self's field of consciousness, just as the soul is the true-Self's primary field of consciousness. The true-Self's field of consciousness is fluid, dynamic and imbued with an array of essential qualities (which will be discussed shortly), but the false-self's field of consciousness is rigid and structured, with no inherent qualities. The false-self has to program the ego to tell it what to do and how to behave in each situation. The ego is programmed with our default reactions to life. If we encounter a situation that is similar to one we have previously experienced, we will already have a default pre-programmed response. That program will automatically activate (unless we have the conscious awareness to intervene), causing us to react automatically (without any conscious involvement). This is the first major problem with the ego – it keeps us on autopilot; it keeps us half asleep.

The second major problem with the ego is that most of its programs (our beliefs, strategies, thought patterns, emotional reactions and automated behaviours) were initially programmed when we were very young, so many of our reactions to life are immature and inappropriate. Some of our programs were updated and re-written as we became older and more experienced, but the deeper ones were created by and created from very young, naïve, immature and inexperienced consciousness. These old patterns are responsible for most of the unnecessary suffering in our lives, but our fear of venturing into the depths of our being allows our immature core (our inner child) to endure, and our unnecessary suffering to continue.

The third major problem with the ego is that it believes we are separate from everyone else and separate from life, rather than an integral part of humanity and an integral part of life. The ego believes we are a separate individual because it is just a thought-form trapped inside our mind and isolated from the rest of the world. The false belief that we are isolated and separate creates fear, which feeds another false belief – that we must protect and defend ourselves psychologically. Many of the ego's programs are concerned with protecting us, defending our position, and counter-attacking anyone who questions us or our beliefs – which brings us nicely onto the next point.

The fourth major problem with the ego is that, deep down it knows it is not real; it knows it was created by the mind; it knows it is just an elaborate thought-form, so it inherently feels insecure, unsteady and unsafe. Any confusing, traumatic or distressing experience shakes the ego to its core. It constantly fears for its "life" so it has to develop coping mechanisms, survival strategies and defensive behaviours to strengthen itself and reinforce its position. Lots of physical, emotional and mental energy is consumed in maintaining the ego's belief structures, coping structures and defensive structures. I call them structures because they are thought-forms that are constructed out of mental "matter".

As the false-self creates new ego structures (beliefs, behaviours, strategies, programs, etc.), it expands into them, identifies with them and becomes one with them. The false-self expands into the structures to create the ego. We then spend the rest of our lives defending our false-self and reinforcing our ego. These behaviours are the cause of all our unnecessary suffering.

Note: Not all behavioural patterns and automated responses are ego structures – many of them are essential to life, allowing us to breathe, move, eat, digest, walk, talk, read and drive without giving them our full conscious attention. These automated patterns start developing as soon as we are capable of learning (i.e. in the womb). But they are not ego structures if we don't identify with them, take them personally or believe they are us.

The Personality

The personality is a blend of authenticity and ego. Our true nature expresses itself through them both, in varying proportions (depending on our current mood and our overall level of development):

- **Authentic Personality** is the true and unlimited aspect of our personality – the parts that are not bound up in ego structures. It is Self-expressive, radiant, generous, compassionate and loving. It comes to the fore when we are relaxed, present, sincere and speak from our heart.
- **Ego Personality** is the inauthentic, limited aspect of our personality – the parts that are bound up in ego structures. It is self-centred, repressed, greedy, fearful and critical. It comes to the fore when we are tense, shallow, superficial and egotistical.

As stated earlier, different areas of our consciousness have different functions, i.e. the head, heart and belly centres are specialised for thoughts, emotions and instincts respectively. Each of these fields of consciousness has numerous sub-areas, each with its own specific abilities. We utilise the area of consciousness that is most appropriate for our immediate requirements. If the required area contains ego structures we will react with the pre-programmed behaviours and false qualities of the ego-personality, but if the area is free and clear we will respond with authenticity.

The degree of authentic personality we are able to express is proportional to the number of ego structures we have, and the degree to which we are identified with them. Our true-nature shines out from the core of our being through our personality. If the personality is full of ego structures the light of our true-nature is blocked, so our expression is inauthentic. If, however, the personality is clear of ego structures, the light of our true-nature radiates freely and our personality sparkles with authenticity. As our consciousness evolves, the ratio of ego to Self gradually shifts in favour of the Self. But the degree of authentic personality we actually express in any given moment also depends upon our mood, energy level, health and circumstances.

Ego Personality > Authentic Personality
(many ego structures = less Self)   (few ego structures = more Self)

Figure 4: The Continuum of Self

So what exactly is the authentic personality? Our true-Self's field of consciousness (our soul) is pure awareness imbued with an array of essential qualities (love, joy, strength, will, peace, compassion, curiosity, creativity, etc.). These aspects of consciousness are called essential qualities because they are the essence of who we truly are. During our childhood, our soul's essential qualities gradually permeate down into our personality where they unfold and develop into a range of usable personal qualities that collectively constitute our authentic personality:

1. Mind-based essential qualities (wisdom, knowing, creativity, clarity, curiosity, etc.) unfold and develop into usable personal qualities in our mental body, primarily in and around the head.

2. Heart-based essential qualities (love, compassion, joy, courage, connectedness, etc.) unfold and develop into usable personal qualities in our emotional body, primarily in and around the chest.

3. Body-based essential qualities (will, vitality, stillness, groundedness, calmness, etc.) unfold and develop into usable personal qualities in our energy body, primarily in and around the belly.

Different areas within these three subtle bodies (fields of consciousness) have specialised functions. For example, we utilise a different area of our heart's consciousness to express compassion than we do to express joy, and a different area still to express courage, and so on. But each area of consciousness, irrespective of its location or function, contains all three types of personal consciousness (mental, emotional and physical).

Each personal quality unfolds at a different time during childhood. For example, Strength starts to develop at about 9 months and Will at about 2 years. But the conditions must be just right for a personal quality to develop optimally, otherwise its unfoldment will be adversely affected or blocked. So parents should try to provide a safe and loving environment for their children, set healthy boundaries with the right balance of freedom and control, and avoid sending mixed messages that might confuse the child's world view.

Our young and undeveloped personal consciousness needs verification that our understanding of reality is correct, so we seek validation from our parents and/or caregivers. If the feedback we receive contradicts or conflicts with our own innocent perceptions and conceptions, the emergent aspect of personal consciousness may not develop properly or fully. This is because the mental confusion and/or emotional turmoil interfere with the natural unfoldment of the personal qualities.

Here are some examples of common parental responses that contradict and invalidate a child's perceptions of reality. They negated our objective perception, our world view and our true sense of Self:

- Shouting at us for no apparent reason (because they are annoyed about something else).
- Saying one thing and doing another (it is natural for children to copy their parent's behaviour).
- Saying "everything is alright" when we are crying and everything is clearly not alright.
- Ignoring us, not listening to us, or not giving us the time and attention we deserve. This makes us believe "I am worthless", "I am not loved" or "I don't exist".
- Saying "don't cry" discourages us from feeling pain and sadness (negating an important aspect of life). It encourages us to repress our emotions and discourages us from releasing them in a healthy way. Note: if our parents attempted to soothe us with food or a toy, as adults we may self-soothe by eating or shopping.

If the distress is intense or persistent, that aspect of consciousness may freeze and stop developing altogether. Generally speaking, the more intense or prolonged our fear and confusion, the less our personal qualities will unfold.

Even as adults fear and confusion can cause us to temporarily freeze – physically or psychologically. When we were young and innocent the effect was much more intense, so even a relatively minor event such as being shouted at could have had an overwhelming effect. Mental confusion, emotional turmoil and physical distress reinforce and validate each other in a feedback loop (see Figure 5), thus increasing the overall fear and trauma. All three elements of the developing personality (mind, heart and body) are affected, so the area of consciousness is traumatised on every level.

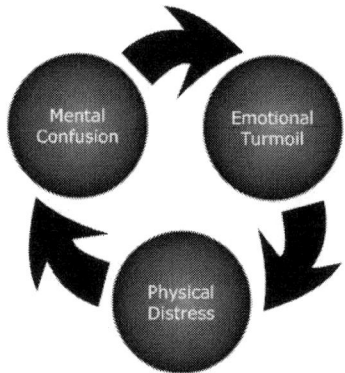

Figure 5: The Vicious Circle of Fear

The traumatised area of consciousness is literally frozen with fear. It is frozen in time and space, so it remains at the age it was at the time of the trauma, and it has a definite location within our body. The piece of consciousness is frozen at the peak intensity of the fear, so it "lives" in eternal fear.

The ego-mind (the part of the mind that is controlled by the ego-self) creates a protective ego structure (thought-form) around the frozen piece of consciousness to protect our ego-self and the rest of our ego from becoming overwhelmed by the trauma, fear and confusion, but in doing so we exile that piece of us. The exiled part feels like it has been imprisoned in hell for eternity. It feels like hell because it is always experiencing the peak intensity of fear, and it feels like eternity because it is literally frozen in time.

A defensive ego structure may also be created nearby and programmed to act as a guard to prevent our conscious awareness from getting anywhere near the exiled part. The pain, fear and confusion have been repressed. They have been buried deep within our subconscious and may become completely forgotten.

We may have "successfully" repressed the trauma but we can't forget about the essential quality that was unfolding into a usable personal quality at the time of the trauma. We need to utilise its functionality in our daily lives but it is not there, or is insufficiently developed. There seems to be a "hole" in our being, so the protective ego structure is programmed to take on the functionality of the missing personal quality, or support a poorly developed personal quality.

If the unfolding of our essential strength is blocked by psychological trauma, we will lack authentic personal strength. This makes us feel vulnerable, so we have to develop ego structures to provide us with false strength. If the unfolding of our essential will is blocked, we will feel anxious and have to develop ego structures to provide us with false will (will-power). These ego structures are coping mechanisms and survival mechanisms that help us to get through life without authentic personal qualities. So psychological trauma changes our entire approach to life: from authentic experience and expression, to defending and surviving.

The functionality of an ego structure can never match up to the real thing because it is a crudely constructed inferior copy of an exquisite essential quality. This is not surprising because most of our ego structures were initially created when we were 6 months to 6 years of age. They were created by an immature and inexperienced ego-mind. So not only are they poor reproductions, they are often immature, inappropriate or even dysfunctional. As we get older, we may refine and develop our ego structures. Ego structures build up in layers like the rings of a tree-trunk – it doesn't matter how highly polished the outer layer is, the frightened infantile core remains buried within. Some people put a lot of time and effort into refining and polishing their ego-personality to help them succeed in life, but that is just masking over the symptoms and ignoring the root of the problem.

Ego structures also form in response to not being fully seen, being seen as inadequate, being ignored or being misunderstood. Such perceptions give rise to false beliefs that we are unimportant, inadequate or have to behave in a certain way to fit in. An ego structure is created around the false belief (to repress it) and programmed to compensate the false belief. If, for example, the false belief is "I should be seen and not heard", we might create an ego structure that restricts our natural expression and makes us introverted. Our false and distorted beliefs are usually copied from our parents or older siblings. If, for example our father believed that people must work hard to succeed in life, and he regularly demonstrated that, or even just said it a lot, there is a good chance that we would have taken on that belief and become a workaholic later in life. We can also rebel against our parents' beliefs and behaviours, in which case we will adopt the opposite belief or behaviour.

These processes occurred countless times during the development of our personal consciousness, so our ego developed in a modular fashion. As the number of ego structures increased they became interconnected and formed a complex super-structure. As the super-structure grew and became more stable, our false sense of self expanded into it – and our ego was born.

Since then the ego has grown, developed, adapted and evolved to help us cope with life's events. Individual coping structures are often updated as we grow older and become more capable. The new layers build up like the rings of a tree trunk (refer to Figure 6).

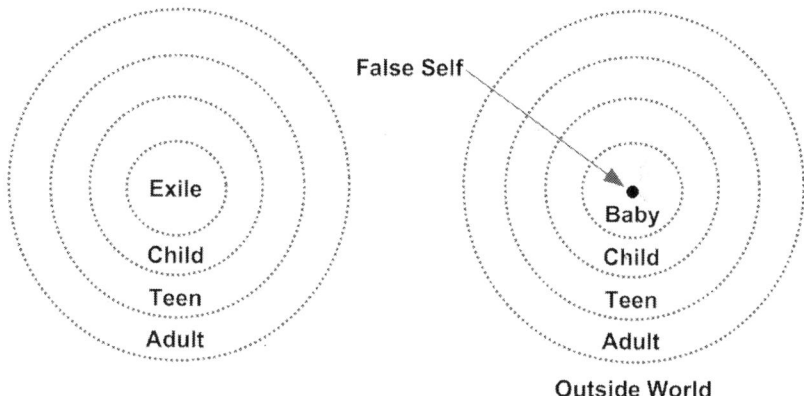

Figure 6: Layers of an Individual Ego Structure
                Figure 7: Layers of the Entire Ego Super-Structure

The more mature and capable outer layers often assume secondary roles of protecting the younger inner layers. These guarding structures don't require updating, so they remain at the age at which they were created.

Collectively, the entire ego super-structure builds up in the same manner as each individual ego structure, with the false-self at its core (Figure 7). The false-self is self-centred; it is the centre of our ego and the centre of our inner-world. But its awareness is usually focussed at the periphery of the ego, because that is where the most capable coping structures are located, because it is far away from the deeply repressed exiles' pain, and because it can get external validation from the outside world.

Every ego is unique and utilises different strategies to help us survive and even thrive in the world we live in. So it is important not to think of the ego as a negative construct that must be purged from our psyche. Although when it no longer serves us it will begin to dissolve naturally. This book is about assisting this natural process, through conscious inner work.

Inner work is not like regular work that requires effort; in fact it is exactly the opposite. Inner work requires us to stop efforting, stop trying, stop seeking, stop grasping, stop clinging, stop resisting, stop fearing, stop over-reacting and stop doing. All it requires us to "do" is just "be". It requires us to become a Human Being instead of a Human Doing.

Different Types of Ego Structures

Different types of ego structures require different approaches to healing and reintegration:

1. Protective Structures are not created to protect the distressed exiled parts of our being; they are usually created to protect us from the distressed exiled parts of our being. They protect the ego-self from becoming overwhelmed by stopping us from getting too close to the distressed exiled parts. The protection comes in two forms:

   a. **Locking it away**: Enclosing, suppressing and repressing the exiled part. Note: Repressing structures are also used to repress unwanted personal qualities (page 44) and primal impulses (page 70).

   b. **Forgetting about it**: Guarding parts are programmed to distract or divert our conscious attention, often by triggering a reactive or compulsive behaviour (i.e. an addiction). Sometimes two or more guarding structures are created to protect one exiled part, and they may have very different strategies for keeping us away. If their strategies conflict, they can pull us (psychologically) in different directions. This forces each "side" to take more extreme measures, which can destabilise our entire psyche and lead to extreme behaviours such as alcoholism, drug addiction, violence and abuse.

Origin: Protective structures are created out of our fear of becoming emotionally overwhelmed.

False Beliefs: Protective structures are built on the false belief that we cannot cope with feeling the distress of the exiled part, so a protective part is programmed to (falsely) believe that the exiled part is a threat. While this may have been true at the time of the original trauma (when we were a young child), it is almost certainly not true now. The protective structure was created and programmed at the time of the original trauma so it is made from very young consciousness and it almost certainly believes that we are still a young child and still unable to cope.

Healing: A protective structure won't relax or dissolve until the perceived threat is gone, i.e. until the exiled part has been healed and reintegrated. But the protective structure probably won't let us near the exiled part until we reassure it that we are a loving, caring and capable adult with good intentions.

2. Coping Structures are programmed to take on the functionality of undeveloped personal qualities (that were not transposed from the soul's essential qualities). They help us to function in the world without our authentic personal qualities.

Origin: Coping structures are created out of a perceived deficiency – to replace a missing or undeveloped quality.

False Belief: Coping structures are built on the false belief that we have lost a part of our soul essence ("soul loss"), but actually we have just lost awareness of it. When we lose awareness of an essential quality it stops unfolding in our personality, so we create an ego structure around the "hole" in our being and program it to take on the functionality of the "lost" part.

Healing: When we stop defending against feeling a hole and actually allow ourselves to feel it fully, we discover that it doesn't feel like a deficiency at all; it feels like spaciousness or pure potential – not unpleasant at all. When we allow this spaciousness to be (i.e. accept its existence and feel it without any resistance), we re-discover the "missing" essential quality and realise that it has been there all along. This reactivates the process that transposes the essential quality into a usable personal quality, so the "hole" fills up with the authentic personal quality.

More about Holes

We create all sorts of reasons to explain the inner pain, anxiety, anger, depression and discontent we feel about these holes in our being. We (incorrectly) believe that we are anxious about a job interview or depressed about a relationship breakup, but we are not. These are not the real reasons; we are just projecting our inner suffering onto an external event because the ego needs to justify its negative feelings. Blaming our suffering on an external cause absolves the ego of any responsibility and diverts our attention away from the true cause. External events don't actually make us anxious, angry or depressed; they just trigger the deeply repressed emotions we already have about the "lost" parts of our being and our "lost" connection to Self.

We try to avoid feeling our pain and discontent by:

- **Doing**: overeating, alcohol, tobacco, drugs, sex, TV, internet, computer games, exercise, work, etc.
- **Objects**: fashion, cosmetics, houses, cars, gadgets, partners, babies, pets, etc.

We believe we are trying to solve an external problem, so we think these external solutions will work. But the real source of our discontent is internal, so only an internal solution will work. The real source of our dissatisfaction is our lack of wholeness – we are full of "holes" so we don't feel whole. The only way we can find lasting fulfilment is to fully feel our holes and allow the "missing" qualities to manifest. This cannot happen while we keep "doing" things to avoid feeling our holes, or keep trying to fill them with "objects".

When we experience the loss or separation of a loved one, we don't feel sad because we miss them; we feel sad because our relationship with them has ended, and the relationship helped to fill a "hole" in our soul.

The relationship helped to mask the pain of our "lost" essence. Now that they are gone, the relationship can no longer fill the hole or mask our pain, so we feel our inherent pain, sadness and grief. The same thing occurs, to a lesser extent, with the loss of objects.

As previously mentioned the only way to effectively "fill" a hole is to feel it as fully as we can, without any resistance; i.e. fully surrender to our pain, sadness or grief.

Another Type of Hole

The self can move around our field of consciousness (which extends beyond the physical body) at will. When it moves out of our body we enter into a state of trance. The self is not present, so we feel absent, detached, dissociated, spaced-out, sleepy or dreamy. We can use this as a subconscious defence mechanism to avoid feeling psychological pain or distress.

The same process occurs, but much faster, when we are startled or shocked. Our self "jumps" out of our body (to protect us from the peak intensity of the anticipated trauma) and immediately back in again. When a psychological trauma is accompanied by a sudden shock, the piece of traumatised consciousness is not only frozen; it can also be ejected from the body. Our self's fear freezes the piece of consciousness and simultaneously carries it out of the body when it "jumps". The self returns to the body a fraction of a second later, but the traumatised piece of consciousness can get left behind – floating in our aura, just outside of our body – the ultimate place of exile. The ejected exiled part leaves a noticeable hole in our psyche (mental, emotional and energy bodies), so the ego's standard coping mechanism comes into play. The hole is encased in an ego structure which programmed it to take on the functionality of the "lost" part.

Ejected exiled parts are responsible for some of the "voices" that some people hear. These free-floating exiles can be healed and reintegrated in one of two ways:

1. If we can sense the presence of the ejected part in our aura, we can move our awareness to its location and consciously merge with it. This intimate connection between our soul's conscious awareness

and the ejected exiled part heals the wounded relationship and allows the ejected exile part to return and fill the hole in our psyche.

2. If we can sense the hole, we can move our awareness to its location and consciously merge with it. The intimate connection between our soul's awareness and the hole heals the wounded relationship and allows the ejected exiled part to return and fill the hole in our psyche.

Freedom from the Ego

Thought-forms are typically short-lived; without concentrated effort and energy to sustain them they quickly dissolve. The same applies to our ego (which is just a very elaborate thought-form); without energy, effort and constant reinforcement it will gradually dissolve. However, we (falsely) believe that we are our ego, so we will do everything we can to maintain it and prevent it from dissolving.

When external events conflict with or invalidate an aspect of our inner model of reality, our psychological structures weaken because the foundations they are built upon (our false or distorted core beliefs) are thrown into doubt. We fear that our sense of self may collapse so we have to strengthen our position by defending against the perceived attack. We zealously defend our position as if we were defending our life, because subconsciously we believe that we are. The ego that started out as a safe place to protect us from the distress of the real world has been defended and reinforced so many times it has become a fortress. But it is a fortress that we cannot leave, so in that respect it is more like a prison.

The false-self (ego-self) cannot permanently leave its fortress/prison because it is an inherent part of the ego super-structure. The ego is the prisoner and the prison, and both are made of the same "material". The ego-self is an ego structure – it can move all around our body and even out into our aura, but it can never escape from being an ego structure.

The true-Self is different; it is made of a subtler "material" (pure-awareness) which is not bound by the mind and mental constructs (ego structures). The true-Self can easily pass through the prison walls of the ego (like a ghost) because pure awareness exists at a higher/subtler level than the mind. So the true-Self is, always has been, and always will be free. To be free, we only have to shift our awareness from the false-self to the true-Self, which is represented graphically in Figure 8.

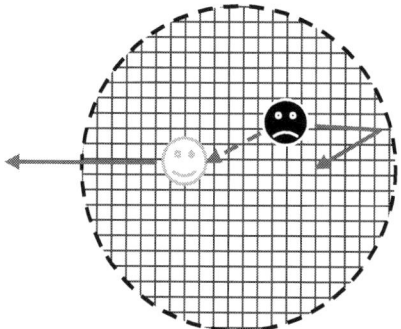

Figure 8: Freedom from the Ego

Our journey to freedom is not an outward one; we cannot escape by pushing outwards against the walls of our prison. Our journey to freedom is an inward one; towards the true-Self. Our journey to freedom is a journey of Self-discovery. We must first get to know our true-Self and then realise that that is who we are and always have been. It is like waking up from a dream; or perhaps nightmare is a more appropriate term? It is like stepping out of a virtual world into true reality. It is like stepping out of the darkness into the light.

Shifting our awareness from the false-self to the true-Self is not easy. The false ego-self has a powerful hold on us because we have been identified with it for so long – we have invested an entire lifetime in being our false-self. So even though we want freedom, we are afraid to leave. The ego's primary objective is to get us through life without feeling the pain of our repressed psychological wounds (exiled parts). The inner work of awakening goes directly against the ego's objective because it requires us to feel into our old hurts and inquire into our false core-beliefs, so we need to proceed gently. Only when our desire for freedom exceeds our fear are we truly ready to enter the path.

The Truth about the False-Self

Up until this point I have described the false-self as a highly elaborate thought-form, and it is, but that is not the whole story. A thought-form does not possess enough self-awareness to convince us that this is who we are, and it does not possess enough processing power to run our entire life. So what else is going on?

The true-Self can directly, intimately and fully experience everything its field of awareness (soul) makes contact with. It literally becomes one with everything it makes contact with. So when the true-Self meets the false-self, the part of the true-Self's awareness that makes contact with the false-self becomes one with the false-self. It is this piece of the true-Self's awareness that vivifies the false-self and literally brings it to life. The true-Self's at-one-ness with the false-self is what makes the false-self appear "real". The true-Self has invested part of its self-awareness in the false-self, so the false-self exists within true-Self, and the false-self's field of awareness exists within the true-Self's field of awareness (as depicted in Figure 9).

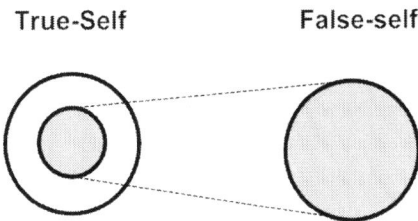

Figure 9: The true-Self perceiving the false-self

The part of the true-Self's awareness that is united with the false-self became identified with the false-self when we were about 6-8 months old. It then forgot that it was part of the true-Self and believed it was the false-self. However, only part of the true-Self is "asleep" in believing it is the false-self; the rest of our true-Self is awake, unlimited and free. The part of the true-Self that believes it is the false-self is so identified (at-one) with the false-self that it is blind to the vastness of its being. If its perception wasn't so limited, it would realise that it is unlimited and eternal. We just need to "wake up" and realise that we are, and always have been, our (entire) true-Self.

The Two-Fold Path of Awakening

Consciously shifting our awareness directly from the false-self to the true-Self is almost impossible, and even if it does occur, it doesn't always last. Before we can permanently enter the "authentic" world of our true-Self we need to neutralise the "inauthentic" charge of our false-self. This is achieved by:

1. **Becoming Self**: This is the psychological/personal aspect of the path. It involves dissolving the psychological material (exiles, holes and ego structures) that block the unfoldment and expression of our true nature.
2. **Being Self**: This is the spiritual/transpersonal aspect of the path. It involves aligning with our true-Self and actively expressing our true nature. This develops our association with our true-Self, so that someday we will come to realise that this is who we truly are.

When we pass through the neutral zero-point, it becomes possible for our sense of identity to spontaneously shift from the false-self to the true-Self; then Being and Becoming unite. This book describes an integrated two-fold path of awakening that can lead us to enlightenment and beyond:

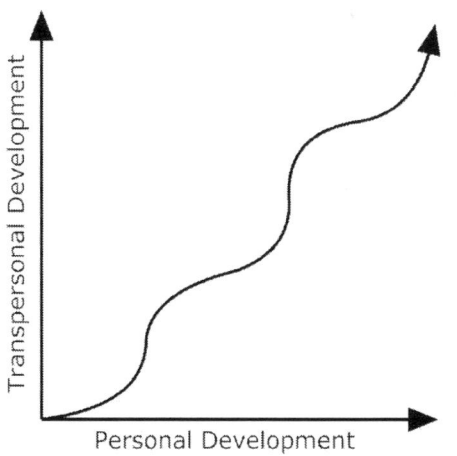

Figure 10: The Two-Fold Path of Awakening

1. Personal Development – Growing Up – Becoming Self

Personal development means "growing up" psychologically; i.e. freeing ourselves from the childish, defensive and egotistical programming and reactions that keep us from living fully conscious lives. Personal development is the journey of perfecting the authentic personality. It involves mastering (not repressing) our thoughts, emotions and bodies to free ourselves from the fears, inhibitions, conditioned behaviours, reactive emotions, critical judgements and limiting beliefs that prevent us from living happy, peaceful and fulfilling lives. This is achieved by dissolving the "negative" psychological material that keeps us trapped in these old patterns, and by actively expressing positive qualities in our daily lives.

There are five main elements to personal development (each of which will be described fully in Chapter 4):

1. **Personal Self-Inquiry** is getting to know and understand our false-self, ego structures and patterns of behaviour so that they can be healed and reintegrated. It is typically done as a standalone practice or therapy, but it can also become an integral part of our life (see point 4).

2. **Body Awareness**: Feeling the blockages, structures and holes in our psyche (with the presence of our soul) to allow our authentic personal qualities to unfold. The associated ego structures then naturally dissolve because they are no longer required.

3. **Healing & Reintegration**: Healing our relationships with our exiled parts (the parts that hold us back and keep us stuck in the past) and re-integrating them (and their associated ego structures) to return our consciousness to wholeness.

4. **Conscious Living**: On-going present-moment awareness to identify the pre-programmed reactive patterns that keep us on autopilot, keep us half-asleep, keep us reacting childishly, keep us from moving on, and keep us from living life fully. It is "live" self-inquiry – identifying issues as they arise in our daily lives so that we can feel into them or inquire into them, and then heal and reintegrate them.

5. **Embodying Essential Qualities**: Actively encouraging more of our soul's essential qualities to unfold in our personality. This is

achieved by actually embodying the qualities we wish to develop. For example: if we want to be more loving, we have to become the embodiment of love and actually be more loving. Consciously choosing to be more loving aligns us with the loving presence of our true-Self and allows it to filter down into our personality.

2. Transpersonal Development – Waking Up – Being Self

Transpersonal development means "waking up" spiritually; i.e. raising our level of consciousness to connect with our true-Self and widening our breadth of consciousness to experience life more fully in the present moment. This is depicted graphically in Figure 11.

Transpersonal development involves re-connecting with, knowing and ultimately realising our true-Self. It is not about transcending the world; it is about bringing higher levels of consciousness down into our being and expressing them in our daily lives. It is about being here as fully as we can in the present moment.

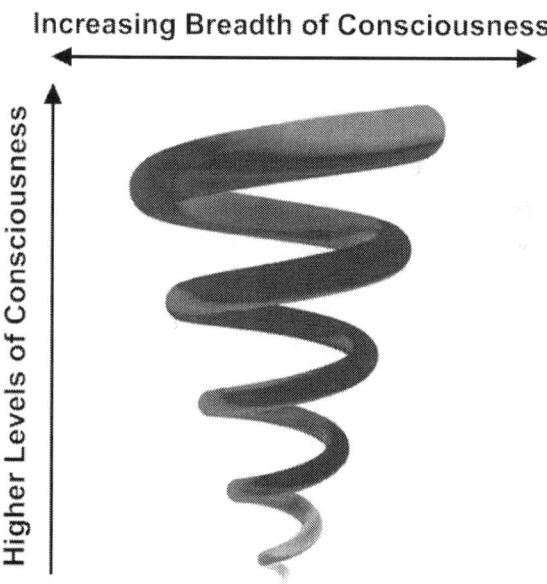

Figure 11: The Spiral Path of Transpersonal Development

There are four main elements to transpersonal development (each of which will be described fully in Chapter 6):

1. **Meditation** is about presence not absence; it is about being fully present in our bodies. It is not about escapism or transcendence. Transcendent states may arise and the boundaries of our physical body may feel indistinct but it is all about remaining present.

2. **Living Presence** is bringing the presence that we discover during meditation into the rest of our lives. It is closely connected to the personal development practices of Conscious Living and Embodying Essential Qualities.

3. **Authentic Prayer**: Conventional prayer is asking for something from God, but authentic prayer is giving something to God. Giving our presence and awareness to God/Life/Universe to help create "what is".

4. **Spiritual Self-Inquiry** is getting to know our true-Self. It is not a path that leads us anywhere – it is a path that stops us in our tracks so that we can rediscover who we really are.

An Integral Approach

Personal development and transpersonal development are distinct but not separate – there is considerable overlap and integration. Developing and integrating the personal aspects of our being (mind, heart and body) helps to develop our spiritual aspect (soul), and developing and embodying the spiritual aspect of our being helps to develop our personal aspects. Or put another way – dissolving our ego structures allows our true-nature to express itself more, and embodying more true-nature helps us to discover and dissolve our ego structures more easily. Both approaches synergistically combine to help us to become more authentic and help our consciousness to evolve. The evolution of human consciousness is optimised by facilitating these natural processes.

Figure 12 (left) depicts Roberto Assagioli's (creator of Psychosynthesis) egg diagram:

- The upper band represents the super-conscious material (insight, intuition, inspiration, etc.) that normally lies above the reach of our conscious awareness. This is the realm of the Self/soul.

- The middle band represents the psychological material (body sensations, perceptions, concepts, beliefs, memories, etc.) that are available to our conscious awareness. The inner circle represents the small part of this that we are normally aware of. This is the realm of the ego-self and the personality.
- The lower band represents the subconscious material (old traumas, memories, repressed emotions, false beliefs, reactive patterns of behaviour, etc.) that normally lie below our conscious awareness. This is the realm of exiles, holes and ego structures.

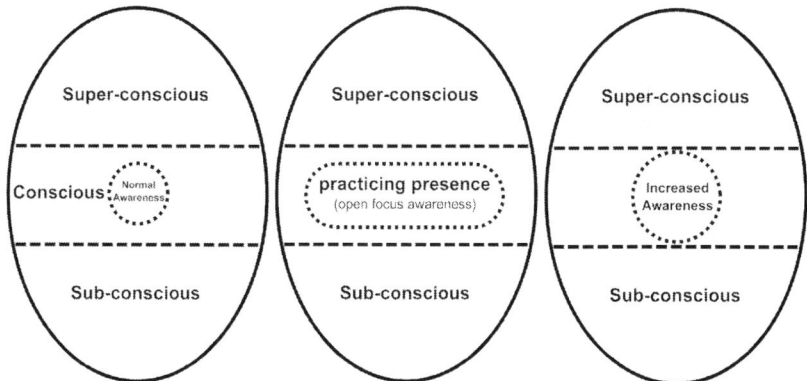

Figure 12: Egg Diagram – Increased breadth of awareness from practicing presence

Figure 12 (centre and right) shows how practicing presence (wide or open focused awareness that encompasses our entire body) expands the breadth of our consciousness, which allows us to experience more of life in the present moment. Our consciousness develops and evolves through experience, so increasing the breadth of our awareness by practicing presence facilitates the development of our consciousness.

Personal self-inquiry is the conscious exploration of the subconscious; it brings sub-conscious psychological material into conscious awareness. If self-inquiry is practiced with open focus / body awareness / presence, it expands the natural breadth of our conscious awareness and increases the "depth" of our conscious awareness (as represented in Figure 13).

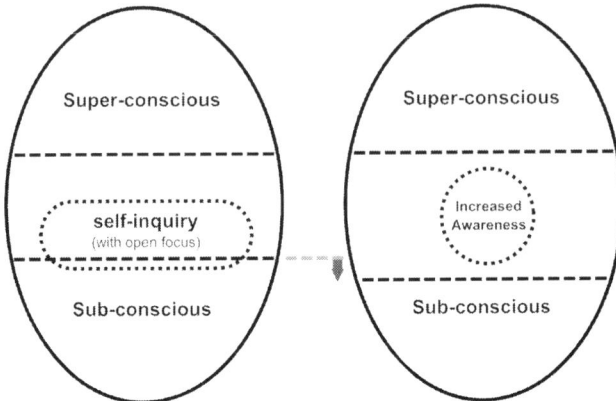

Figure 13: Egg Diagram – Increased breadth and "depth" of awareness from self-inquiry

Meditation and spiritual Self-inquiry are the conscious exploration of the super-conscious; they bring super-conscious insights into conscious awareness. If meditation or spiritual Self-inquiry are practiced with open focus / body awareness / presence, they expand the natural breadth of our conscious awareness and increase the "height" of our conscious awareness (as represented in Figure 14).

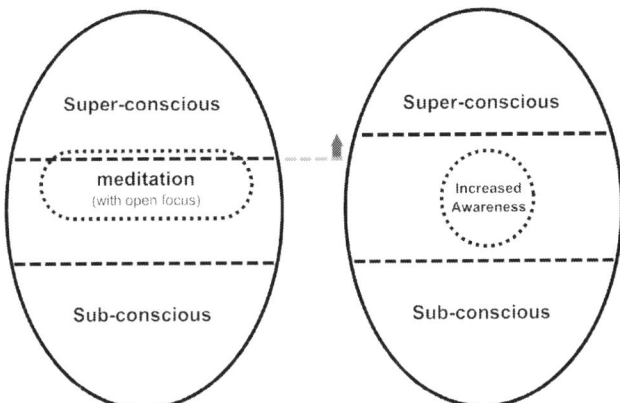

Figure 14: Egg Diagram – Increased breadth and "height" of awareness from meditation

The Dynamic Evolution of Consciousness

Consciousness is alive – it needs to flow – and if it doesn't flow it stagnates. Consciousness needs to flow inwards and outwards, which is the two-fold path. Focusing only on one aspect of life (inner OR outer) means that consciousness cannot flow freely, and the result is an unbalanced life:

- **External Focus**: Only focused on the ego and the material world, with no interest in the inner (psychological and spiritual) world.

OR

- **Internal Focus**: Only focused on the spiritual Self and transcendent states, which are of little use in the external world.

Simultaneously focusing on both aspects of life (inner AND outer) creates polarities between which consciousness can flow:

- **External to Internal Focus**: The personality focuses inwards to become more aligned with the Self so that the blockages (ego structures) between the two dissolve. This aspect of the path is known as personal development (Becoming Self).

AND

- **Internal to External Focus**: The Self expresses itself and its essential qualities outwards through the personality and into the external world. This aspect of the path is known as transpersonal or spiritual development (Being Self).

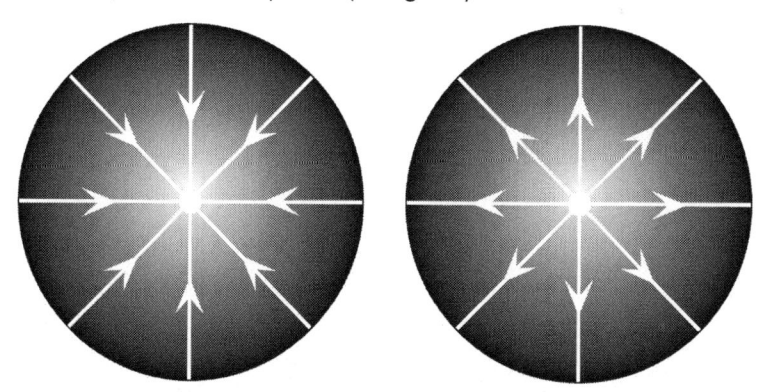

Figure 15: Personal Development (Becoming Self)
and Transpersonal Development (Being Self)

Consciousness flows more freely as we progress along the two-fold path because there are less ego structures to obstruct the flow. The major milestones on the path are as follows:

1. **Progressive Awakening** occurs as ego structures are gradually dissolved and exiled parts and essential qualities are gradually reintegrated. This process of refining the personality is ongoing, but it cannot be completed from within the personality.

2. **Enlightenment**: Just as you cannot demolish a building while you are still inside it, the last of the ego structures cannot be dissolved while the Self is centred in the personality. The Self has to transcend the personality in order to dissolve the final ego structures and perfect the personality. The Self moves up from the personality triad (body, heart and mind) to the soul triad to complete this final stage of human evolution. The three components of the soul triad don't have English names, but in Sanskrit they are known as Higher Manas, Buddhi and Atma.

3. **Beyond Humanity**: When the personality is clear of ego structures, the polarities that drive the human stage of the evolution of consciousness have been neutralised. The lack of polarity means that the Self must move onto the next stage of its evolution. The human kingdom is transcended when the ego has been completely transcended, i.e. all ego structures have been dissolved. From here on, physical incarnation in a human body is optional.

These topics are described further in Chapters 4 and 7. For fuller and more technical description of the soul triad, enlightenment and beyond please refer to my first book, *The Science of Spirituality*.

Chapter 2: **The Human Condition**

Human Beings

A human being is not a single entity; we are composed of several different yet fully integrated components. Each component (or body) is an independent consciousness yet they are all integrated and work in harmony, much like the different parts of a car all work together to get us from A to B. The Self is the driver (or at least it should be) and the mind, heart and body are components of the vehicle that carry us through life.

Component	Perceptive (Yin) Side	Expressive (Yang) Side
Self/Soul	Pure Awareness	Essential Qualities
Mind	Mental Perception	Cognitive Thinking
Heart	Emotional Perception	Emotional Expression
Body (physical + energy)	Sensory Perception	Physical Action/Will

Figure 16: The Composition of a Human Being

Each component exists and operates on a different level (or dimension) of reality. Each element has perceptive (yin) qualities which allow us to perceive our environment, and expressive (yang) qualities which allow us to interact with our environment.

The three non-Self components (mind, heart and body) are not "us", but they are aspects of our being. Because the various aspects of our being are so well integrated, it is very easy for us to become identified with them – which is what usually happens. This misidentification provides us with a lot of different opportunities for psychological and spiritual growth that we wouldn't otherwise experience, but it also creates a lot of self-inflicted and unnecessary suffering.

The three non-Self components are highly programmable – once they have learnt a pattern of behaviour they tend to react automatically in similar situations. This is great because it allows us to carry out complex tasks without using all of our conscious attention, but it can encourage us to switch off and miss out on the fullness of life. It can be compared to a car that can learn to drive itself – it encourages the driver (Self) to fall asleep – which is what usually happens. We half open an eye when something major happens (like hitting a metaphorical tree), but most of the time we live our lives on autopilot and wonder why things don't always go the way we would like.

This book is about awakening from the semi-conscious state that most of us live in most of the time, and the first step of the process is to look at the things that keep us "asleep" and the things that we do when we are "asleep". The reason I am dedicating a whole chapter to these "negative" aspects of the human condition is so we can identify which ones affect us and understand how they adversely affect our lives. This not only helps us to know ourselves more fully, it also disempowers our subconscious patterns by bringing them into the light of our conscious awareness. This gives us a choice – we can allow them to keep happening or we can consciously stop doing them and free ourselves from a lot of unnecessary suffering.

The Personality

An average personality is a blend of authentic personality (the true-Self operating through the Mind, Heart & Body centres) and ego personality (the false-self operating through the ego structures). This is depicted graphically in Figure 17.

The Self's field of consciousness (soul) operates freely and clearly through the authentic elements of the personality, allowing authentic expression of our true nature. But true nature is blocked and distorted by the egoic elements of the personality, resulting in inauthentic, reactive, childish, selfish and even evil behaviour. The proportion of authenticity we express is directly related to our level of awakening. The two-fold path is about dis-identifying from, disempowering and dissolving the ego personality, and associating with the true-Self to develop the authentic personality. Note: I am not saying that the ego-personality is inauthentic, just that it isn't our true nature; it is our conditioning.

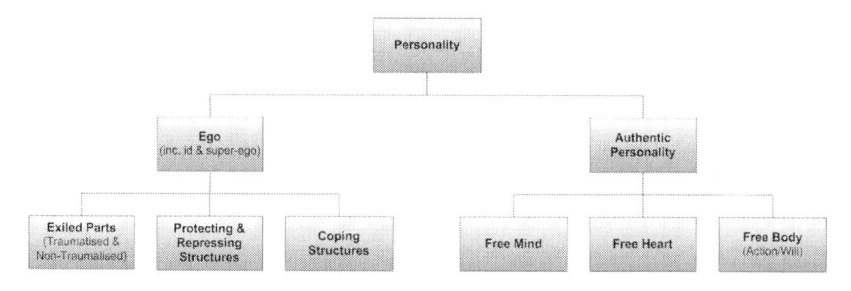

Figure 17: The Two Sides of the Personality

As we gradually dissolve our ego structures (through inner work), the balance of power shifts, allowing more of our authentic personality to be expressed. A great personality is not achieved by refining, polishing or re-programming our ego structures; it is achieved by dissolving them. Note: The personality does not disappear when we attain enlightenment; it just becomes more authentic.

Imagine that ego structures are made out of ice. When the ice (ego structure) melts, the structure dissolves and the water (consciousness) is released and reintegrated into our authentic personality. The same applies to exiles, which are literally made out of "frozen" consciousness. When the warmth of our soul merges with an exiled part, the "frozen" consciousness is liberated and reintegrated into the wholeness of our being.

Sub-Personalities (or Parts)

We don't have one single ego personality – it is a system of many parts. In most people the system is reasonably well integrated, i.e. all the parts of the ego super-structure are connected together to form one integrated system. Even so, the individual ego structures within the super-structure can still think, feel and act independently from the whole. They are individual units AND they are part of a larger system – just as a finger is an individual unit, but it is also part of a larger system called a hand, and part of an even larger system called the body.

Individual ego structures (and localised clusters of ego structures) are sub-personalities or "parts" that combine to form our ego super-structure. They are called "parts" because we often say "part of me wants to do it and part of me doesn't".

Multiple or Split Personalities

The technical term for a "split personality" is Dissociative Identity Disorder (DID). It was previously known as Multiple Personality Disorder (MPD). People with this condition have created a number of distinct ego super-structures (sub-personalities) that are disconnected from each other. This prevents the intense pain and trauma that are held in each part from overwhelming the entire personality. Multiple personalities are our second line of psychological defence:

1. **The first line of defence** is the creation of separate sub-personalities (individual exiled parts and ego structures). These are sufficient to protect us from the mild to moderate psychological traumas that most of us experience in life.

2. **The second line of defence** is the creation of separate personalities (large constellations of exiled parts and ego structures). These are only required to protect us from severe traumas and persistent abuse.

The ego-self moves between the different personalities, utilising whichever one is most appropriate. Since each personality is utilised for a different aspect of life, it is not surprising that different personalities have very different traits. The treatment of multiple personalities is beyond the scope of this book, but the principles for reintegration are the same as for individual ego structures.

The Wounded "Inner Child"

The ego is largely "constructed" from innocent, immature, inexperienced and impressionable young consciousness, which is why we often behave like children when things don't go our way. We try to give the impression that we are grown-up and mature, but that is just the outer layers of the ego that were added later in life; underneath the mature façade lies a wounded inner child. The inner child is not a single "entity"; it is a collective of many parts that formed over the course of several years in response to numerous confusing and distressing events. During inner work, it is very common to encounter (through inner vision or a felt sense) a young version of ourselves who is scared and confused. This inner child may be an individual part or it may be a cluster of inter-related parts:

- **Individual Parts**: Three different types of parts can present as an inner child. They are usually still at the age they were when they were originally created:
    - **Exiles** are pieces of scared, confused and distressed consciousness that were exiled (deeply repressed) to protect our ego-self from becoming overwhelmed. This is perhaps the most common type of wounded inner child that we are likely to encounter.
    - **Protective Ego Structures** are pieces of consciousness that were programmed to protect our ego-self from an exiled part by distracting our attention or "physically" preventing access. Distracting parts may present as a younger child having a tantrum, and protecting parts may present as a protective older child.
    - **Coping Ego Structures** are pieces of consciousness that were programmed to supplement the functionality of undeveloped personal qualities, caused by "lost" contact with our soul's essential qualities. A coping structure will occasionally present as an inner child, but usually as a responsible and capable, yet somewhat inflexible, older child.
- **Cluster of Parts**: A cluster of related exiles or ego structures may present as an inner child. If they present as a single entity they must be treated as one and can often be healed as one.
- **The Collective**: The inner child is the collective consciousness of all the individual parts (inner children). Its age is the average age of all the individual parts. It cannot be healed as a whole because it contains countless un-related traumatised and programmed pieces of consciousness.

I have described the different types of inner children for reference purposes only. In practice we don't always know which type we are dealing with and we don't really need to know. Whether we are working with an individual part, a cluster or the collective, each inner child needs to be treated as an individual and needs to be treated with love, compassion, understanding and respect. The Talking to Parts Technique in Chapter 5 describes an effective method of healing and reintegrating wounded inner children.

The Repressed "Soul Child" or "Wonder Child"

In many ways a soul child is very similar to a wounded inner child, except that a soul child is not wounded; it is merely repressed.

When we were young (typically between the ages of 2 and 4), if one of our newly embodied personal qualities was ignored or not always well-received by our parents, we may have repressed it in order to maintain their love and approval (or keep ourselves safe). It is not possible to repress an entire personal quality because they permeate our entire field of personal consciousness, but it is possible to repress the part of our consciousness that most fully embodies (and therefore principally expresses) a particular personal quality. So that is what we did – The part of us that expressed a new personal quality was repressed if our parents didn't acknowledge it (which made us believe that it was unimportant), or if our parents actively disliked it (which made us believe that it was unacceptable).

A soul child is basically a non-traumatised exile. It is a piece of our consciousness (which embodies an authentic personal quality) that is encased in an ego structure to repress that quality. The repressing ego structure is not just a containment structure; it is also programmed with the opposite quality to neutralise the effects of the authentic quality. If, for example, our playfulness was not encouraged we may have encased it in seriousness, which would have caused us to be serious and sensible at times when we could have been playing and having fun.

We didn't always encase the unwanted part in the opposite ego quality; e.g. a playful part in seriousness, or a loving part in hatred. Sometimes our parents' misperceptions and misjudgements determined which ego quality we encased our unwanted part in. In such instances, we encased it in the opposite of what our parents perceived. For example: If they misperceived our openness as weakness, we may have encased it in false strength. If they misperceived our tranquillity as laziness, we may have encased it in striving. If they misperceived our tenderness as neediness, we may have encased it in boisterousness.

No matter what an authentic personal quality is encased in, it can never be completely contained; some of its energy will always seep out and influence our personality. However, the repressed personal quality will be tainted by its own frustration at being repressed, and it will be distorted by the ego structure that encases it. So our repressed playful nature will be distorted by its own frustration and by the seriousness that encases it, resulting in spiteful undertones.

If we grow up in a repressed environment (e.g. due to an overbearing parent) many of our authentic personal qualities will be repressed in this way, and lots of repressed parts equals lots of repressed frustration. The repressed frustration continually seeps out and adversely affects our personality, resulting in some or all of the following underlying issues: irritability, impatience, restlessness, general unease, anxiety, insomnia, boredom, discontent, etc. In addition to these underlying issues, the repressed frustration will occasionally erupt as an angry outburst.

Incidentally, you may be wondering why a repressed part of our personal consciousness (that is composed of mind, heart and body consciousness) is called a soul child or a wonder child? The unwanted personal quality was still emerging (i.e. being transposed from the soul to the personality) at the time the part was repressed. This means the soul was intimately merged with the part when it was repressed. So a soul child is a wondrous blend of radiant <u>soul</u> consciousness and innocent <u>child</u>-like personal consciousness, hence the term soul child.

We don't know that we are dealing with a soul child until we make intimate contact with it. Our initial contact is with the encasing ego structure, so we feel its false quality (e.g. hatred or seriousness). It is only when we feel deeply into the false quality that we discover the wonderfully radiant soul child in the centre. The Soul Child Reintegration Technique in Chapter 5 describes an effective method of liberating and reintegrating repressed soul children.

The Ego

The ego is a definition of who we think we are. It is a giant elaborate thought-form that takes a lot of energy and effort to sustain. Like any thought-form, it has no enduring reality and will eventually dissolve. All definitions are limiting and the ego limits us in many ways. It limits who we think we are, it limits our experience of life, and it limits our expression of life. The ego obscures direct contact with Self and reality.

The remainder of this chapter is about understanding the things that we do, often subconsciously, that hinder our development and prolong our unnecessary suffering. Bringing these subconscious reactions into the light of our conscious awareness is the first stage of the healing and reintegration process. Subsequent chapters describe the steps we can consciously take to optimise our development but for now it is back to the ego and its many "flaws".

1. Narcissism

Narcissism is an exaggerated sense of self-importance, and the ego is incredibly narcissistic. The ego believes *it* is very important, its thoughts are very important, its feelings are very important and every aspect of its life is very important. Basically, the ego believes it is the centre of the universe. But in the grand universal scheme of things our personal problems, issues, hurts, beliefs and opinions are practically meaningless. We need to learn to see our lives from a more objective philosophical perspective rather than a subjective personal perspective. We also need to realise that our ego-self is not the true centre of our universe.

We can practice tirelessly and meditate for years, but we will never make any real progress while we are operating from an egocentric position that is only concerned about "me". To make real progress we need to move away from our ego's self-centred positionality and move towards our true-Self, which is a part of everything. Everything then becomes the centre of our universe. From there we have the power of the entire universe at our disposal, and then almost anything becomes possible.

2. Identification

The ego is about identity; it is not about who we really are. The ego identifies with just about everything that is important to us – our body image, our possessions, our family, our culture, our country, our beliefs, our cause, our religion or even our favourite sports team. We feel their ups and downs almost as if they were our own. We are highly identified with them because we have invested part of our (false) self in them.

Our body is the one thing that we all became identified with (to a greater or lesser degree) at a very early age. Body-identification can turn into vanity and cause us a lot of unnecessary suffering. For example, the identity of being fat causes us a lot more distress than simply being aware that our body is overweight. The identity of being ugly causes us a lot more distress than simply being aware that our face is not as beautiful as some others.

We are not our thoughts, emotions or impulses; if we were, they would always obey us. This simple realisation can profoundly transform our lives. When we stop acting on every impulse, when we stop getting caught up in every emotion and when we stop believing every thought, we can begin to find our true-Self.

In order to know what we truly are we must first know what we are not. In order to claim back our freedom, power and true sense of self, we need to dis-identify from anything and everything that is not us. I don't mean distancing ourselves from life and the people we love; I mean re-establishing healthy boundaries so that we don't get too caught up in anything that doesn't directly relate to our present moment experience.

3. Separation

The ego is not hardware (like a computer); it is software (like a computer program). It is a way of processing information that leads us to believe that we are separate individuals – separate from each other and separate from the world. The false belief that we are an isolated individual creates fear, which gives rise to another false belief – that we must defend ourselves; psychologically if not physically.

We distance ourselves from reality to protect our ego-self from being hurt and disappointed. It was a great coping strategy and survival mechanism when we were very young, but as adults it creates far more suffering than it protects us from.

4. Controlling

The ego fears for its survival so it wants everything in life to be safe, predictable and controllable. New experiences are rarely predictable or controllable so the ego generally dislikes change. The ego can never relax or be happy while it is constantly resisting life, trying to control everything and trying to make things the way they "should be". If it can't maintain control, the ego will try to pretend that everything is under control, even if everything is falling apart around us and we have no idea what to do about it.

The truth is we have no control over life because we never know for sure what is going to happen next. Even though we have no control over life the thought of losing our illusory sense of control fills us with great fear. But even that fear is an illusion because we can't really be afraid of losing something we never had.

5. External Validation

The ego is always seeking validation to reassure itself that it is still valid (legitimate and acceptable). The ego formed early in our childhood in response to external mirroring, feedback and validation from our parents and caregivers, so it is not surprising that the ego continues to seek this external validation to reassure itself that it is still worthy of existing.

When someone invalidates our beliefs or disagrees with us it can feel like they are invalidating our sense of self; our very existence. This makes us feel disempowered and we generally react in one of two ways:

- **Actively**: we get angry and fight back (psychologically or physically).
- **Passively**: we close down and wallow in self-pity.

Neither reaction is appropriate or necessary, but the ego's insecurities make us believe they are.

Deep down the ego knows it is standing on shaky ground, so it seeks external validation to shore up its unstable foundations. The ego's sense of self is intimately linked to the thoughts, beliefs and concepts we have about ourselves and world around us. So the ego seeks validation by trying to make other people think, feel and act the same way that we do. If they agree with our point of view, then we must be real and we must be important. But we have all had different life experiences so we all have different views and opinions. So getting everyone to agree with us and validate our sense of self is never going to succeed. No wonder the ego is never happy or contented.

Every ego believes that its own views and opinions are better than everyone else's and more important than everyone else's. We are all the same in this respect, and since we can't all be right, we must all be wrong! No one's thoughts or beliefs are any more significant than anyone else's, and no one's thoughts or beliefs really matter. We are all equal in that respect – equally deluded!

All conflicts and arguments stem from one root cause, which is that we, as human beings, believe the thoughts in our minds. If we thought them they must be real and they must be true. But most of our thoughts are spontaneously generated by our mind (mental body). The mind generally reacts to present events based on our past experiences of similar events. So our thoughts (and associated feelings) are the result of our past programming. Our thoughts are rarely anything new; they are usually rehashed old thoughts and beliefs.

Most of our core programming occurred when we were young children, so many of our beliefs are actually our parents' beliefs (or the opposite of their beliefs). And because most of our thoughts and beliefs originate from immature parts of our psyche it is no surprise that many of our thoughts are reactive, childish and immature; yet we still believe them to be true. No wonder there is so much disagreement and conflict in the world.

6. Invalidating Others

If someone says "I really like chocolate ice cream" and our favourite flavour is vanilla, we can't just accept their opinion; we have to respond with "No, vanilla is the best". We have to validate our beliefs (and our sense of self) and it doesn't matter if we invalidate others in the process.

As I have already stated, our opinions, preferences and beliefs have no more importance or validity than anyone else's. We know that logically, but logic goes out the window when we are identified with our beliefs, because we are not just defending a belief; we are defending our sense of self – and attack is often the best form of defence. The above example is quite trivial but people will often go to any extreme to defend a belief that is really important to them.

7. Polarised

The ego is often polarised in its point of view. It is either "I am great and I am right (and you are wrong)" or it is "poor wounded me, I have been victimised (and you have attacked me)". There is rarely any middle ground where the ego is concerned so we frequently flip between these two extreme self-images. The ego doesn't like neutrality because that lacks energy, and energy is what the ego needs to sustain itself. Also neutrality doesn't require any resistance (in fact it implies acceptance); and the ego equates that with giving up.

Another type of polarity that exists within us is the polarity between conflicting ego structures. The ego is constantly fighting against itself – different parts pull us in different directions, so we never really get anywhere. The only way forward is to drop our ego-agendas and stop resisting life. Life is inevitable, so we may as well work with it. Conscious awareness neutralises the polarities and extreme views of our ego and brings us into balance and alignment with our true-Self. Defending our ego-self demonstrates that we are more aligned with our ego-self than our true-Self. It shows that we are more interested in staying the same than we are with psychological or spiritual development.

8. Defensive

The ego and its structures are inherently unstable thought-forms, but because the ego forms our entire (false) sense of self we defend it vigorously. We become defensive in response to perceived psychological attacks to protect and reinforce our weakened ego structures. Our first line of defence involves justifying our position (beliefs, decisions or actions). This can serve two purposes:

1. It reaffirms to our ego-self that we were justified and correct. This self-validation shores the weakened ego structures.

2. If we are lucky we may also convince the other person that we were correct, in which case we get external validation too, which strengthens our ego structures even more.

If the other person doesn't buy into our story we may respond with a counterattack. This is intended to psychologically weaken the other person in the hope that it will stave off further attacks. But the ego forgets that it is battling with another ego, so any counterattack is bound to be met with yet another attack and things can quickly get out of hand.

When we defend ourselves, we are attempting to stop the psychological material from penetrating deep into our ego because there it will resonate with other deeply repressed material that we are too afraid to face. When we are open and undefended there is nothing to hinder that material from coming up so it is perfect for unearthing and healing our old repressed hurts. We simply have to set our intention to uncover our repressed psychological material and it will start revealing itself to us (when the time and circumstances are right). It won't necessarily be pleasurable but it won't be as bad as we might imagine. This is because our subconscious fears about facing this material originated when we were young and incapable of handling it. So the fears still affect us as if we were a frightened and confused young child. But now that we are an adult we are much better equipped to deal with our old repressed psychological material.

9. Passive–Aggressive

Ego structures are created to compensate for undeveloped authentic personal qualities. They are crudely constructed mind-created imitations of our soul's essential qualities. Depending on our state of mind at the time of their creation, ego structures are imprinted with an underlying passive or aggressive temperament:

1. **Passive**: introverted, weak, victimised, timid, submissive, compliant, depressive, etc.
2. **Aggressive**: extroverted, over-compensating, hostile, assertive, proud, hyperactive, etc.

Ego structures are hardly ever neutral because we are usually in a state of turmoil when they are formed, and it is this emotional tone that gets imprinted into the ego structure. The underlying temperament of our ego structures shapes the general temperament of our ego and therefore our personality.

10. Feeling Special

The ego has self-esteem issues because deep down it knows that it isn't the Self and can never live up to the Self. To overcome these feelings of inadequacy the ego tries to make itself feel special. It does this by assigning value to goals and objects, so it can feel good about itself when it achieves them. It can say "I did that; I am great" and bask in its self-created feelings of pride, superiority, importance and grandeur. Success, power, wealth, possessions and vanity are all just façades – they are attempts to make up for the inadequacies (holes) we feel inside. If we were whole and complete we wouldn't need any of these things to feel good about ourselves.

If we can't believe stories about ourselves that make us feel superior, the ego will create stories about ourselves that make us feel inferior (which is feeling special in a negative way). Then the ego can wallow in its self-created feelings of pity, inadequacy, shame, stupidity or failure. An even better way of feeling special in a negative way is to be a victim of injustice or ill-health. This is even better than self-pity because we can wallow in other people's pity too; and we can "milk it". Only the ego could "get off" on feeling bad!

11. Credit and Blame

The ego is extremely quick at claiming it is the cause of everything good in our life, and equally quick at blaming someone else for everything bad in our life. Neither of these beliefs is true because the ego isn't really the doer of anything; it notices things after they have occurred and takes the credit or apportions the blame, as appropriate.

All conscious wilful acts are initiated by the Self (which does include the ego-self). The Self activates the appropriate area of consciousness – if it contains an ego structure we act from its programming, and if it is clear of ego structures we act from our true-nature. The ego merely notices our actions after they have been initiated. The ego is a semi-autonomous puppet that takes all the glory for putting on a good show (and offloads all the blame when things go wrong), but it is the Self that writes the script and pulls the strings.

12. Projecting

When we get upset, irritated or angry we usually blame someone else for making us feel that way – this is a typical ego defence mechanism. Because society classifies anger as a negative trait, the ego doesn't want to take the blame and shame for being angry, so it blames someone else for "making" us angry. We project the "cause" of our anger outwards onto an external source. The other person's words or actions may have given our anger an opportunity to arise but the other person is not the cause of our anger. They did not make anger arise within us; we allowed it to. We must take 100% responsibility for everything that happens in our life because some part of us attracted it into our life for a reason – for us to experience, learn and grow.

Every time a part of us gets triggered is an opportunity for us to feel it and heal it. Rather than trying to get rid of the emotional charge it is better to stay with it, feel it and accept it. Our emotional reaction is a call for help from an exiled part or an ego structure that just wants to be noticed, understood, related to and reintegrated.

13. Reactive

The ego's nature is reactive. Ego structures react rather than respond, and their reactions are based upon past experiences. So the ego reacts to present events with behaviour from the past. The past never completely corresponds with the present so a pre-programmed reaction from the past is never going to be completely appropriate in the present.

Many of the ego's core strategies and programs originate from perceived survival situations in our early childhood. In a survival situation we don't have time to think; we must react instantly. By the time we are consciously aware of such a reaction it has already occurred, so we can't stop the ego from reacting. As long as we have ego structures they will react, but with awareness we can learn to catch them early enough to stop them being fully acted out. For example, if we notice that we have become offended we can intervene before the next step of the reactive program is triggered (e.g. feel offended > get angry > defend our self > counterattack the offender). Without awareness and conscious intervention, one reaction will trigger another, and so on, resulting in a chain reaction. The further along the chain we get the more we get caught up in the drama and harder it becomes to stop the process.

Reactions are perfect in survival situations but modern adult life doesn't involve many life-threatening situations. Our lives aren't threatened when someone says something that offends us, so we don't need to react angrily. We need to learn to respond to the now, from the now (not from the past) – only then can our responses be truly appropriate.

There is no point resenting the ego's reactivity, feeling ashamed of it or trying to change it. We have to accept that "it is what it is" and "it does what it does". All we can do is stop its reactions from snowballing out of control and engulfing our personality. When we catch a reaction early enough, instead of becoming consumed by it and acting it out, we can feel into it, begin to understand it, and maybe discover what triggered it and why? From there we may be able to determine the original cause of the reactive behaviour (which is usually from our childhood). By giving the reaction the space to "be" in our consciousness, we are not rejecting it and we are not encouraging it. In this "allowing space" we can feel its energy and inquire into it to understand what is going on inside of us. We are making a subconscious reaction conscious and in doing so we are disempowering it.

Bringing subconscious beliefs and behaviours into conscious awareness allows us to challenge them. Our conscious mind will not allow us to keep believing negative beliefs or keep acting out negative behaviours (unless addictions are involved). The negative programs went unchallenged when they were subconscious, so they would activate automatically. When the programs become conscious we can choose to run them or not, which gives us control over our programs and reactions to life. With conscious awareness we can learn to respond to the present from the present, rather than reacting from the past.

Our identification with the ego can blind us from the inappropriateness of its reactions. We are looking through the distorted veils of our ego structures so it is not surprising that (at the time) we often consider our ego's reactions to be appropriate. Inquiry helps us to see through this distortion and discover the truth – that it wasn't the other person's fault. If a reaction is arising within us, it is to do with us; not them. When we take ownership of a reaction (i.e. accept that this is about us; not them), we can inquire into it openly, begin to understand it, take responsibility for ourselves, free ourselves from our programming and discover more of our true nature. The ego's reactions are messages from the past that can become our teachers in the present.

14. Childish

Age regression is when we suddenly start exhibiting the behaviour of a child. We may display the body language of a child or speak in a childish manner. It is caused by a young part (exile or coping structure) being activated. Something in the present resonates with something from our childhood so we become identified with that part. Our expression originates from an immature piece of consciousness so our expression is childish.

15. Repressing and Numbing

When the repressed emotions that we have stuffed down into our belly call out for our attention we may interpret the message as hunger, and eat food in an attempt to numb it down. Similarly, when other exiled parts of our being cry out, we may try to numb them down in other ways, e.g. cigarettes, alcohol, drugs, etc. Our coping ego structures are trying to repress their cries to protect us from facing the painful emotions that we repressed all those years ago.

These coping parts that are afraid of feeling the pain were programmed when we were very young, so they probably believe that we are still very young. They don't know that we are adults now and are much better equipped to deal with our repressed psychological material, but we can tell them and we can show them. We can start by developing a loving and caring relationship with those parts. Then we can help them to release their fears and invite them back into the wholeness of our being.

16. Doing and Not Doing (Avoiding)

Doing things and keeping busy are great distractions; they are classic ego strategies for keeping us from connecting with our exiled parts. When we stop doing we become more able to perceive the pain of our exiled parts. This makes us feel uncomfortable and agitated, which motivates us to do something to avoid these uncomfortable feelings. Doing often becomes habitual and addictive, e.g. OCD, fitness-freak, workaholic, etc.

We sometimes decide that the best way to avoid psychological pain or to avoid feeling inadequate is to avoid life, i.e. withdraw from life and remain isolated. If we don't put ourselves in challenging situations our painful repressed material cannot get triggered. If the ego's inadequacy is experienced as an inability to interact with other people we may even abandon personal relationships altogether and become a recluse.

17. Trance

We live much of our life in a state of trance; i.e. when we are not "present" because our consciousness is caught up in an ego structure or is taking a break out-of-body. We find it difficult to stay present when "negative" feelings arise so we distance ourselves from our feelings by spacing out, but in doing so we reject an important aspect of life.

If we had the courage to fully feel into our repressed emotions we would discover that they are actually opportunities for healing, and we would realise that they are not nearly as bad as we think. It was our avoidance of these feelings as young children that led to our current issues. We repressed them because we didn't have the capacity to deal with them at the time. As adults we do have the capacity to deal with negative feelings – the only reason we think we don't is because the same childhood beliefs are still operating today.

18. Dissatisfied

We usually discover that the satisfaction and fulfilment we experience after achieving a goal is less than we expected and relatively short-lived, especially compared to the time and effort we put into achieving it. This is because most goals are ego-driven; they are not authentic; they are not what we truly want. Dissatisfaction is a core quality of the ego because it was imprinted with a negative belief (e.g. I am not good enough) at the time of its creation. So the ego will never be satisfied for very long, no matter what we achieve. Our only hope for lasting satisfaction is to transcend the ego and awaken to our true-Self.

The Self/soul is the source of all our positive qualities, including happiness, joy and fulfilment. When we truly realise this all external wants and desires fade away and we discover that everything we could ever want is already within us. The ego has no inherent positive qualities so it has to look outside of itself to find happiness and satisfaction. The ego projects value, worth and specialness onto external things and rewards itself with happiness and satisfaction when it attains them or achieves them. This false happiness is short-lived. Authentic happiness is permanent and unshakable because it isn't dependent on external circumstances; it is our true nature. It is available to all of us, right here and now!

You might think that experience would tell us that goal achievement and material acquisition are not paths to lasting happiness and fulfilment. The sensible thing would be to change our strategy and try something different. But most of us just carry on with the same old strategy in the hope that one day, if we achieve enough or acquire enough, we will eventually find lasting satisfaction. This strategy is not only destined for failure; it frequently results in addiction as we crave one short "fix" of satisfaction after another.

19. Addicted

Ever since we first became identified with our false concept of self, maintaining and defending our ego has been our number one priority in life. It has driven us to adopt a range of different strategies that distract and protect us from feeling the pain of our psychological wounds and the "holes" in our being. We try to fill our holes with the pleasant feelings that accompany achievements, acquisitions and/or substance use. But the effect is only short-lived and the intensity of relief diminishes over time, so we have to keep doing it. We need more of it and more often, so our coping mechanism becomes an addiction. It can be alcohol, drugs, food, fashion, sex, romance, cars, gadgets, work, fitness, sports, religion, spirituality, fantasy or anything that gives us a short-term buzz. Addictions initially provide short-term pleasure but ultimately they only ever result in dissatisfaction and unhappiness.

We mistakenly believe that addictive behaviours benefit us in two ways:

1. Decreased negative feelings, i.e. less sadness.
2. Increased positive feelings, i.e. more happiness.

Both of these strategies are ways of avoiding "what is" – and that is the problem. Freeing ourselves from any addiction requires us to feel "what is"; it requires the courage to go "cold turkey". If we stop feeding our habit we will soon feel "what is" (withdrawal symptoms), and that is just what we need to heal ourselves. Fully feeling our psychological and/or physical discomfort, without any judgement or resistance, connects us directly to the root of the issue. We can then heal our relationship with the exiled part and re-integrate it into our consciousness. The addictive behaviour (our coping mechanism) is no longer required so the coping structure dissolves and with it the addiction.

20. Resistance

The ego is resistant to "what is". It can't just accept things as they are. It wants to control life because it fears life. It fears being invalidated by life, and it fears death. The soul may be eternal but the ego certainly is not!

The ego is also resistant to change, and this keeps us from developing and growing. It keeps us "who we have been" instead of being "who we are" and becoming "all that we can be". The ego does this by projecting what it "knows" from our past experiences onto our present experiences and anticipated future experiences. New experiences are not predictable or controllable so they make the ego fearful and anxious.

There are three main types of psychological resistance:

1. **The ego actively resists Life**: The ego wants to control everything and change everything to its liking because it fears for its survival. The ego fears death, so it fears almost everything in life.

2. **The ego passively resists Life**: Life naturally flows through us but ego structures impede the flow. When life flows though us freely and easily, our life flows freely and effortlessly. But when ego structures impede the flow of life, our life does not flow freely. When things don't go our way in life we should contemplate whether our (ego's) chosen path is aligned with our life's purpose (universal will).

3. **The ego resists the ego**: Inner conflict occurs when different parts of us want different or conflicting things.

Psychological resistance is a clear sign that something within us is out of balance. It is an invitation to inquire within, to discover the source of the resistance and to heal it. Softening our resistance through conscious awareness softens our ego structures, which allows our life to flow more freely.

When we resist anything negative (e.g. a false belief, a negative emotion or a destructive behaviour) we are inadvertently reinforcing it, because we are confirming its existence as something that must be avoided. By resisting it we are actually making it stronger and more enduring – hence the saying "what we resist persists". Life carries on regardless whether we accept it or resist it, but it is a whole lot easier, happier, richer and fulfilling when we accept it.

We miss so much of life because we are too busy moaning about it and trying to change it. The simple act of letting go of resistance and criticism can have a profoundly positive effect on our lives. We easily get caught up in the self-created drama of our subjective reality, so we can never truly know peace. True peace comes from fully experiencing "what is" and fully accepting "what is". This allows the mind to relax and the heart to open, which allows clearer perception and clearer expression.

21. Subjective

The ego can't be objective; it has to take a subjective position. It can't see things exactly as they are; that would be pure awareness. The way we normally see the world is not the way it really is, because we are looking through the subjective filters of our ego structures. Our ego structures filter, colour and distort our perceptions (on the way in), and they distort our expressions, speech and actions (on the way out). Our perceptions and expressions are coloured by our likes and dislikes, distorted by our fears and judgements, and influenced by our ideas of how we think things should be. In order to see things objectively we need to look at the world from a different perspective – from the perspective of pure awareness. Unfortunately, most of us don't know the difference between thinking and awareness.

The Mind

Thinking doesn't block awareness; pure awareness is always there (in the background), but we are usually drawn to the mental activity in the foreground. We are rarely just aware of our thinking, i.e. quietly watching our thoughts. Instead, we identify with our thoughts and we identify with being the thinker, and consequently we believe everything we think. But a thought is just a thought – we don't have to believe it or buy into it. Thoughts are not the truth – just because we believe them does not make them true. Any thought that comes from the ego-mind is likely to be distorted to some degree, because it originated from a part of us that is rooted in fear and confusion. We can't think straight when we are scared or confused, so let's stop buying into the thoughts that come from our scared and confused parts.

Thoughts are conceptual representations of reality; they are not reality – so in that respect there is no such thing as a true thought. If thoughts are not real, we don't need to believe any thoughts – we can just notice them and let them pass. We don't need to hold onto them or buy into them. We don't need to incorporate them into our world-view. When we believe a thought, that thought becomes part of our "reality", because it gets incorporated into our virtual inner-world. If we don't believe any thoughts our false "reality" gradually falls away to reveal true reality. Our virtual-world dissolves to reveal the real-world, and our false sense of self dissolves to reveal our true-Self.

Spontaneous Thoughts

Most thoughts seem to occur spontaneously; they just pop into our minds without any conscious intent to think them. They spontaneously arise from the mind's past programing in response to present events, and many of them are trivial, meaningless and unhelpful; e.g. labelling thoughts, critical thoughts, associative thoughts, reactive thoughts, and thoughts about other thoughts. These thoughts generally arise without us consciously deciding to think them, because it is the mind's nature to think, associate and remember. The areas of the mind that contain ego structures can only think, associate and remember things that are related to their programming and experiences. The free areas of the mind are much more objective, flexible and capable. The Self can use these free areas of the mind to consciously think, plan and analyse, but most of our thoughts don't consciously originate from the Self; they spontaneously originate from the ego-mind's past programming.

Identification with Thoughts

Often when we are talking, we are expressing our thoughts without consciously knowing what we are going to say – the words just seem to flow out. But because the words came out of our mouth we identify with them and we believe them. Identifying with everything we think, feel, say and do increases our identification with our ego-self. Simply noticing every thought, feeling, word, impulse and action increases our identification with our true-Self.

The ego identifies with the content of our minds (i.e. thoughts) whereas the soul is the space in which the content is occurring. This still and silent space isn't the absence of thought; it isn't the absence of mind; it isn't "no mind" – it is something completely different to mind. It is the soul; the true-Self's primary field of awareness; the ground of our being – it is who we truly are. And this is what we should be identifying ourselves with; not the content. Our thoughts, emotions and sensations are just passing phenomena that come and go – they are impermanent so they cannot be us, because what we are is eternal. What we truly are is beyond thoughts, beyond emotions, beyond sensations, beyond actions and beyond words.

The mind, heart and body are aspects of our being, but they are not the essence of who we are. The mind, heart and body are tools that we (our true-Self) can utilise for perception and expression. They are tools that enable us to interact with life, and as such they are tools that can help to develop our consciousness. But if we keep buying into our thoughts and keep getting caught up in our emotions, they will continue to run our lives and we will continue to suffer unnecessarily. For example, when we dwell on a thought we become identified with it and start thinking from its perspective. From the perspective of a vindictive thought we start thinking more vindictive thoughts. If we are not careful this vindictive positionality can develop into a grudge or a feud and create a lot of suffering for everyone involved.

In addition to identifying with our thoughts we generally also believe them. We believe that our thoughts, opinions and beliefs are true, and if anyone else's are different to ours, they must be wrong. Because we identify ourselves with our thoughts, opinions and beliefs, we consider alternative views to be a psychological attack on ourselves. Then we become defensive or aggressive, which strains our relationships and leads to more unnecessary suffering.

Easily Programmed

Our subconscious mind continually feeds our conscious mind with thoughts, feelings and impulses that our conscious mind assumes are its own. And our conscious mind continually feeds (programs) our subconscious mind with bad habits, illusions and fictions. So negative thoughts and fictitious concepts are continually recycled between our conscious and subconscious minds, which reinforces our ego. This vicious cycle can be only broken by continued awareness of our thoughts and feelings to ensure that we only give attention to (and reinforce) positive influences and dismiss the negative ones.

Every time we subconsciously repeat a particular behaviour we are reinforcing an ego structure. The stronger our ego structures become, the more difficult they are to overcome. Automated behaviours make us less conscious, and our goal is to become more conscious. By consciously behaving in a manner that is different to our normal pre-programmed ego reactions we can gradually re-program them. But this won't dissolve their structure – ego structures can only be dissolved through inner work.

Mental Overlay

When the ancient traditions talk about us living in a dream world, they don't literally mean that objective reality is a dream; they are talking about the subjective mind-created (imagined) inner virtual world that we live in (and project out over the objective real world).

Our mental overlay is the sum of all of our thoughts and beliefs about our self, other people and the external world. Even though our mental overlay isn't real, we make it our reality by continually feeding it with unchallenged false, distorted, judgemental and egocentric thoughts. It is our identification with our inner world that gives us our uniquely distorted view of life and makes us take life personally. We all see the world through our own unique, yet broadly similar, set of filters and distortions.

Our mental overlay changes our objective perception into subjective perception. It colours and distorts our expression and perception, turning objective reality into a subjective reality. Seven billion people look out into the same world yet we all see it slightly differently – we all see life slightly differently.

Blindly buying into our thoughts is one of the main factors that maintains our mental overlay. In order to free ourselves from this distorted and egocentric world-view we need to challenge our thoughts. We can't suddenly stop thoughts from arising but we can notice them, question them and stop buying into them. By consciously screening our thoughts and rejecting those that are reactive, egocentric and false, we not only disempower the thoughts, we also disempower our mental overlay. With ongoing awareness, the number and intensity of false thoughts will decrease, as will the influence of our mental overlay; allowing us to see reality more objectively and live more in the present moment (instead of being triggered by fear-based patterns from our past).

Running Commentary

Have you ever noticed a quiet voice inside your head that narrates the world for you? It labels people and objects; judges them and categorises them. We already know what it is because we have seen it, heard it or sensed it; so we don't really need our ego-mind to tell us what it is. So why does it do it? The ego-mind does this to bring the outside world into the inner realm of our mind. Basically, it re-creates the external world inside our mind by mentally labelling everything we encounter. Living in our mind's virtual world makes the world seem safer because an inner mental concept is more manageable, predictable and controllable than the real external world, but it distances us from reality and direct experience of life.

Our inner world will continue to be reinforced as long as we allow this narration to continue unchallenged. If we don't consciously challenge these narrative thoughts they will enter our subconscious mind and reinforce our inner virtual world. We must be careful not to actively resist our narrative thoughts because "what we resist persists". We just need to quietly notice them without giving them any conscious energy. Then they will have been noticed (with pure awareness) but not bought into or validated by the mind. Over time, our inner world will gradually soften to give us a clearer and deeper perception of reality.

Inner Critic (Super-Ego)

Whenever a thought contains a subjective judgement or comparison we can be pretty sure it comes from the ego-mind (not the authentic-mind). The ego-self is inherently unstable, so it needs to protect itself from threats. Anyone or anything that is better than you (or your things) is a potential threat. The ego-self has an early warning system to spot potential threats so that we can take action before they become actual threats. This dedicated ego structure (or part) is known as the super-ego or the inner critic.

In order for our ego-self to remain safe and secure we must feel confident, competent, intelligent, strong and in control, or at least give that impression to the world. If we don't do this our super-ego criticises us for putting our ego-self's "life" at risk. It is the super-ego's job to evaluate everything we perceive: to label it, categorise it, assess it and determine its level of threat (psychological and/or physical). The super-ego also evaluates everything we think, say and do, and it criticises us if we do not live up to its expectations. The super-ego's high standards are primarily based on the critical feedback we received as children; from parents, teachers and other authority figures.

We originally created our super-ego to spot potentially problematic behaviours in ourselves before our parents did. It was designed to keep us from getting into trouble with our parents, so we internalised their beliefs, standards and judgements. It helped to keep us out of trouble and keep us in their good books, so that we received more love and positive attention than we might have otherwise received. But as adults we have our own discerning mind and moral standards, so we no longer need the internalised beliefs of our parents.

Standards are necessary to maintain a civilised society, but the critical judgements that the super-ego attacks us with are totally unnecessary and unhelpful. Besides, the super-ego is often too late – criticising us after we have messed up, just as our parents did.

The ego automatically and subconsciously responds to super-ego attacks by repressing the attacked parts of the personality, like a victim hiding from a bully. The ego can never win an outright fight with the super-ego because it is far too strong and intelligent, and there is always an element of truth in its arguments and judgements. So we need to learn to deal with super-ego attacks in a different way – by consciously and intentionally inquiring into the mechanics of the super-ego to discover what triggers it and what its exact motives are. This can be facilitated by the "Changing Chairs Technique" that is described in Chapter 5. With conscious awareness we can also learn to respond appropriately instead of reacting inappropriately (and then criticising ourselves for doing so).

We need to remember that the super-ego is defending our false sense of self. The super-ego wants us to be all that we can be, but its strategy is fundamentally flawed. It wants to transform the ego-self into the true-Self because then it would be happy, free and eternal; but this is simply not possible. Our only hope of becoming all that we can be is to realise that we already are our true-Self. For this to happen we need to heal and reintegrate our exiled parts, but they will not reveal themselves while the super-ego is active. So working on the super-ego is an essential aspect of psychological and spiritual growth.

The Spiritual Super-Ego (a Self-like part)

As we become more awakened and spiritually aware, the super-ego becomes "spiritualised" and judges the rest of the ego as unspiritual. The spiritual super-ego is a part of the ego that is trying to be like our true-Self; hence the term "Self-like part".

Many spiritual people mistakenly believe that their super-ego is their true-Self. This can be a hindrance to their development because inner work is ineffective if the true-Self is not present. The spiritual super-ego will take us through the motions but no real work is being done. It is deluding us; we are deluding ourselves.

One method that can be used to gauge how much Self is present is to notice whether we are expressing essential qualities such as love, compassion and curiosity, but the Self-like super-ego can mimic these qualities quite convincingly. The only way to be certain that the Self is actually present is to feel its presence in our body. This is achieved by expanding our awareness into our entire body and feeling its palpable presence – it feels like a fullness or subtle energetic swelling. Presence in conjunction with essential qualities confirms that the Self really is present.

Mental Suffering

> "What disturbs men's minds is not events,
> but their judgements on events" – Epictetus

Happiness is determined less by our physical and environmental circumstances and more by what our mind tells us about them. The same applies to relationship issues – it is less about what the other person did or said and more about what our mind tells us about it. We would be a lot happier, and suffer a lot less, if we stopped buying into our thoughts. If we continue to allow our negative thought patterns, emotional reactions and conditioned behaviours to activate automatically, how can we expect anything to truly change? We can only create an optimum life for ourselves if we create some space for change. Doing the inner work to dissolve our ego structures literally creates the space for our true nature to unfold. Refer to Chapters 4 and 5 for further details.

Other Tricks of the Mind

Other common false or distorted thought patterns include:

- **Assuming & Expecting**: Assuming other people have the same standards, morals and beliefs that we have, and expecting them to live up to those standards (which they are probably not aware of).

- **Mind Reading**: Assuming that we know what other people are thinking; e.g. She would never go on a date with me.

- **Fortune Telling**: Assuming that we know what is going to happen in the future; e.g. I won't get that promotion.

- **Catastrophising**: Believing that our life will fall apart if something happens or doesn't happen; e.g. I won't be able to cope if he leaves.

- **Blaming**: Attributing someone else as the source of our issues; e.g. He made me so angry.

- **Jealousy**: Focusing only on people who are doing better than us (and ignoring everyone who is worse off than us); e.g. Why does she always succeed? It's just not fair!

- **Glass Half Empty**: Only seeing the "negative" aspects of our lives, and ignoring everything that is positive; e.g. health, family, friends, home, income, car, vacation, etc...

To overcome these negative thought patterns we simply need pure awareness, because consciously checking them stops them from being subconsciously reinforced, so they gradually lose their power.

The Emotions

Emotions can be compared to waves washing up on the shore – they come and they go, and they can be gentle or powerful. If we identify with an emotion (e.g. I am sad, as opposed to I feel sad) we will tend to hold onto it because we believe it defines us. If we hold onto a powerful emotion, such as anger, we become flooded with it and the emotion overwhelms us. If we hold onto a gentler emotion, such as shame, we tend to wallow in it. If we try to hold onto a positive emotion such as happiness, we will probably lose it quicker, because in the back of our mind we will be worrying about losing it. Holding onto any emotion is never a good idea, but nor is resistance. Emotions are natural responses and we must learn to feel them without resistance or identification.

Emotional Signposts

We need to learn to feel our emotions fully and then release them. Emotions are messages that guide us along life's path. They are signposts that keep us on track and heading in the right direction:

- **Positive Emotions**: e.g. joy, peace and love inform us (and reward us) that we are going in the right direction; i.e. our level of consciousness is going up.

- **Negative Emotions**: e.g. fear, guilt and shame inform us (and punish us) that we are going in the wrong direction; i.e. our level of consciousness is going down.

Negative emotions highlight the error of our ways, so they actually serve a positive purpose – they wake us up, turn us around, and get us back on track. It is only our identification with them that causes us to hold onto them and results in unnecessary suffering. With pure awareness we can feel our emotions and release them before we get caught up in them.

The True Source of Negative Emotions

When we feel anxious, the thing that we think we are anxious about is rarely the root cause. It is merely a trigger that activates our ego's inherent anxiety. The ego-mind projects our inherent anxiety onto an external cause so it doesn't have to look or feel into the true cause of our anxiety. The root of all anxiety is the "loss" of our true-Self. This typically occurs at age 6-8 months when we become identified with our ego-self and lose our connection with our true-Self. This momentous event fills us with fear, anxiety, regret, anger, self-hatred, depression, shame and grief. If you have children, you may have noticed a change in their behaviour around this time as they changed from pure beings into egocentric beings. We all hold all the aforementioned negative emotions within us, at the very core of our ego, but one or two will predominate. This means that some of us will be more susceptible to anxiety, while others will be more susceptible to anger, depression, shame or self-pity.

The True Source of Positive Emotions

When we feel happy, the thing that we think we are happy about is rarely the root cause. It is merely a trigger that activates our true-Self's inherent happiness. The ego-mind has to project our happiness onto an external cause because it cannot perceive the true cause (our true-Self). The degree to which we are affected by the creation of the ego-self sets our baseline level of happiness in life. The only way we can improve our baseline level of happiness is to re-develop our connection with our true-Self (and dis-identify from the ego-self).

To summarise: Positive emotions originate from the core of our true-Self, and negative emotions originate from the core of our ego-self. We generally try to avoid the core of our being because it houses the deep psychological pain, trauma and distress associated with the creation of our ego-self. For this reason the ego likes to look outwards rather than inwards, so it projects the cause of our emotional state onto external people and events.

Repressed and Trapped Emotions

Emotional energy can become trapped in the spaces between ego structures. Our field of consciousness (which contains our matrix of ego structures) closes and contracts in response to fear, anger and anxiety, and opens and expands in response to love, compassion and joy. Fear-based "negative" emotions cause our ego structures to contract, which traps the negative emotional energy inside. If we are constantly tense and stressed, the negative energy can remain trapped indefinitely. These blockages put our entire system out of balance and can lead to psychological and physical illness.

As children, many of us were taught to repress (not feel and not express) our negative emotions. We did this by stuffing them down into our belly, away from the heart and the mind, where they could not be felt and could easily be forgotten. Our repressed negative feelings keep trying to get our attention so that they can be released. But we don't want to feel them, so we resort to comfort eating, alcohol, tobacco, etc. to numb our uncomfortable feelings, or enjoyable activities to distract us from them.

Conscious fluid physical movements, particularly of the belly and pelvis, can help to loosen things up and allow the trapped emotional energy to dissipate naturally. Trapped emotions can also be released by techniques such as the Sedona Method™ and Release Technique™, which encourage the ego structures to relax. More forceful methods can also be employed such as catharsis (shouting and bashing), re-birthing (circular breathing) and holotropic breathwork. These techniques charge up the body with subtle energy, which forcibly discharges the trapped emotional energy.

Such releases can be very beneficial because repressing and holding onto emotions for extended periods of time is very unhealthy; resulting in stress, illness and disease. So releasing trapped emotions by any means is beneficial, but it is only part of the healing process. Once the excess emotional energies have been released, they will gradually build up again because the exiled parts and ego structures that create and trap the emotional energy are still there. The second stage of the healing process is to address the root cause of the issue (e.g. exiles, holes and ego structures) using the methods described later in this book.

The previously mentioned techniques do a wonderful job at stage 1 and often result in powerful emotional releases which provide welcome relief, but many of them ignore stage 2 – healing the root of the problem. The symptoms may have gone but the root cause remains – the exiles, holes and ego structures remain. These are the root cause of all our issues in life, and they will continue to cause us a lot of unnecessary suffering until we reintegrate these aspects of our being.

The Body (and Energy Body)

Primal Drives and the Id

We have a range of primal impulses and survival instincts that have not been discussed yet. They include the survival instinct, the social instinct, sexual libido, pleasure seeking/pain avoidance, immediacy, assertiveness and competitiveness. These instinctual drives are necessary for survival in a sometimes harsh physical world. These instinctual qualities are different to essential qualities because they have nothing to do with our soul; they are intrinsic qualities of our energy body (the energetic template around which our physical body develops). They originate from the belly centre (the nucleus of the physical-energy body) and are expressed primarily through the lower three chakras (base, sacral and solar plexus). They unfold during the first three years of life but some aren't fully activated until adolescence.

Just as essential qualities are transposed "downwards" from the soul into the personality, these instinctual qualities are transposed "upwards" from the energy body into the rest of the personality. If they unfold optimally they infuse the authentic personality with vitality, optimism and healthy instinctual drives. But if their unfoldment is disrupted these natural drives become distorted, which results in dysfunctional behaviour traits such as impatience, aggression, greed, selfishness, callousness or brutality. These dysfunctional (repressed or overly-expressed) drives are the aspect of the psyche that Freud referred to as the "id".

In the Soul Child section (on pages 44-45) I explained that if an emerging personal quality was not well-received by our parents we encased it in a repressing ego structure. We employ a similar mechanism to repress our primal impulses. If an emerging primal impulse was not well-received by our parents, we may have encased it in a repressing ego structure. The consequences are essentially the same as with the soul child; namely repressed energies seep out and adversely affect our behaviour.

Repressed primal impulses can cause people to become violent in an attempt to reconnect with their primal drives, and repressed libidinal energies can cause people to have affairs in an attempt to rekindle their repressed passion. If as babies we were forced to wait to feed (e.g. while a bottle of milk was prepared or because we were on a 4 hour feeding schedule), several of our primal drives could have been affected. Our impulses for survival, pleasure seeking/pain avoidance, competitiveness, assertiveness and immediacy could have all been repressed or distorted, resulting in anxiety, impatience, greed, frustration and/or anger. These distortions are so deeply rooted that they often stay with us our entire life. A frustrated feeding impulse can also create an energetic blockage in the mouth/throat, which can cause difficulties in expression, e.g. shyness or stammering. On a related note: The pleasure and nourishment we get from feeding can create an association that pleasurable things are good for us. This can further distort our feeding impulse and result in cravings and addictions.

The repression of a primal impulse can be partial or almost total. If it was almost total, we would have soon missed its functionality in our life. So we would have had to develop a coping ego structure to provide us with a false version of the repressed primal impulse. False impulses are never as effective as authentic primal impulses, so we had to keep increasing the power of the false impulse in the hope that it would eventually be effective. But if we over did it we would have been left with an out-of-control false impulse that would often trigger dysfunctional behaviour.

So unwanted primal drives are either repressed (by a repressing ego structure) or acted out (by a coping ego structure that is attempting to compensate for the repression). Both of these strategies prevent us from feeling the natural energy of our natural primal impulses. Being with a primal impulse and feeling it fully means that we don't have to repress it or act it out. Allowing a primal impulse to simply "be", without resisting it or expressing it, allows it to return to a state of balanced equilibrium.

Parental and Generational Influences

- **Conception**: The sperm and egg are not just physical – like us they also have energetic, emotional and mental counterparts. These subtle bodies are infused with our parents' traits and qualities, and they are absorbed into our own subtle bodies when we incarnate.

- **Gestation**: As the embryo grows within our mother's womb we are also influenced by her physiological and psychological state. Our mother's fears and anxieties in particular exert a strong influence on our developing subtle bodies – predisposing us to certain traits and qualities. These subtle energetic influences are reinforced by bio-chemical and hormonal influences through the umbilical cord.

- **Childhood**: Young personalities are very impressionable, so we commonly copy traits, behaviours, emotions and beliefs from our parents and other important people in our lives. If we don't like one of their traits (e.g. laziness) we may rebel against it and adopt the opposite trait (e.g. drivenness).

These parental influences didn't just affect us, they affected our parents, and their parents, and their parents, etc. so they are also generational. These qualities and traits can be processed in the same way that we process our own psychological material – refer to Chapter 4 for details.

Pain

Pain and discomfort are the body's way of alerting us to a physical problem, so that we can take action and heal it, but often pain has no physical cause. For example: 80% of back pain has no physical cause, 70% of stomach pain has no physical cause, and 60% of chest pain has no physical cause. So what are our bodies trying to tell us? Non-physical pain and discomfort are the body's way of alerting us to non-physical (i.e. psychological) problems so that we can take action to heal them. To put it simply, the body energetically records what the mind and emotions cannot handle during moments of intense psychological stress, fear or trauma. The body then sends us signals to remind us about our psychological wounds in the hope that we will heal them – restoring harmony and wellbeing.

The ego-self has a natural tendency to move our consciousness away from painful experiences, but unfortunately avoidance is the very mechanism that locks the trauma in place. Our nervous system tenses up and a piece of our consciousness becomes frozen with fear at the peak of the traumatic experience. This mechanism protects the rest of our consciousness from having to experience the full psychological force of the trauma. Our consciousness "freezes" the traumatic moment, which creates an energetic blockage in our psyche. This causes imbalances in our body, heart and mind, which can manifest as pain and disease.

Forgetting or repressing a trauma does not release the piece of consciousness that is energetically frozen in time; it remains trapped and separated from the rest of our being, continually reliving the trauma moment. The separated piece of consciousness yearns to be reintegrated again so it tries to get our attention by sending us a series of increasingly perceptible messages on the intuitive, mental, emotional, sensory, and eventually physical levels. The messages are subtle at first, but if we disregard them (as most of us do) they will get louder and coarser in the hope of eventually getting our attention. We commonly ignore or repress these messages because we are afraid to face our traumas head on. Sometimes we are so "deaf" that a message has to manifest as a serious disease in the physical body in order to get our full attention.

Whenever we encounter a situation in life that resonates with one of our existing psychological wounds our body reminds us of the original trauma with some subtle (or perhaps not so subtle) body sensations. These body sensations can also be triggered by simply thinking about a past trauma. The psychological blockage can be healed by reversing the mechanism that stored the trauma in the first place; i.e. by being fully present and really feeling the body sensations (and any associated emotions), rather than trying to avoid them. It can be acutely painful when cleaning out our emotional wounds, but it is chronically painful when we ignore them and allow them to fester for years.

What Eckhart Tolle refers to as the "pain body" is the collective energy/ consciousness/pain of all our wounded/exiled parts, and the negative emotional charge we hold within the matrix of our ego structures. Eckhart's method for healing the pain body is very similar to some of the methods described in this book, i.e. holding it in conscious presence. He calls this "The Power of Now" – for further details please refer to his book of the same title.

Pain Does Not Equal Suffering

We generally associate pain with suffering, but there are times when we feel pain but don't suffer (e.g. when we are happy or busy), and there are times when there is no objective pain but we still suffer (e.g. rehashing past events or holding grudges). Pain does not equate to suffering, and suffering does not equate to pain, so we must learn to recognise them as independent phenomena. It is true that sometimes we experience them together and sometimes there is a causal link, but generally pain is something that happens in the body and suffering is something that happens in the mind.

Pain is physical and suffering is psychological, which means that two people who are experiencing the same level of physical pain could be experiencing very different levels of suffering. This is due to their different levels of psychological resilience; i.e. their ability to deal with adversity. If we are overly identified with the victim parts of our ego we will suffer a lot. If we are more aligned with our Self, we will suffer less. This is because the Self simply notices things as they are, without labelling them as suffering, without wallowing in self-pity and without catastrophising.

The Buddha experienced intense back pain for much of his adult life, but he didn't suffer from it because he didn't resist it. Awakening and enlightenment are not about freedom from pain and suffering; they are about freedom in the midst of pain, then there will be less suffering. The "I" that experiences suffering doesn't actually exist; so does our suffering really exist?

Pain and disease are inevitable consequences of inhabiting a physical body. Most physical conditions occur in parts of the body where our awareness is not normally present (avoidance). Consciously focussing our awareness/presence on the troublesome area can provide some relief (because it demonstrates that we are not resisting it), and it may even heal it.

So if you are experiencing pain, really feel into it. That is the only way to fully accept the situation and stop resisting it. By "really feeling it" I mean feeling it with the presence of Self; not just noticing it with the mind.

The next step is a bit tougher – It involves loving the situation and being truly thankful for it. Being thankful that life has provided us with exactly what we need for our consciousness to develop. We don't need to understand the reasons from the personality / mind perspective; we just need to trust that our life is going to plan.

Why?

Why is life designed this way? Why is it so painful and challenging to be a human being? Because the Self/soul can experience, learn, develop and evolve in ways that would not be possible if it remained pure, whole and integrated. By becoming fragmented and limited the Self/soul becomes less capable and life becomes more of a challenge. It allows us to experience life from the perspective of a completely separate individual and it allows us to experience duality. This opens up new dimensions of experience, new opportunities for growth, and deeper understanding of ourselves.

So even though life may seem difficult at times, it is actually perfect (exactly the way it needs to be). Becoming "imperfect" for a while is "perfect" for the development of the Self. Our journey of Self-discovery, our reawakening, our return to wholeness is what life is all about – it is the meaning of life. So embrace life, welcome life, love life, live life fully and live life consciously.

Crisis Point

We may reach a point in life when nothing really satisfies us. We have "been there and done that" and learnt the hard way that achievement and acquisition do not bring us lasting happiness or fulfilment. Even the thought of achieving more or acquiring more leaves us cold, and we begin to wonder if we are ever going to find lasting peace, happiness or fulfilment. We become disillusioned with life as a sense of meaninglessness pervades our usual activities, and we don't even know what we truly want. We have reached a crisis point; where something in our life must change. It is during these challenging times that people often develop an interest in the transpersonal side of life, as they earnestly seek new meaning and purpose. Great transformations can occur during these unsettling times.

Transformation

Personal transformation is not the result of "doing" – it is the result of "being". Being present to whatever is occurring in our life – internally and externally. Transformation can only occur when we allow ourselves to be present with all the feelings that threaten and scare our ego. This requires us to develop the courage and curiosity to explore our inner world and truly get to know ourselves. Our outer world won't change until our inner world changes. We can move house, take a vacation, get a new job or find a new partner, but we will still be the same person – nothing will have really changed. We will still be on life's merry-go-round, not actually going anywhere.

Stuckness is the result of our inability to let go of the beliefs and behaviours that obscure opportunity from us. Life's difficulties are not obstacles on the path; they are the path. They are the challenges through which we experience, learn and evolve. Our development is slow when nothing new happens in our life, so we should regularly step out of our comfort zone, try new things and live life fully.

Accepting What Is

Everything that exists and everything that occurs has a fundamental rightness to it and is inherently perfect. I am not using the word "perfect" in the subjective sense (e.g. I think this is perfect); I am using it in the objective sense. From the perspective of the Self, everything in existence is complete and perfect, just as it is. Acceptance is absolute co-operation with "what is".

Complaining about things we cannot change is a waste of effort, and not acting when we can change things for the better is a wasted opportunity. This sentence may appear to contradict the previous paragraph about everything already being perfect, but inherent perfection does not mean that everything has to remain static and unchanging. Life is a journey after all, and every step is perfect. Life isn't passive; it requires activity and engagement. Life isn't static – change is required for consciousness to evolve. When change is occurring, change is "what is". Every moment of life is perfect because every moment is a perfect opportunity for our consciousness to develop.

Chapter 3: **Human Potential**

Introduction

We come into this world with nothing and we leave it with nothing, so it is pointless trying to acquire lots of material possessions while we are here. Our material balance sheet is always zero at the start of our life and it is always zero at the end of our life, and no one is ever going to change that! But it is a different story with our spiritual balance sheet. If we end our life with a higher level of consciousness than we began with, then we have had a successful life. Adding to our spiritual balance sheet by developing our consciousness is the one purpose that remains the same in each and every lifetime, no matter who we are.

All living beings possess an inherent drive to evolve, to become the highest possible expression of life and to fully realise themselves. Psycho-spiritual development is the wilful co-operation with this natural process. Consciousness only develops through experience; it does not develop through theoretical learning. For example, seeing the word "fear" in print is not the same as experiencing it first-hand – this is why we incarnate.

Life is all about developing our primary field of consciousness (our soul). The soul is pure awareness imbued with a range of essential qualities, so purifying our awareness and developing our essential qualities are the meaning of life:

- **Pure Awareness** is the perceptive quality of the Self/soul. Even though pure awareness is intrinsic to our true nature, it can still be refined. More refined, subtler and purer consciousness has two major benefits: (1) Clearer perception of higher/subtler dimensions of reality. (2) Fuller, richer and more objective life experiences. Awareness is refined through inner work, meditation, practicing presence, conscious living, etc.

- **Essential Qualities** are the expressive qualities of the Self/soul. Even though essential qualities are intrinsic to our true nature, they can still be developed and refined. The more developed our essential qualities are, the fuller, richer and more direct our interaction with life is. Essential qualities are developed by embodying them, expressing them and being them. During our childhood, our soul's essential qualities were transposed into usable personal qualities. Due to the intimate unity between the soul and the personality, any personal qualities that we develop and refine during this lifetime are immediately paralleled in our soul's essential qualities. Better-developed essential qualities transpose more easily and effectively into personal qualities in our next incarnation. This will (probably) result in a better life next time around because we will have more authentic personal qualities and less ego structures.

Skandhas: The Seeds of the Ego

"Skandhas" is a Sanskrit term meaning "aggregates". Skandhas are the seeds of our ego structures from our past lives. They predispose us to certain mental, emotional and behavioural traits, so consequently shape our general character and outlook on life.

Ego structures "contain" our psychological issues. The issues that are not fully resolved in a particular lifetime are stored as skandhas so they can be addressed in a future lifetime. When our subtle bodies dissolve at the end of an incarnation, the ego structures are converted from actuality into potentiality; i.e. the structures dissolve but their informational patterns are stored in skandhas. Difficult childhood experiences in a subsequent lifetime (that resonate with a stored pattern) transform that potentiality back into actuality. So basically, our skandhas influence how our ego structures and character develop.

At about 6-8 months old we all go through the same distressing psychological event: ego-formation (when our awareness shifts from the true-Self to the false-self), but we all handle it differently. The way we psychologically deal with this (e.g. feeling imperfect, afraid, unloved, etc.) is heavily influenced by our skandhas – our general disposition to life.

Part of the reason why young children are so psychologically vulnerable is so that their skandhas can be reactivated to create an ego that broadly resembles the ego from the last lifetime. Childhood is essentially setting us up psychologically where we left off last time. Skandhas give the Self/soul continuity between incarnations, allowing its development to continue where it left off last time. Not all of the skandhas from previous lives are reactivated in each incarnation – it depends what the soul is here to experience and learn. But eventually they will all need to be reactivated and resolved.

Death and Reincarnation

Our fear of death is not just a physical fear; it is also a fear of the ego dying. When our physical body dies the ego doesn't immediately die. The ego is a complex blend of thoughts, emotions and energies, and they gradually peel off and dissolve layer by layer (as if we were getting undressed for bed). The physical body is shed first, then the energy body, then the emotional body, then the mental body (which includes our mental concept of self) until all that remains is our soul body (or causal body). We generally "sleep" for a few hundred years before beginning our descent into a new physical incarnation. During the descent, most moderately developed souls are involved in making choices and decisions about their impending physical life.

The first "garment" we put on during our descent is the mental body, then the emotional body, then the energy body. The energy body temporarily merges with the energetic template of the new physical body sometime after conception. The Self (in the soul body, mental body, emotional body and energy body) comes and goes while the physical body grows in the womb, but the Self does not "permanently" merge with the physical body until birth.

In the first few months after birth, all the bodies are incredibly authentic and pure because they have not been "polluted" with ego structures. The skandhas (seeds of the ego from past lives) gradually get reactivated by early life experiences and act as catalysts in the development of the ego. Our skandhas and childhood experiences combine to develop an ego that perfectly meets our soul's developmental needs.

Why Do We Need An Ego?

Life is a drama in which part of our true-Self gets lost. But this is all part of the learning experience; there is nothing wrong with it – it has to be that way. The fact that it is that way means it has to be that way. The ego will naturally be relinquished when the soul has experienced and learned all it can from this set up. Trying to rush things, striving to become free, struggling to awaken only slows the soul's progress. It is proof that we haven't yet learned what we need to learn from ego-identification. So just relax and go with the flow – live life and enjoy it – because you chose it – you chose to come here and experience this life!

The ego is a natural and necessary stage in the development of human consciousness – there is nothing wrong with it or bad about it. It has served us well for many years and has got us to where we are today. It served us particularly well when we were very young and found it difficult to cope in an unpredictable, confusing and sometimes distressing world.

The ego was initially formed from very young consciousness, and much of it is still very young today. All the exiled parts remain at the age they were when they were exiled, and many of the coping structures remain at the age when they were first formed. So the ego is not an enemy that must be vanquished; it is a collection of innocent isolated parts of us that yearn to be reintegrated into the wholeness of our being. These parts must therefore be treated with great care and compassion.

When the Self has experienced and learned all it can from the separate and limited perspective of the ego, it will begin the process of dissolving the ego and awakening to wholeness. This is a natural process and there is nothing we can do to make it happen – we can only cooperate with this natural process by following the two-fold path.

The ego is a tool that the Self uses to develop its consciousness, just as a book is a tool that a reader uses to develop knowledge. There is nothing the book can do to make the reader more knowledgeable, and there is nothing the ego can do to make the Self more evolved. Inner work is not about making changes happen; it is about creating opportunities for healing, reintegration and growth to occur naturally.

We judge a book or a movie by how engrossed in it we become. It is the same with life – it is most successful when we engage with life and live life fully. But there comes a time when we start getting a bit bored with life; when we start to realise that it isn't really that engaging any more. This could be a sign that we are awakening to the possibility of a new way of being?

Awakening From The Ego

The part of us that wants to awaken is the ego (because the true-Self is already awake). But the ego is just a thought-form; it is a false entity, so it cannot wake up to true reality. The ego's desire to awaken is futile and impossible because its dream can never become reality – we have to awaken *from* the dream in order to see reality. Nothing we do within the dream has any effect on the real world. It is not until we stop striving (within the dream) that we can wake up and realise that we are in fact the dreamer – the Self; not the ego.

The only reason the ego wants to awaken and become enlightened is because it thinks this will end its suffering. The spiritual quest is just another of the ego's long list of strategies to end its suffering. The ego is inherently unhappy and it desperately seeks relief, so it tries everything it can in the material world to try to find happiness. When those strategies fail, the ego turns its attention to psychology or spirituality to try to find happiness, but they won't achieve the desired success either. The only strategy that will work is for the ego to get out of the way – to step back and allow the Self to come to the fore.

So by all means, set your intention to become enlightened but don't try too hard, because striving comes from the ego, and it reinforces the very thing that we are trying to dis-empower and dis-identify from. So forget about the quest and just enjoy the journey. The only thing that is really important in life is to live the life we have now. If we rush towards enlightenment we will never get there, because we won't have learnt the most important lesson of all: We need to forget about our self in order to find our Self.

Self-Image

We all have a self-image; a conceptual view of who we think we are and how we want to be seen. A self-image may include our appearance, our clothes, our behaviour, our intelligence, our work ethic, our fitness, our sense of humour, our sensitivity and our spirituality. No matter what our self-image is, it takes a lot of effort and energy to maintain, and it creates a lot of anxiety and suffering when we don't live up to our self-imposed ideals. So why do we do it? Basically, we believe that maintaining our self-image makes us happy. And without it we would feel vulnerable and exposed, and maybe even worthless.

Our self-image is driven by our attachment to things that we believe will make us happy, and our aversion to things that we believe will make us unhappy. They key word here is "believe" – we are back to false and distorted beliefs again. If being rich truly makes people happy, why aren't all rich people happy? If being successful truly makes people happy, why aren't all successful people happy? If being attractive truly makes people happy, why aren't all attractive people happy? Because none of these things are sources of genuine happiness – the happiness they provide is hollow and short-lived. And while we continue to chase these external fixations, authentic happiness will continue to elude us.

When our actual image changes slowly (e.g. growing old), our self-image has time to adapt, but if our actual image changes quickly (e.g. in an accident), our self-image conflicts with our actual image, which causes a lot of suffering for the ego-self. If we must have a self-image it is important that we keep it up-to-date, otherwise it will lead to a lot of unnecessary suffering. For example, holding onto a youthful self-image drives people to Botox® and facelifts as they desperately try to keep their actual image close to their desired self-image.

Our self-image doesn't just apply to our physical characteristics. If, for example, we have a successful self-image we will suffer when we fail, and if we have a spiritual self-image we will suffer when we are seen to be unspiritual.

A self-image is like a label that we apply to ourselves to define who we are, but it is also a standard that we must live up to. When we fail to live up to our self-imposed standards our super-ego attacks us, which may leave us feeling angry or deflated. A self-image can only ever lead to one thing – unnecessary suffering; so it is in our best interests to let go of ours. A self-image is not necessary – it is who we think we are; not who we actually are. So we don't lose anything by dropping our self-image; we actually gain something. Without a self-image to live up to we gain the freedom to be ourselves; without any labels, standards or limitations. We don't have to "do" anything to be ourselves; we can just "be" ourselves. Dropping our self-image is the first step in freeing ourselves from the virtual inner-world that we live in (and project out over the real world). Letting go of our virtual-self allows us to discover our true-Self.

So how do we let go of our self-image? Through present moment awareness. Whenever we become aware of a self-centred thought or emotion (e.g. I am good looking or I am happy) we can discard it by saying to ourselves "that's not me". This stops us from identifying with it, buying into it and perpetuating our (false) self-image. All "I" thoughts and emotions are false because we are not thoughts and we are not emotions – we are pure consciousness. So even if we have an IQ of 155, the thought "I am clever" is still false. "I am expressing intelligence" or "I am experiencing happiness" are more accurate, but there is still no point in expressing what we already know. Labelling and commentating on our lives keeps us in our heads, perpetuates our virtual world and stops us from experiencing life directly. So we ideally want to avoid all "I" thoughts, labelling and mental narration. The only "I" thought that is 100% true is "I am" (as in I exist), which can actually help us to connect with our true-Self.

If we have a particular image of our self that we want to present to the world, be it a spiritual person, a geek, a hippy or a bad-boy, our ego will want to defend that self-image. While we remain defended, we will continue to hide certain parts of our personality and falsely exaggerate others. This keeps us from accepting our true nature, which keeps us from being our true-Self.

A Taste of True Nature

Take a moment to close your eyes, go within and contemplate your self-image. Allow yourself to sink below it and you will probably discover that there is nothing there – just a spacious field of emptiness (but a whole-emptiness rather than a deficient-emptiness). There is no self-image; there is only pure beingness. Many people would rather hold onto their false sense of self than feel this "no sense of self", but it is actually very pleasant and soon feels like home. It is a relaxing space in which we don't have to "do" anything; we can just "be". It is pure beingness – beingness that is content within itself. It doesn't have to do anything, be anyone or present a façade to the world; it just "is".

The Façade of the Persona

All self-images are just concepts of ourselves that we create and hold in our minds – they have no inherent reality and they are not who we truly are. Our true nature is whole, complete, perfect, happy and fulfilled. We are all these things and more; we have merely forgotten. Because we don't know who we truly are, we create a façade of who we imagine ourselves to be. Without a true sense of self, we create a false sense of self; a false self-image.

Our false sense of self is inauthentic, which leaves us feeling unsettled and insecure. We don't know who we truly are and we can't feel who we truly are because we have lost our connection to our true-Self. One of our strategies for dealing with this psychological instability is to create a persona to present to the world so that no one else can see how lost and insecure we feel on the inside. We usually try to hide our insecure and inadequate feelings by presenting a façade of confidence, capability and control.

The persona that we present to the world is the outermost layer of our ego, which is where our consciousness is focused most of the time. We work hard to polish our persona so that we are seen how we want to be seen, but there is no depth to it – it is just a shallow and superficial façade. Many of our relationships are shallow and superficial because the relationships are between two false façades, not two authentic Selves. We can let down our façade and reveal our authentic personality simply by being authentic and deep, instead of superficial and shallow.

What are we trying to Protect?

The Self cannot be hurt or wounded; it is immortal and indestructible, so it doesn't need to be protected. It is the false self that is unstable (because it is just a thought-form), so this is the part of us that needs psychological protection.

Figure 18 is an image from Chapter 1 that has been re-labelled to more clearly illustrate the arrangement between our true-Self, false-self (ego-self) and self-image. Our self-image is a mind-created concept of who we think we are. Part of our Self becomes identified with our self-image, i.e. believes it is the self-image, thus creating the ego-self. It is our identification with our self-image that keeps it (the thought-form) from dissolving. When our self-image is shaken, our ego-self feels threatened and may fear for its existence. So we protect our self-image in order to keep our ego-self feeling safe and secure.

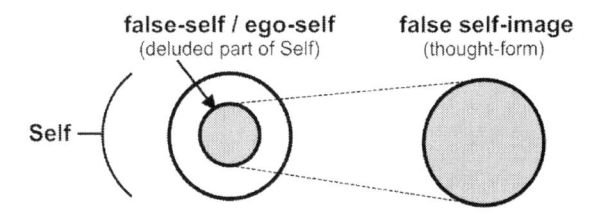

Figure 18: The ego-self's identification with the false self-image

When someone offends us or puts us down, the ego has to respond (automatically react) to reinforce the self-image thought-form. The ego may also launch a counterattack on the aggressor to weaken their self-image and redress the balance of power. These psychological defence mechanisms are triggered in order to maintain something that isn't even real – our concept of who we think we are. These defence mechanisms are responsible for much of our unnecessary suffering in life, and it is all self-inflicted (ego-self-inflicted). Our self-image is not really the problem because we need a sense of self to live in the world and interact with other people. The main problem is our over-identification with our self-image. Our intense belief that we are our self-image makes it seem more real than it really is.

Ego Ideal

In addition to our self-image, we also have an ideal self-image of who we aspire to be – this is our "ego ideal". Like our self-image, our ego ideal is just a thought-form. Our ultimate goal in life is to realise our ego ideal –

to become our ideal, whatever that may be. The problem is that in trying to reach our ideal we are separating ourselves from our present reality. We are not living in the present moment and we are rejecting who we are right now. In short, we are so focused on "becoming" that we have forgotten all about "being".

Not being happy with "who we are" makes us want to be something else, which is why we create goals and ideals. We would be better off living in the present, being who we are right now and accepting ourselves as we are right now. At any moment we are "who we are" – there is no need to be anything different – we are already perfect, complete and whole.

If we don't accept who we are right now we are bound to feel inadequate and deficient. It is this sense of inadequacy that fuels so many of the ego's neuroses (as described in the last chapter). If we can't accept who we are right now, how can we ever expect to know true happiness, peace or contentment?

Soul-Identification and Self-Realisation

The development of the human consciousness spans thousands of different lifetimes. The entire journey can be broken down into 5 distinct stages, each of which is characterised by a different identification:

1. **Body Identification**: During the "primitive stage" of the soul's development it is primarily identified with the body.

2. **Lower-Emotional Identification**: During the "cultured stage" of the soul's development it is primarily identified with negative emotions.

3. **Higher-Emotional Identification**: During the "developed stage" of the soul's development it is primarily identified with positive emotions.

4. **Thought Identification**: During the "humanistic stage" of the soul's development it is primarily identified with thoughts.

5. **No Identification/Soul Identification:** It is not until the "enlightened stage" of the soul's development that it fully awakens to its true nature and transcends all identification with the personality.

Self-realisation occurs naturally when sufficient ego structures have been dissolved to allow the Self to dis-identify from the ego and realise its true nature. Sometimes this occurs prematurely (when many ego structures are still present), in which case it will only be a temporary state because the influence of the ego structures will soon pull the person back into ego-identification. This is most likely to occur at the transition from the "developed stage" to the "humanistic stage" because emotional identification has lost much of its grip and mental identification has yet to become firmly established.

The Truth about the Soul

Just as the ego-self is a misidentified part of the true-Self, the ego is a collection of misidentified parts of the soul. The ego is soul consciousness that believes it is mind consciousness, emotional consciousness and/or body consciousness. Because the soul consciousness believes it is these "lower" forms of consciousness it also takes on their limitations. If, for example, a piece of soul gets bound up in an exiled part, the piece of soul will believe it is traumatised and exiled. If a piece of soul gets bound up in an ego structure, the piece of soul will believe it is constrained by inflexible automated programming.

Psychologically it can feel like the misidentified piece of soul is missing (i.e. a hole), but it is not. It has simply forgotten that it is soul because it is misidentified with an exiled part. It still has all of its essential qualities but it cannot utilise them because it has forgotten it is soul. When the piece of soul wakes up to the truth that it is (and always has been) soul, the "missing" essential qualities are immediately rediscovered.

The above process affects souls at all levels of development but the degree of dis-identification with true nature and mis-identification with psychological "objects" is greater in less-developed souls. This explains why less-developed people are more likely to get caught up in rigid beliefs, overwhelming emotions and habitual behaviours. It also explains why they are not interested in psycho-spiritual development – they have little or no sense of their true nature, so why would they be interested in pursuing it?

More-developed souls generally have a stronger connection with true nature and are less identified with psychological "objects". This means they are better able to dis-identify from "objects", connect with their true nature and awaken to wholeness.

Evolution of the Soul

If you place a sponge in a bowl of water, the water infuses the sponge and becomes one with it, but the water is not changed by the sponge experience. The process is slightly different for the soul: The soul merges with the "object" it experiences, but the soul's essential qualities are developed and refined by the experience. The soul evolves as a direct result of metabolising its experiences.

Conscious awareness is the focal point of our Self's consciousness, so things that we experience with full conscious awareness make more of an impression on our soul than things that we experience with only partial awareness. Life makes more of an impression on our soul when we live consciously, so we experience more and our consciousness develops faster.

Conscious living (in the now) is so beneficial because the greater depth of experience provides more nourishment for the soul and thus promotes spiritual growth. New and challenging experiences nourish the soul more than repeat experiences (things we have experienced before). Processing exiles, holes and ego structures is especially nourishing for our soul, not just because it provides intense experiences, but because it also liberates and reintegrates misidentified pieces of our soul.

Our soul experiences everything; even things that we are not consciously aware of. So the soul does evolve through semi-conscious and sub-conscious experiences, but to a lesser extent than it does through fully conscious experiences. The soul experiences less and develops less when our awareness is not focused directly on the experience, because less soul is present to have the experience.

The soul experiences less and therefore develops more slowly when it becomes identified with "parts" (e.g. exiles and ego structures) because less "free" soul is present to have the experience. Each piece of soul that is identified with a part forgets that it is soul, so its experiences are not fully conscious. Its experiences are also less clear because they are diminished, distorted and coloured by its identification with the part.

The benefit of identification is that the soul gets to experience life from many different perspectives, which increases its <u>breadth</u> of experience.

But its <u>depth</u> of the experience is reduced due to the fact that its experiences are not clear or fully conscious. So a misidentified soul requires more time to acquire the necessary depth of experience, which means it develops at a slower rate. Living consciously in the present moment increases our presence and awareness, which optimises our soul's rate of development.

Happiness

The one thing that we are all seeking in life is happiness. We might say that we are seeking fame, fortune, success, sex, excitement, adventure or spirituality, but all of these things are just strategies to find lasting happiness. None of these things actually make us happy; it is the value we put on them that makes us feel happy or not. If, for example, we put a high value on relaxation, a weekend at a luxury spa will make us feel happy, but if we put a high value on excitement a spa weekend will feel very boring. If "things" were genuinely a source of true happiness the effect would be universal (i.e. everyone would enjoy the spa weekend). But it doesn't work that way – happiness from "things" is not objective, it is subjective; it is based upon the value that we assign to them.

Life is a constant search for happiness but we rarely find anything that lasts. We are all looking for the same thing but we are going about it in different ways. We are all looking for happiness in different places, but all the different places share one thing in common – they are outside of ourselves. When we look outside of ourselves for happiness, our level of happiness will go up and down like a rollercoaster in response to external events. We can never achieve lasting happiness while we continue to look outside of ourselves because we can't control what Life sends our way.

Throughout our evolutionary journey we have tried just about every strategy imaginable and searched almost everywhere in our quest for true happiness. We have had some great experiences and learnt a lot along the way, but we have never found what we are searching for. Eventually, we grow tired of searching and turn our attention to the one place we haven't looked so far – inside ourselves.

True happiness is not something that can be sought and acquired; it is our soul's natural state of being and we can only connect with it by going within. We cannot connect with our inner happiness while we are busy looking for happiness externally. We cannot connect with our inner happiness while we are trying to do, achieve, feel, heal, fix or change anything. We can only connect with our inner happiness when we drop all that doing and just "be" (abide in the inherent joy of our true nature). We discover a deeper, longer lasting and more fulfilling kind of happiness when we stop trying to make ourselves and our lives different, because authentic happiness is not dependant on external conditions or feeling good emotionally.

We will not find authentic happiness by making it our goal ("destination happiness"); we will find it by appreciating the journey (our present moment experience of life). Life is a journey, not a destination. So we need to slow down and enjoy the ride rather than madly rushing to get "there" (wherever we mistakenly believe happiness can be found). True happiness can only be found right here (within us) and right now (in the present moment).

Even if our present moment circumstances are not particularly pleasant we can still connect with our inner happiness, but only if we don't allow ourselves to get carried away (from here and now) by external circumstances. Authentic happiness is all about being present; it is not necessarily about being emotionally or externally happy. Authentic happiness is experienced when we embrace everything that life sends our way. We can never attain lasting happiness if we are always screening life – clinging to the "good" and rejecting the "bad".

Our lives will not transform just because we read something inspiring or have a peak experience. Such things may change our thoughts and beliefs about life, but a new life cannot manifest until we address the deep-seated conditioning of our ego structures. A new life may begin in the mind with a new outlook on life, but until it filters down through our heart and into our body nothing much will change. A new life requires a new way of being – being in our body and feeling life fully (good and bad). It requires us to feel our reactions to life in our bodies in the present moment, without any judgement or agenda. Instead of trying to eradicate our flaws we must embrace them, because developing an intimate relationship with every aspect of our being is our only hope of reintegrating our being and awakening to wholeness.

I Am Entitled To Be Happy

We all generally believe that we should be happy, we believe that we are entitled to be happy, and we believe that something must be wrong if we are not happy. If we feel sad we do things to stop ourselves from feeling the sadness, and if a friend feels sad we will try to cheer them up. The ego does everything it can to try to control life in the hope that we can always feel good and avoid feeling bad. If the ego's strategies fail it will blame the sadness on some external cause and wallow in victimhood. The ego can feel justified in believing it has been wronged (even if this increases our suffering), because any amount of suffering is better than being judged a failure (by our self or others). For the ego, failure is not an option because it invalidates the ego's reason for being.

While we remain identified with the ego it is inevitable that we will sometimes feel a victim of life's circumstances. This is a false view of life because we are actually agents of Life – we are agents through which Life flows. This involves embracing (not resisting) everything that Life sends our way; be it "good", "bad" or indifferent. We must learn to take responsibility for everything that Life sends us because it is what our soul needs for its development.

I Would Be Happy If...

There is no doubt that many subjective experiences in life do make us feel happy, temporarily. The ego extrapolates this view into a (false) belief that if one good thing in my life makes me a little happy, then lots of good things in my life will make me very happy. This eventually develops into a belief that if I can make everything in my life "just perfect" then I will be very happy forever. The only flaw with this ego strategy is that it cannot control everything in life! It can't even control its own thoughts, so what hope does it have at controlling the whole world and everyone in it?

Holding onto the false belief that "I would be happy if..." gives the ego hope. Hope that one day all of its striving and struggling will eventually pay off, but it never will. The ego has followed this strategy for countless lifetimes and dropping it would mean that the ego is a failure for wasting countless millennia on a futile strategy. So the ego holds onto the hope that things will be better in the future, rather than actually living the life that we have right here and now.

After the ego has tried all the material and sensual paths to happiness, it will eventually try the spiritual path. Not because the ego is spiritual, but because all the other paths have failed and spirituality or religion are all that remain. So the ego wastes many more lifetimes searching for happiness and fulfilment from some external God or saviour (there are plenty to choose from). During this period, the ego holds onto the (false) belief that "if I pray hard enough or meditate long enough, then I will be happy". This ego strategy is just as futile as all the others because once again the ego is looking in the wrong place. It is not until we look within, to the very core of our being, that we will discover the true source of authentic happiness.

False Beliefs and Expectations

Our authentic happiness is blocked by our (false) belief that life is not how it should be; i.e. how we want it to be. This unfulfilled false belief gives rise to negative emotions – the negative emotions make us feel uncomfortable – the ego equates the discomfort with unhappiness – so the ego tries to alleviate the discomfort by seeking happiness elsewhere. But the discomfort is only a symptom; it is not the root cause – the root cause is the false belief that life must be how we want it to be. The expectation that accompanies this false belief sets us up for failure, disappointment, frustration, anger and unhappiness.

Our expectations of other people also affect our happiness. Let me give you an example to clarify the point. If we had a partner who took us for granted, we would probably feel a bit sad. But if our partner was very loving and attentive, we would probably feel very happy. It is not our partner's actions that make us feel happy or sad – it is our beliefs and judgements about their actions that determine how we feel:

- We believe that our partner should demonstrate their love. When we see evidence of their love, we feel loved. When we feel loved, we feel happy.

- We believe that our partner should demonstrate their love. When we don't see evidence of their love, we feel unloved. When we feel unloved, we feel sad.

It is all too easy to blame our partner for our sadness but the common denominator in both of the above examples is "we believe that our partner should demonstrate their love". If we dropped that false belief we could be happy whether our partner demonstrated their love or not.

When we create expectations of other people and they fail to live up to them, we feel disappointed, sad or angry. People rarely live up to our expectations because they are our expectations, not theirs. They are our standards, not theirs. We are expecting them to live their lives according to our standards – standards that we may not have even communicated to them. If we really loved them, we wouldn't impose our standards on them; we would give them the freedom to be themselves. That is true love; that is unconditional love.

Some other common false beliefs that block happiness include:

- Believing we have to control everything in order to be happy.
- Believing we have to change in order to be happy.
- Believing other people have to change in order for us to be happy.
- Believing other people are responsible for our happiness.
- Believing external circumstances are responsible for our happiness.

Initial Judgements and Secondary Attacks

We often compound our suffering by judging unpleasant emotions as bad. By equating an uncomfortable feeling with suffering we become a victim, and victims suffer. For example, if we are feeling anxious we will judge it as unpleasant (the initial judgement), then we will identify with the unpleasantness (the secondary attack), which adds to our suffering. So we double our suffering by negatively judging our feelings.

With conscious awareness we can catch the judgemental thought and prevent the secondary attack. If we don't buy into the thought that anxiety is bad, the secondary suffering cannot manifest.

Is It Happening Right Now?

The mind loves to rehash the past and worry about the future, but this can adversely affect our happiness in two ways:

1. We can't access our true-Self's inherent happiness unless we are fully present, and we can't be fully present if we are rehashing the past or worrying about the future.

2. Our inherent happiness is masked by the unhappiness that we create through moaning, judging, blaming, worrying, fantasizing, regretting, over-analysing and over-planning.

It is almost impossible to stop our mind from thinking because thinking is its nature, and it is difficult to change what our mind thinks about (e.g. past or future) because our thought-patterns are often deeply rooted in our subconscious. But with conscious awareness we can screen our thoughts and decide whether to buy into them or not. So when we are afflicted by unpleasant or unhelpful thoughts about the past or future we can consciously decide to not buy into them and remind ourselves that it is not happening right now.

What Is Blocking My Happiness Right Now?

Happiness is an inherent quality of our true nature. Happiness is always present within us, but our perception of it is blocked by psychological material, in much the same way that clouds block our perception of the sun. The sun is always there but we can't always see it, and happiness is always there but we can't always feel it.

We can ask ourselves "What is blocking my happiness right now?" Don't put too much emphasis on the mind's answer; instead focus on how your body is responding. Scan your body for anything that feels unsettled, unnatural or uncomfortable (e.g. pressure, pain, blockages or emotions) and allow yourself to feel it fully, without trying to change it or make it go away. Surrender to it and relax into it, without any resistance. If there is physical discomfort, breathing into that area may help (i.e. imagining your in-breath flowing into the area). Doing this simple practice for a few minutes a few times a day can have a profound effect on our lives.

Cultivating Happiness

The secret to being happy is to _be_ happy; to actually embody happiness. Just smile and notice what happens – you are instantly happier. Being happy requires us to be happy with everything just as it is; right here and now. If we can't be happy now we can never be happy, because _now_ is the only time there is. Our physical body might live for 100 years, but the only time we actually live is in the present moment. Life is a seamless series of present moment experiences, and it is up to us to live them. To be happy in the present moment we must stop resisting life and stop trying to make everything the way we think it should be. When we embody happiness, express happiness and keep choosing happiness, it becomes our natural way of being and connects us with our true nature.

It's Not Personal

The ego-self is in the habit of taking everything personally. It over-identifies with everything it perceives, and in doing so it confuses its sense of self with the "object" it is perceiving.

Emotions are the most polarised aspect of our being; i.e. they carry the most charge. So the more emotion we experience the more difficult it is to keep things in perspective and remain objective. The more emotion that accompanies an experience the more we identify with it and the more we take it personally.

Our thoughts and emotions feel very personal and very unique to us, but actually we all have similar things going on inside of us, so they aren't really that personal or unique. We all have similar exiles and ego structures, so we all see things in broadly the same way. We are all living in the same world, walking similar paths, having similar experiences and reacting in similar ways. So is life really that personal? From an objective point of view it all seems pretty generic and universal.

We can learn to take things less personally by expanding our outlook and seeing life as an integrated universal process, rather than a purely personal experience. Life is a vast, impersonal, universal process that doesn't belong to any one individual. Life happens and we are simply someone experiencing it. Seeing life from this impersonal viewpoint gives us the space and perspective that can help us to avoid getting too caught up in personal issues.

The more we can de-personalise our experiences, the more we will dis-identify with our ego. A simple way to do this is to not think "I am happy" (or sad or angry or whatever), but to simply notice "I am experiencing happiness". By not identifying with the emotion we are not confusing our sense of self with it. By simply noticing that we are experiencing an emotion, our experience is less personal and our sense of self remains clear. Our experience doesn't change, but our relationship to the experience changes radically. We change our perspective from the feeler (ego-self) to the witness (true-Self).

When we cultivate a more accepting relationship with our experiences (i.e. they become less personal), we will also find that we are better able to cultivate more accepting relationships with other people.

Striving

We often try very hard to succeed, but don't fully intend to succeed. Consciously we may want to achieve something, but subconsciously other parts of us want us to fail, so they subconsciously sabotage our conscious efforts. We strongly believe that we want to succeed, but deep down we are afraid of success. We all have subconscious parts with conflicting interests, energies, wants and desires that pull us in different directions. Unless all the aspects of our being are united and aligned we will probably never achieve our full potential, no matter how hard we try.

Striving does not work, because it creates "distance" between where we are now (in the present) and where we what to be (in the future). This temporal distance causes impatience, anxiety, self-criticism, self-pity, etc. To achieve our full potential we have to stop striving and relax into our being.

"Becoming" is the natural unfoldment of "being". Becoming occurs in the present moment (in a seamless series of present moments), so there is no temporal distance between being and becoming. Life is the seamless series of present moments in which we can simultaneously "be" and "become".

If we live our lives consciously in the present moment we will be aware of every step we take along life's path. But if we focus only on the destination (the future) we will feel anxious and impatient because we will have lost sight of where we are right now (the present moment). But more importantly, an unconscious life is not a full life, so we will experience less and therefore develop less. Striving to develop actually slows our progress, so forget about the destination and enjoy the journey – and before you know it you will be here.

Wanting

Whenever we want something, we generally start suffering. We tell ourselves "I will be happy when I get what I want". We are basically telling ourselves that we cannot be happy or contented until we get what we want. We believe that getting what we want is the only way we can end the discomfort of wanting, and if we believe that, that is what we will experience. But even if we get what we want it won't satisfy us for long, and we will soon want something else. Wanting doesn't just apply to material possessions; it applies to wanting to be seen, heard, understood, respected, loved, wanted, attractive, successful, famous, rich, enlightened, etc.

The happiness that we associate with getting what we want actually has nothing to do with getting it – we are happy and contented because we don't "want" anymore. We have incorrectly associated happiness with getting what we want, but actually it is "not wanting" that makes us happy. We are happy because the burden of wanting has been temporarily lifted.

The Self is whole, so it wants for nothing and is always happy. The ego-self, on the other hand, wants because it feels inadequate and lacking. The ego is trying to make up for its feelings of lack by acquiring things – hence all the wanting. External things cannot actually fill an internal hole – it is the value we put on these things that satisfies us, for a while at least. But when we realise that these things don't actually have any meaningful value, the illusion quickly wears off. Rather than learning from this experience we still mistakenly believe that something else will satisfy us, so we keep making the same mistake over and over again.

Wanting is a sense of lack, and "getting" is the ego's way of avoiding that sense of lack. Being comfortable with the lack/wanting is the first step in realising that there is no lack. It is a way of connecting with our Self, who knows no lack. So don't try to resist or repress your wanting – if you want something: feel the wanting. Then you may discover that you don't have to get what you want in order to feel good.

We feel good when we stop believing that wanting is bad and getting is good. We feel good when we simply allow the wanting to be. We feel good when we simply allow ourselves to be. It is the inner turmoil we create around wanting and getting that keeps us from feeling our inherent happiness and contentment.

Everything we truly want, we already have in abundance. We don't truly want a big house, a fast car, lots of money and our perfect "soul-mate" – what we truly want are the good feelings that we associate with having these things (e.g. peace, happiness and contentment). No matter what we think we want, what we all ultimately want is peace, happiness and contentment. We already have these essential qualities in abundance because they are aspects of our true nature; we have just lost sight of them. Wanting is a natural process that can help us to rediscover these "lost" essential qualities, but only if we really feel the wanting (and assign less importance to actually getting).

Wanting doesn't have to be a thread that we must follow until we get what we want. If we break the link that we have created between wanting and getting, we can simply allow our wanting to be; without feeling compelled to do anything about getting it. If we sit in our field of wanting and just "be" we will discover that everything we truly want is already present within us. When we break the link between wanting and getting, we discover a new link between wanting and already having. So don't try to deny your wants, and don't try to satisfy your wants – just feel them and discover that you already have what you truly want. Like everything else in life, wanting is a direct invitation to discover more of our true nature.

Unlike the ego's wanting, the soul's wanting is not motivated by fear and lack; it is driven by a longing for wholeness and unity. The soul can sense its own potentiality and has a natural desire to transform that potential into reality. This authentic wanting is what drives authentic psychological and spiritual development. In contrast, the ego's "spiritual" wanting (e.g. psychic powers and abundance) leads us away from the authentic path and impedes our authentic development.

Motivation

If our motivation for personal or spiritual development is to ease our personal suffering and feel happier, we may achieve some short-term success, but we won't succeed in developing our consciousness. If our motivation comes from the ego-self we will never succeed. In order to succeed the motivation has to come from the true-Self and it has to be for a higher purpose. We will only succeed in our development when we are not doing it for personal gain. We will only succeed when we align ourselves with the universal goal – the evolution of consciousness as a whole. When our personal will is aligned with universal will we cannot fail to succeed.

In the grand scheme of things our personal insecurities, fears, worries and problems are insignificant. The universe exists for consciousness to develop and evolve, and it can do that through any medium. The personality is the medium that the Self uses to develop its consciousness (the soul). So the personality doesn't have to be perfect from a subjective point of view, but it is always perfect from the soul's point of view (i.e. it perfectly fits the soul's current developmental needs).

The evolution of consciousness is so slow because different parts of us often have conflicting interests and motivations. Consciously we may want to grow and evolve, but the wounded parts of us that we have exiled or repressed don't want us to move on because they don't want to be left behind. This can adversely affect our motivation to do the inner work. We make occasional efforts to overcome our negative patterns, but most of the time we continue feeding them (usually subconsciously). Without presence and conscious awareness our progress will be slow.

Our journey of Self-discovery is partly motivated by our soul's natural desire to evolve and partly motivated by our ego's desire to be free from suffering. The ratio largely depends on our overall level of development (i.e. how far along the path we have travelled), but it also varies from moment to moment depending on our personal circumstances.

Once we realise that the evolution of consciousness is our very purpose for living, we have discovered the meaning of life. This "knowing" activates a latent drive within us – a drive to realise our true-Self and to clear whatever prevents us from doing so. It awakens our curiosity to uncover our subconscious psychological material and activates the courage we need to face it.

Resistance

On the face of it the ego wants to develop and grow – it wants to become all that it can be. But deep-down the ego knows that psycho-spiritual development will eventually result in its dissolution, so it subconsciously resists. Basically, part of the ego wants to evolve (because it is suffering) and part of the ego wants to stay the same (because it is safe and known). This makes our journey of awakening much more challenging than we might imagine. But the ego gets off on hard work – it gets off on "doing" because it doesn't like "being". And while we are busy "doing" we are probably not "being", which keeps us identified with our ego-self and not our true-Self. So the ego's resistance prolongs its existence.

The ego's resistance cannot be tackled head on. The more force we exert against the ego, the more it will resist. The ego's resistance can only be overcome with a passive, non-confrontational approach. We have to gently bypass the ego's defences rather than launching a full-frontal assault. If we don't threaten the ego, it won't feel threatened, so it won't resist as much.

The most effective way of gently overcoming the ego's resistance is to become supremely conscious – to bring all of our subconscious psychological material into the light of our consciousness. Practices such as self-inquiry, meditation, body-awareness and conscious living all help with that. Once we make our subconscious material conscious it loses much of its power because the conscious mind will not allow detrimental subconscious patterns to be acted out unchallenged.

Suffering

The true-Self is an active agent in the natural unfoldment of Life – it actively goes with the flow of Life. The false-self, on the other hand, resists the natural unfoldment of Life and tries to manipulate Life to its own selfish and short-sighted ends. If seven billion egos actually had the power to directly manipulate Life, life on Earth would be a living hell. Fortunately, Life isn't so easily swayed, and the consequences for trying to control Life are suffering. I am not talking about some external karmic punishment; I am talking about self-inflicted suffering that is the result of resisting "what is". It is comparable to a little boy having a tantrum when he doesn't get his own way – his suffering is entirely self-inflicted.

We can end our suffering right now – we just have to drop our beliefs, stop believing our thoughts, stop buying into our emotions, stop trying to control everything, stop reacting to everything, and stop resisting everything. In short, we have to drop everything we think we are, because none of it is who we truly are. All these things are ego and we are Self.

Our entire self-image is wrong: "who we think we are" is just a figment our imagination, and we aren't completely sure that "who we really are" actually exists. We are blind to our true-Self because we are so identified with our false concept of self. To awaken to our true nature we have to give up our (false) concept of self. We have to let go of "who we think we are" because it is not who we truly are. We cannot discover our true-Self until we drop our identification with our ego-self.

We have to at least be open to the possibility that we are not who we think we are; that we may have got it wrong for all these years. We have to be open to the possibility that things may be different to how we think they are. We have to be open to the possibility that we may know absolutely nothing about the true nature of our Self or reality. Unless we open ourselves to these possibilities we have zero chance of awakening to wholeness.

Life can be compared to an ocean wave – we can be carried along almost effortlessly on the crest of the wave, or we can be dragged along in the wake, kicking and screaming and struggling to keep our head above the water. The crest of the wave is the present moment, and to ride it requires conscious active engagement with Life. If it weren't for the ego's resistance we could be living on the crest of Life's wave all the time, instead of struggling and suffering unnecessarily.

Acceptance

Acceptance is more likely to bring about a shift than resistance, because acceptance allows things to move on, whereas resistance causes them to stand still. Acceptance means fully experiencing "what is" without any resistance, judgment, analysis or agenda. When our consciousness is fully experiencing "what is" without any resistance, judgment, analysis or agenda, we are fully present. When our consciousness is identified with something that we are experiencing, we are not fully present. When we are fully present there can be no resistance, because resistance comes from the ego. When we are fully present there is no ego; only Self/soul.

Acceptance means we don't have to be anyone or do anything – we can simply "be". This type of radical acceptance can be challenging for some people because "not doing" can be confused with being lazy, passive, fatalistic or giving up on life, but the only thing we are giving up is our ego's resistance.

Acceptance doesn't mean that we have to be a passive victim; nor does it mean that we have to fight back aggressively – the world is only black and white to the ego. If we are genuinely present our Self will intuitively guide us as to what approach is required. When we stop strategising, struggling and resisting we can tap into the intuitive guidance of our Self. When we stop listening to the ego we are better able to hear the silent voice of our Self. Acceptance allows us to transcend the thinking mind and enter into the non-conceptual world of direct knowing and direct experience.

The more we practice being present, especially when life is challenging or boring, the easier it becomes to accept Life without resistance. The problem is never with Life (Life is perfect); the problem is with our perception of Life (we are just not seeing the inherent perfection of Life).

Life's Inherent Perfection

Life is the dynamic unfoldment of potentiality into actuality. Life unfolds as it interacts with Self. Life animates each individual Self, so we are all one, but we are also individual.

Life is a dynamic process that moves with grace, direction and purpose. Each moment of Life gracefully follows that direction and is attuned to that purpose. So each moment of Life is inherently perfect, no matter what the ego-self may think about it. Whenever we resist Life we are separating ourselves from the perfection that is unfolding.

Life is a journey not a destination, so where we are right here and now is far more important than our final destination. Wherever we are on our journey right now is perfect – perfect for our soul's development. Striving to get "there" or attain enlightenment takes us away from Life's inherent perfection in this present moment and it takes us away from <u>our</u> inherent perfection in this present moment. When our attention is focussed on the past or the future we are depriving our soul of the perfect experiential growth opportunity that is right here and now.

"What Is" Is Meant To Be

If we want to awaken, we must stop resisting "what is", i.e. let go and allow life to unfold naturally in this very moment, without analysing it, judging it, resisting it or trying to control it. This doesn't just apply to the present (what is); it also applies to the past (what was) and the future (what will be):

- **The Past**: Believing (in the present moment) that a past event shouldn't have happened or was wrong is resisting "what was". Changing the past is impossible, so resisting the past is futile – it can only result in unnecessary suffering. The same is true of continually rehashing or regretting past events. Accepting what has happened is the only way to find peace.

- **The Future**: Manipulating matters (in the present moment) to affect the future is resisting "what will be". Putting all our efforts into trying to manipulate one particular future is a big gamble – if it comes off we will be happy for a while, but if it doesn't we will be disappointed for a lot longer.

Whatever has happened, is happening or may happen doesn't have to be judged as good or bad. Be it pleasant or unpleasant – "it is what it is" and it is meant to be that way. If we judge it as "good" we will be sad when it ends, and if we judge it as "bad" we won't be happy until it ends. But more importantly, judging implies that we want everything to be good and nothing to be bad. This sets us up for more unnecessary suffering because we can't control life enough to make that happen – Life simply happens.

If we put all of our effort into trying to achieve something and it happens, it doesn't mean that we have succeeded; it just means that it was meant to be that way. If we put all of our effort into trying to achieve something and it doesn't happen, it doesn't mean that we have failed; it just means that it wasn't meant to be that way. No matter how life turns out it is exactly how it is meant to be. Life gives us the experiences that we need for our development. What actually happens in our lives is meaningless (from a cosmic perspective); it is what we get from the experience that counts.

Trust (or Faith)

When we resist Life by saying "this should be happening" or "that shouldn't be happening", we are trying to limit Life's infinite potential. We are sanctioning only one outcome out of countless possibilities, and in doing so we are setting ourselves up for unnecessary suffering:

- **"Success"**: If things turn out how we wanted, the ego takes all the credit and puffs itself up with pride. This strengthens our ego, which is detrimental to our development and prolongs our unnecessary suffering.

- **"Failure"**: If things don't turn out how we wanted, the super-ego judges us a failure and we feel bad. This weakens our ego, so we have to reinforce it through some other egotistical behaviour. This too is detrimental to our development and prolongs our suffering.

The only way to stop resisting Life is to trust it – to be open to Life, with an open mind and an open heart. With trust we can learn to accept "what is" without any judgements agendas or strategies, to fully feel "what is", and to be grateful for "what is". We may have no idea why life is leading us along a particular path, but we don't need to know. When we have an open heart and an open mind, we are open to the truth of reality. We are open to perceiving objective reality instead of the subjective overlay that we usually project out onto the world. We are open to perceiving "what is" rather than trying to control everything.

Complaining about our circumstances only increases our suffering because we are expressing our resistance and putting it out into the world. We are trying to turn a subjective opinion into objective reality. The more "reality" we give it, the more we will suffer. It is healthier to simply notice and feel whatever is happening within us (in response to life's events) because that demonstrates our acceptance of Life and our trust in Life.

In biblical times, trust was called "faith", and Life was called God. God is not a being that controls the universe; God is the dynamic process that is the universe unfolding, so that consciousness can evolve through direct experience.

Gratitude

Gratitude is very important because it demonstrates that our acceptance and trust are total. It demonstrates that we know Life is doing its best so that our consciousness can evolve.

It is easy to feel thankful or grateful when something good happens, but are we supposed to feel grateful when something bad happens? Are we supposed to feel grateful when we are bored? Are we supposed to feel grateful when someone annoys us or insults us?

- **Yes**: If we are not grateful for what we have and how things are, we must want things to be different. And resisting "what is" inevitably leads to unhappiness and suffering. Gratitude takes acceptance to another level – it is not merely accepting "what is"; it is being truly thankful for "what is"; it is being truly thankful for Life.

- **No**: If we tell ourselves that we should be grateful we are just creating another thought-form that will block us from our true-Self. So gratitude has to be authentic – it has to come from the heart – it cannot be forced. If we don't feel like being grateful to Life it means our consciousness is currently caught up in an ego structure. But if we go within and connect with our soul, we can connect with all of our essential qualities, including gratitude.

Gratitude is not something that many of us do, but practicing gratitude on a daily basis can help us to connect with our soul's essential qualities (even those that haven't been transposed into usable personal qualities).

Proponents of Positive Psychology suggest that we should review our day each evening and identify three things that we are grateful for. They can be specific things such as enjoying lunch with a close friend, or general things such as being grateful for waking up in the morning or getting through the day. Gratitude also gives us a more positive outlook on life – focusing on the positive helps us to align with our soul, whereas focussing on the negative keeps us rooted in the ego.

If we stop judging, we can be grateful for everything and make gratitude a way of life. Gratitude gives us a bigger perspective on life, it allows us to experience the full spectrum of life, and it enables us to find genuine happiness that is not dependant on external circumstances.

Life's Challenges

Our reactions to challenging events and challenging people show us where we are stuck. When difficult people "push our buttons" they show us our reactive behavioural patterns; they show us what we still need to work on. So instead of getting angry and resentful we should really thank them and love them.

We have a choice to keep feeding the reactive behaviours that block our happiness or, with conscious awareness, we can catch these patterns before they take hold of us. We have a choice to see difficult people and situations as opportunities for growth (ultimately resulting in genuine happiness), or we can wallow in self-inflicted pity or stew in self-created anger. You decide.

As long as we continue to hold onto ego-based expectations about how life should be and how other people should behave, we are setting ourselves up for a life of disappointment and unhappiness. If we drop our expectations and actively accept what life sends our way, then we can be happy. We can learn to live our lives with child-like curiosity, fully engage with life in the present moment and be truly thankful for all of our experiences. Or we can keep trying (in vain) to make things go our way, keep worrying about what might happen if they don't, and keep feeling bad when they don't. Again, it is your choice.

Destiny (Our Chosen Life Path)

Our destiny is not the product of our past – our past actions do not propel us into the future; our past actions hold us back and impede our development. It is the potential energy of what we have chosen (our intent) that creates our destiny and leads us through life.

Our choices create a "vacuum" in front of us that pulls us along our chosen life path. It is in this "void" of pure potentiality that our life unfolds. We have already chosen our destiny (prior to this present moment), so now we must let go and allow it to manifest in this eternal present moment. I don't mean that we should just sit back and passively wait for a new life to fall into our lap. We have to engage with life in the present moment to ensure we don't miss life's opportunities for growth.

Our past actions and our old limiting beliefs prevent us from achieving our full potential. The parts of us that are stuck in the past (exiles and ego structures) are the resistance that hinders our development. In order to move forwards freely we need to heal the parts that are holding us back.

Free-Will

Our approach to life can influence our destiny but we cannot directly control what Life sends our way – we simply decide how we are going to respond to it. This is where our free-will comes into play. But just how much free-will do we really have if we live most of our life on autopilot? Will is not free if it is bound by the effects of our conditioned behaviours. Will is only free if we have sufficient conscious awareness to use it in a considered manner. Without conscious awareness we cannot respond, we can only react.

Will is an essential quality of the soul. If that aspect of our soul is ego-identified we will not have access to our essential-will; we will only have access to the ego's mentally constructed version of will (false-will). False-will is rigid and stubborn, and is better suited to resistance than positive action. False-will is based upon the ego's fears and coping strategies, which often conflict with Life (universal will). We can consciously exert our will to work with the natural flow of Life, or we can consciously exert our will to resist the natural flow of life, or we can unconsciously sit back and do nothing:

- A wise fish actively swims with the flow and makes great progress.
- A stupid fish actively swims against the flow and gets nowhere (except very tired).
- A sleeping fish passively goes with the flow, but learns nothing because he is asleep.

The development of consciousness requires awareness <u>and</u> action (will). Getting the balance right requires continuous awareness of the subtle changes in Life's currents. When we become attuned to Life and actively engage with it, our lives open up with a sense of flow, ease and grace. Grace occurs when we allow Life to naturally unfold within us and flow through us without any resistance.

Will is not a force to be exerted upon the world. There is no outwards expression of true-will or trying to make things happen. True-will is the firm yet flexible ground on which our true being stands. It is from this unshakable core that our intention flows through us in full alignment with Life.

Intention is consciously committing to how we are going to live our life. Every morning, we can simply state our intention to evolve spiritually, psychologically, creatively, intuitively, peacefully and patiently into an awakened and enlightened being. Once our intention has been set, we must drop any agenda about how or when it will occur. We must drop all investment in the outcome and leave that up to Life.

Karma

Karma is a Sanskrit word meaning action, but it is generally understood to mean the consequences of our actions. The word karma is commonly used to indicate bad karma and the word merit is often used to indicate good karma. The Law of Karma is often described as "cause and effect", because every action (or cause) has a corresponding consequence (or effect).

Ego structures are one of the main mechanisms through which karma operates, in two ways:

3. Human Potential

1. Ego structures are the primary <u>cause</u> of our bad karma; i.e. they are responsible for the "bad" behaviour that generates bad karma.
2. Ego structures are the mechanism through which we experience the <u>effects</u> (or consequences) of our bad karma; i.e. our unnecessary suffering is the result of our ego structures getting triggered.

Suffering that results from ego structures is unnecessary because it is not directly related to the Self's evolution. The Self may choose to experience "suffering" (e.g. a terminal illness) in order to grow and evolve – this is necessary suffering – it is not karma.

- The Self's chosen path through life is the optimum path for the development of our consciousness. It is fast and direct, taking us only to the places that we need to go. And provided we learn from our experiences we won't need to go there again. It involves only the pain that is necessary for our growth (no more, no less).

- The ego's path through life is slow, indirect and repetitive. It results in lots of unnecessary suffering – suffering that we bring upon ourselves as a consequence of choosing the ego's path. Now there's a great definition of karma: the suffering that we bring upon ourselves as a consequence of choosing the ego's path.

Karma is not divine justice or retribution. It is not "an eye for an eye" or "what goes around comes around". Karma is the universe seeking to restore balance, but not in the way that people commonly think. Karma is stored within us, by us. Karma is the stuff that we choose to hold onto (beliefs, stories, justifications, principles, thoughts, emotions and hurts). This is the mechanism by which karma is stored. Karma manifests as a result of our negative emotions and thoughts (e.g. fear, shame, guilt, anger, regret, hatred, loathing), not towards other people, but towards our self. If we let go of all this stuff, we can be free. If we fully accept and fully forgive ourself we can be free.

The thing that makes a murderer feel the subconscious need to be murdered in a future lifetime is his own subconscious guilt, shame and regret. He mistakenly believes that he can only forgive himself once he has suffered the same fate as his victim. But it doesn't have to be that way. If the murderer can heal his own guilt, shame and regret with loving-acceptance then there is no need for him to suffer the same fate. He has already learnt his lesson – the easy way. The hard way involves all the unnecessary suffering that we subconsciously impose on ourselves. The continuing cycle of: victim > attacker > victim > attacker, etc. The hard way doesn't actually restore balance; it just keeps the pendulum of karma swinging from one side to the other. Balance is only truly restored when all the negative beliefs and emotions associated with our actions have been neutralised. Please note: I am not in any way implying that all murder victims must have been murderers in past lives; I am merely using a scenario to illustrate one of the main mechanisms of karma.

The Root of All Evil

The world is the perfect environment for the development of human consciousness. Everything that occurs in the world happens for a reason, and that reason is the development of consciousness. So we should stop resisting life, stop judging everything, and stop wanting things to be different, because it is all perfect and it all serves a higher purpose. Everything, no matter how wrong or evil it may appear to be, happens for a reason and that reason is the development of consciousness. The ego-mind can rarely comprehend the intricate reasons why "bad" things happen, so it resorts to judging, blaming and condemning.

Evil behaviour is the result of highly disturbed ego structures. Ego structures are the result of childhood traumas and confusion. Traumas and confusion are the result of the innocence, immaturity and incapacity of our young consciousness to deal with challenging events. So the origin of evil is innocence!

We can't go back a generation and blame our parents for inflicting our childhood traumas because they were the product of their parents and their childhood. And their parents were the product of their parents and their childhood, and so on... So ultimately there is no one to blame. We simply have to take responsibility for our own lives, our own behaviour, our own impulses and our own actions.

While I am on the subject of "evil", I will take a few moments to explain about heaven and hell from a psycho-spiritual perspective:

- **Hell** is the world of the sub-conscious. We descend into the depths of our sub-conscious to release our exiled parts from their eternal suffering, and reintegrate them into the wholeness of our being.
- **Purgatory** is the world of ego consciousness. We spend most of our time in this semi-conscious world of lust, gluttony, greed, sloth, wrath, envy and pride (the seven deadly sins). This is the world we are attempting to awaken from.
- **Heaven** is the world of the super-conscious. We ascend into our super-conscious to connect with and realise our (divine) Self. This is the world we are attempting to awaken into.

A New Way

Before we ever feel the compulsion to look within we first have to exhaust all the external sources of peace, happiness and fulfilment. It is only after we have tried them all and have learned (the hard way) that they don't satisfy us for long that we can eventually call off the search. It is only after we have exhausted every other avenue that we can finally stop striving, strategising and resisting. Only then can we accept life fully and relax into our true being.

It seems that we have to discover "who we are not" before we can discover "who we are". The more familiar we become with our inner terrain, the more we will come to realise that nothing actually needs fixing, because we are not actually broken — we have just forgotten that we are whole.

Our conscious awareness is used to being focused at the periphery of our being, because it has been outwardly focussed for thousands of lifetimes, so it takes time to re-orient our awareness inwardly. Our true-Self resides at the very core of our being, beneath all the subconscious layers of psychological material that we have repressed over the years. Our inner world can seem like a labyrinth at first, full of dark and scary places that we don't really want to go. It can seem very challenging but it is all part of the process of Self-discovery. Demonstrating that we have the courage to face our shadow side is an important milestone on our path because it shows that we are truly ready to awaken.

When we look within we don't immediately awaken to our true-nature or instantly achieve lasting peace, happiness and fulfilment. First we have to explore the inner terrain of our psyche, to discover and dissolve the psychological material that impedes our pure awareness and pure expression. We have to become aware of our reactive psychological patterns and overcome them. We have to get to know our soul and align ourselves with it. We have to learn to stop resisting and trust life. This inner quest can take many lifetimes, so patience, perseverance, courage and curiosity are required. Even then our progress will be slow and we will keep slipping back into the ways of the ego. We need to remember that we are attempting to undo the habits of thousands of lifetimes in only a handful, so it is important not to try to rush or put pressure on ourselves to succeed, because these ego strategies will lead us away from our true-Self.

We achieve our full potential by allowing our consciousness to unfold naturally through living consciously (being), and by proactively working with that natural process (becoming):

- **Being** is where we are on Life's path, right here and now. It is the inherent perfection of the present moment. It is our own inherent perfection; just as we are, and it is Life's inherent perfection; just as it is.

- **Becoming** is the natural unfoldment and evolution of consciousness that comes from proactively engaging with Life. It is our inherent perfection becoming even more perfect. It is the living journey.

Western spiritual people tend to be more focussed on "becoming", i.e. striving to improve themselves and get somewhere. Eastern spiritual people tend to be more focussed on "being", i.e. being content with where they are spiritually. These are our natural propensities, so we may need to focus on the opposite one to ensure our development remains balanced. Western people often need to slow down and relax into their being, while Eastern people often need to become more proactive rather than just sitting in blissful meditation or devotional prayer.

If we focus purely on "being" – being content with ourselves and our lives exactly as they are, then things will stay the same. If we focus purely on "becoming" – becoming awakened or enlightened, then we will never achieve it, because there will always be distance between us and our goal. Our approach to life must involve being and becoming. Our goal (becoming) is the dynamic unfoldment of consciousness that continually manifests in the present moment (being). We are perfect just as we are right now, and we will always be perfect whatever we become in the future. By "perfect" I mean the perfect psychological and spiritual configuration for the development of our consciousness; I do not mean subjective perfection.

Being and becoming can be compared to surfing the crest of a wave (of life). We are standing still (being), yet we are moving through life (becoming), and it is almost effortless. The flow of life carries us along in a seamless series of present moments.

The ego is generally dragged along (kicking and screaming) in the wake behind the wave of life. The ego is reacting to life (after it has happened) rather than engaging with life (as it happens). The ego is trying in vain to control events that have already happened; it is trying to change what has already happened. This is why the ego suffers so much – because all of its struggling, striving and resisting are futile.

There has to be a better way, and there is. The ego-self just needs to step back and allow the true-Self to take care of things. The true-Self is an instrument of universal will and a channel through which Life can flow without resistance. Without resistance there is nothing to prevent our intention from becoming our reality. When we align with Life all the different parts of us become aligned (like iron filings in a magnetic field) and stop pulling us in different directions. All of a sudden we are living in the flow of Life; we are living in grace.

We are all unique so we all choose different paths through life, none of which is better or worse than any other – everyone's path is perfect for them. We all choose to journey at different paces, and fast isn't necessarily better than slow. Everyone's pace is perfect for them because we have all the time in the world. However, each of us does have an optimum path and an optimum pace, and it is up to us whether we choose to live it. All it takes is conscious living – living in the present moment with pure awareness, absolute acceptance and total trust.

Chapter 4: **Personal Development**

Introduction

Personal development means "growing up" psychologically, i.e. freeing ourselves from the childish, defensive and reactive ego programming that keeps us from living fully consciously. Personal development is the journey of perfecting the authentic personality. It involves mastering (not repressing) our thoughts, emotions and bodies to free ourselves from the fears, insecurities, conditioned behaviours, reactive emotions, critical judgements and limiting beliefs that keep us from living happy, peaceful and fulfilling lives. This is achieved by dissolving the "negative" psychological material (exiles, holes and ego structures) that keep us trapped in these old patterns and prevent us from moving forward. Michelangelo tirelessly chipped away all the unnecessary marble to reveal his masterpiece – David. We must do the same to reveal our own inner beauty.

The methods of personal development described in this book do not involve reprogramming, reinforcing or rebuilding our ego structures, as is common with NLP (neuro-linguistic programming), affirmations and some forms of coaching and psychotherapy. Such methods avoid the root of the issue and strengthen the ego – which is the exact opposite of what is required. The primary purpose of personal development is the healing and reintegration of exiles, holes and ego structures. The more ego structures we heal and reintegrate, the more objective our perception becomes and the more authentic our expression becomes.

Personal development is not about worldly success; it is about on inner worldly success – peace, clarity, harmony, love, joy, compassion, creativity and authentic expression. It is about clearing the obstructions that impede the natural unfoldment and development of essential qualities in our personality. As we clear our ego structures we make space for essential qualities to unfold, and in doing so we become more authentic – more of who we truly are. Of course, a well-integrated personality is also very effective in the external world, which can result in worldly success – but that isn't why we do it; that is just the icing on the cake. There are five main elements to personal development:

1. **Personal Self-Inquiry** is getting to know and understand our false-self, ego structures and patterns of behaviour so that they can be healed and reintegrated. It is typically done as a standalone practice or therapy, but it can also become an integral part of our life (see point 4).

2. **Body Awareness**: Feeling the blockages, structures and holes in our psyche (with the presence of our soul) to allow our authentic personal qualities to unfold. The associated ego structures then naturally dissolve because they are no longer required.

3. **Healing & Reintegration**: Healing our relationships with our exiled parts (the parts that hold us back and keep us in the past) and re-integrating them (and their associated ego structures) to return our consciousness to wholeness.

4. **Conscious Living**: On-going present-moment awareness to identify the pre-programmed reactive patterns that keep us on autopilot, keep us half-asleep, keep us reacting childishly, keep us from moving on, and keep us from living life fully. It is "live" self-inquiry – identifying issues as they arise in our daily lives so that we can feel into them or inquire into them and then heal and reintegrate them.

5. **Embodying Essential Qualities:** Actively encouraging more of our soul's essential qualities to unfold in our personality. This is achieved by actually embodying the qualities we wish to develop. For example: if we want to be more loving, we have to become the embodiment of love and actually be more loving. Consciously choosing to be more loving aligns us with the loving presence of our Self/soul and allows it to filter down into our personality.

There is a considerable degree of overlap between these five elements of personal development. There are also many similarities between this material and the transpersonal development material in Chapter 6. The one thing that unites and underpins all the material in this book is the Self/soul – in particular its pure awareness and intimate presence.

Intimate Presence and Pure Awareness

Carl Jung wrote in *The Undiscovered Self*, "You cannot solve a problem with the same level of consciousness that created it". The ego is a mind-created "problem", so it cannot be "solved" by the mind. We have to use a higher level of consciousness – the pure awareness of our soul (our Self's primary field of consciousness). It was the absence of presence and pure awareness that resulted in parts of our consciousness being exiled and their associated ego structures being created. Our young and innocent personal consciousness simply did not have the capacity to cope with these distressed parts, so we exiled them out of conscious awareness. Being with these parts fully (i.e. giving them our full presence and awareness) is all that is required to heal the separation and reintegrate them back into our being. We are simply doing now what we couldn't do at the time of the original distressing event. This type of healing only works if our awareness is <u>pure</u> (i.e. no agenda, judgement or fixing) and our presence is <u>intimate</u> (i.e. no resistance, avoidance or suppression).

Alice Bailey wrote in *Esoteric Healing* "cures are brought about [when] the soul pours through to the point of concentrated awareness". This means that the healing process is activated by simply focusing our soul's presence and awareness on the appropriate area of our body. The soul's presence has to intimately merge with the part (exile, hole or structure). Merely putting our awareness on the part is not enough because there is still separation. Healing and reintegration can only occur when there is intimate contact; when the Self/soul and the part become one.

Exiles, holes and protective ego structures are "negative" thought-forms bound up in "negative" emotions and "negative" energy (note: coping ego structures are generally just thought-forms). The thought-form is the core of the "part" but that is not what holds it together or gives it life. The thing that holds a part together and brings it to life is a piece of our soul – a piece of soul that has become misidentified with the part – a piece of soul that believes it is that part and has forgotten it is soul.

The presence of the rest of our Self/soul is absolutely vital for the healing and reintegration process because its intimate union with the part allows the misidentified piece of soul to reunite with the rest of our soul (causal body). Without the piece of soul to hold it together, the part dissolves and its constituent elements reunite with the mental body, emotional body and energy body.

Discovering and Practicing Presence

Presence is fundamental to personal development and transpersonal (spiritual) development, and it is a pre-requisite for most of the practices and techniques described in this book. Presence has a palpable feeling – it feels like a subtle energetic swelling or presence within the body (or part of the body). It has a sense of fullness; like something within us is expanding and trying to get out. This pretty much describes what our soul is doing – manifesting more fully within us and coming to the fore.

Presence requires us to be present spatially (right here) and temporally (right now). Presence requires us to "be" – right here, right now. It should be easy to just "be"; it is our natural state after all, but it is far from easy. We have spent decades practising "doing" and we have forgotten how to "be". We need to put less emphasis on "doing" and re-learn how to "be"; both of which require practise and commitment. Thankfully, they can both be achieved through one simple practice – Practicing Presence, which is described below:

- Spread your awareness throughout your entire body and sense the subtle but palpable presence of your soul.

- Watch, notice and feel whatever arises, without any agenda. You are an impartial observer.

- Don't try to do anything or achieve anything during the practice.

- Don't analyse, assess, judge or criticise anything, including yourself, during or after the practice.

- All you have to "do" is feel your awareness spread throughout your body and notice what arises – that is it – if you are doing anything more, you are doing too much.

The first few times you practise the exercise, you may not be able to actually <u>feel</u> your soul's presence in your body. But it will happen, when you relax and stop <u>trying</u> to feel it. You will probably notice that there are areas of your body where it is more difficult to feel presence than others. You will probably also notice that there are areas of your body that feel out of balance or feel like blockages – these are the areas where most of your psychological material is stored (exiles, holes and ego structures).

Presence is central to most of the practices and techniques described in the next few chapters, so practise it as much as you can. I do it while driving my car, reading, watching TV and lying in bed. With practise it can be done whilst walking or performing simple tasks. I really cannot stress how important and beneficial this simple practice is:

- It gets us out of our heads and into our bodies, which allows us to experience life more objectively and live life more fully.
- It takes us deeper into ourselves – deeper into our body, senses, emotions, desires, behaviours and beliefs.
- It helps us to become less reactive, so our relationships with other people improve.
- It helps us to develop an authentic relationship with our Self/soul.

1. Personal Self-Inquiry (Psychological Exploration)

The truth is not "out there"; it is within us. To discover our own truth we must to get to know ourselves (true-Self and ego-self) by exploring our psychological and spiritual terrain. When we meditate our conscious awareness expands "upwards" into the super-conscious levels of our soul, and when we get triggered it contracts "downwards" into the sub-conscious levels of our ego. Effective self-inquiry requires a combination of the two; i.e. expanding our soul's pure awareness down into our sub-conscious.

Self-inquiry is about exploring our subconscious to bring our repressed parts (exiles and ego structures) up into conscious awareness to liberate them from their perpetual suffering and to liberate ourselves from their reactive behaviours.

Self-inquiry requires awareness, curiosity, openness, courage and trust – trust that we see what we need to see and feel what we need to feel at the right time. But it is not just about finding answers; it also involves identifying the right questions (i.e. questioning our beliefs, attitudes and strategies).

Self-inquiry is the intelligent application of presence and mindfulness, and it begins with a holistic awareness of our entire being (soul, mind, emotions and body). Then, while maintaining that holistic awareness, we focus our awareness on a particular body sensation or emotional issue and feel into it as fully as we can and see where it takes us. It can be a very subtle process, so our body must be relaxed to sense what is arising, and our mind must be open to receive the insight. Whatever arises, we must completely surrender to it (i.e. feel it and allow it without any resistance) before inquiring into its origin. If it didn't want to be observed it wouldn't have shown itself in the first place.

Self-inquiry can begin with the mind (e.g. deciding to enquire into our underlying anxiety) or the body (i.e. feeling and inquiring into whatever is arising in the present moment). No matter where we begin our inquiry, our objective is always the same – to follow the subtle signs to discover how, when, where and why the issue originated.

Self-inquiry can be incorporated into our daily practice (like meditation), or it can be done on an ad hoc basis when we notice a part of us getting triggered. Every experience in every moment is an open invitation for us to understand ourselves better, to inquire into the depths of our being, to rediscover our true nature and become who we truly are.

In his book *Brilliancy*, A.H. Almaas describes inquiry as: "When we are inquiring, we are holding the content – the various facets of experience – and then inter-relating those elements, seeing relationships, and analysing and synthesising. But our consciousness not only holds the whole interrelated field, it also sees through things; it sees through the veils, defences, and resistances to underlying meanings, to underlying parts of our experience. We notice that our perception not only has a wider vision, but also that it can have a penetrating capacity. The penetrating capacity goes directly to the essence of the matter through brilliant illumination that pierces as it illuminates. Our consciousness is so smooth that it can move through little cracks, into tiny, subtle places. Brilliancy can seep into and penetrate those little subtle cracks and allow our consciousness to see things we wouldn't normally see."

The key to self-inquiry is witnessing whatever arises with "new eyes" and feeling it with a "new body", as if we were experiencing it for the very first time, with innocence and wonder, and without any preconceived ideas, agendas or expectations:

- **Do** feel it as completely and intimately as possible. Be curious about it – What are its attributes, e.g. size, shape, location, colour, density, texture, temperature, emotional tone, age and gender? Does it have anything to tell you or show you? Accept it fully, thank it, and love it. These are qualities of Self/soul.

- **Don't** fear it, avoid it, judge it, label it, identify with it, cling to it, justify it, explain it, interfere with it, try to change it, tell yourself a story about it, or do anything that colours or distorts your direct perception. These are qualities of ego.

Our desire to discover our own truth comes from the heart not the mind. The mind can be a useful tool to see the connections and piece it all together, but it is the heart's desire to be whole again that fuels our self-inquiry. If too much attention is focused on working things out in our mind, our awareness will move out of our body and into our head. Our pure awareness will be pushed aside by our mind, and our agenda-less inquiry will suddenly have an agenda. This is ok for short periods of time, but it is important to return to pure awareness as soon as possible. With the mind out of the way the answers often come to us effortlessly.

As previously stated, each part of the ego (exile, hole or ego structure) is a blend of thought, emotion and energy, but the proportions vary:

- **Thought**: Most holes and ego structures are primarily thought-forms (false, distorted or limiting beliefs). When we identify a false or limiting belief we stop believing it, feeding it and reinforcing it, so it gradually dissolves and we are no longer identified with it. This process may take a while, especially if the belief has been with us since childhood.

- **Emotion**: Most exiles are primarily emotional (fear and trauma), but they often have a false or distorted belief at their core. Inquiring into the belief behind an emotional trauma gives us another "handle" to connect with the issue more fully.
- **Energy**: The energetic aspect of exiles, holes and ego structures is largely a by-product of the mental and emotional aspects. Energetic imbalances and blockages can put our entire system out of balance, which can amplify or suppress the effects of exiles, holes and ego structures. Energetic imbalances can also affect us on the physical level. Sudden imbalances can produce acute physical symptoms, and long-term imbalances can produce chronic physical symptoms.

Section 2 of this chapter (Body Awareness) describes a sensory approach to self-inquiry that focuses on the energetic and emotional aspects. The remainder of this section describes a more insightful approach to self-inquiry that focuses on the false, distorted and limiting beliefs. It might initially sound like a mind-based approach to self-inquiry, but the mind isn't the primary tool and it doesn't require us to think of the answers. It is much more intuitive; drawing on the penetrating, perceptive, intuitive and insightful qualities of the Self/soul's pure awareness. The Self/soul is the key to all inner work.

Intuitive Insight

The false, distorted or limiting beliefs that lie at the centre of many of our "parts" exert a massive unseen influence on how we live our lives. Self-inquiry can help us to bring these subconscious and semi-conscious beliefs and strategies into the full light of our conscious awareness.

The biggest false belief that we hold onto is that we are our ego-self, but we also have a primary belief that shapes our fundamental approach to life, and a collection of core beliefs that influence our different strategies for life. Discovering these false beliefs is the key to liberating ourselves from the ego's narcissistic, controlling and fear-based strategies. Discovering these false beliefs is the key to a better life.

We all have lots of false, distorted and limiting beliefs buried in our sub-conscious, and they have been highly influential in shaping our attitude to life. Their influence goes unchallenged because they operate outside of our conscious awareness. They distort our perceptions of reality and they only allow us to remember things that reinforce their false and distorted beliefs. Consequently, a lot of the burdens we carry in life are imaginary – the results of false beliefs. So freeing ourselves from our false, distorted and limiting beliefs can profoundly affect our self-image, our world view and the way we live our lives.

Most of our false beliefs originate from our early childhood, when our personal consciousness was insufficiently developed to be objective, rational and wise. Our limited mental capacity made lots of incorrect assumptions, interpretations and conclusions which gave rise to lots of false, distorted and limiting beliefs. These in turn gave rise to lots of naïve, ineffective, conflicting and distressing strategies which still subconsciously influence and direct our lives today.

Rehashing our childhood traumas can be very helpful when healing and reintegrating exiled parts, but it isn't always very helpful in exposing the false beliefs of our ego structures. Insight and intuition are far more effective, and these faculties work better when we are not caught up in painful emotions. Reconnecting with the past is obviously necessary, but the soul's pure awareness can give us intuitive insight without getting caught up the story. Inquiry requires us to be in an open and receptive state, and only bring in the mind after an insight has been gained, to discern its relevance and validity.

Identifying and invalidating the false and distorted beliefs we have about our childhood, enables us to see our childhood in a much more positive light. Aspects of it may have seemed bad from the subjective perspective of the ego, but from the objective perspective of the soul it was all perfect. The one thing that we tend to forget in psychological work is that we chose our lives. We chose them because they would provide our souls with the perfect opportunities we need to develop and evolve. Resenting our childhood or blaming our parents is detrimental on a number of levels: it causes us to suffer, it makes us feel helpless, it blocks our intuitive inquiry and it keeps us trapped in the past.

Primary Beliefs

Our primary belief is the false or distorted seed thought around which our entire ego super-structure developed. When we were only a few months old something happened (a primary wound) that caused us to incorrectly believe that "I am not good enough" (or something similar). Our entire ego super-structure grew around that primary belief, so many of our coping and survival strategies in life are concerned with addressing the feeling of lack that is associated with our primary belief. Even our desire to improve ourselves and progress spiritually comes partly from the false belief that is imprinted into our ego-self (and partly from our Self/soul's natural impulse to evolve and express itself fully). But no matter what we achieve, nothing will ever alleviate the primary belief that we are not good enough. We can never be truly satisfied or happy while we hold onto our primary belief. But we can't completely let go of it until we realise our true-Self, because our primary belief is imprinted into the core of our ego-self. Nevertheless, identifying our primary belief can significantly reduce its influence over us and help us to understand ourselves better.

We all have slightly different primary beliefs, such as: I am unlovable, helpless, lost, abandoned, unsafe, powerless or unworthy, but the principle is the same. Our ego's need to overcompensate for the insecure feelings that are associated with our primary belief determines our entire approach to life. For example, someone whose primary belief is "I am powerless" will subconsciously strive towards attaining power (often at any cost). Someone whose primary belief is "I am unlovable" will do anything they can to be loved (even if it means putting up with abuse). Basically, the ego wants to prove the primary belief wrong.

The programming of a primary belief is so deep and so strong that it can override all other aspects of our personality, including our morals. We may be a kind, considerate, sensible and ethical most of the time, but in matters relating to our primary belief our good nature may go out the window.

Core Beliefs

Our primary belief is surrounded by a number of associated beliefs that are also very close to the core of our ego-self. A primary belief is quite generic (e.g. I am not good enough), but core beliefs are a bit more specific (e.g. I am stupid, I am not important, I am invisible, nobody likes me, I can't do it, etc.). Further out from the core beliefs are countless other inter-related peripheral beliefs that connect together to form a larger network of beliefs – our belief system.

Most elements of the ego (exiles, holes and structures) are based around a false, distorted or limiting belief. Yes, they often have emotional and energetic qualities too, but the false or limiting belief is usually the core of the issue. The goal of personal self-inquiry is to discover these false, distorted or limiting beliefs and see through them.

Our core beliefs formed early in our childhood, when our ego was small, young and innocent. If we grew up in a balanced, safe and loving environment each new layer of our ego would have become more aligned with the truth. But if we grew up in an unstable, confusing and traumatic environment each new layer of the ego would have become more distorted from the truth. Growing up and learning to survive in a difficult environment may lead us to believe that "Life can be difficult" (which is objectively true). But the ego may distort this into "Life is difficult" (which is not true). The ego may distort it even further into "Life has to be difficult", which may cause us to subconsciously manifest unnecessary difficulties in our lives. This belief can give rise to associated beliefs such as "I feel at home in difficult environments", which can distort into "I feel uncomfortable in safe and caring environments". Such beliefs can make it difficult for people to stay in personal or therapeutic relationships.

Some of the ego-structures and belief patterns that are furthest away from our core may have become so distorted that they are the polar opposite of our primary or core beliefs. These parts of us may believe that "I am great" and "Everybody loves me" whereas the core parts of our ego believe that "I am nothing" and "nobody loves me". This can result in a lot of inner conflict and unnecessary difficulties in life.

Discovering Primary, Core and Other False Beliefs

Discovering our primary belief involves awareness (noticing when beliefs pop into our mind, and why) and self-inquiry (inner detective work). Our peripheral beliefs can lead us to our core beliefs, and our core beliefs can lead us to our primary belief. This is depicted in Figure 19.

```
Peripheral Belief ┐
Peripheral Belief ├ Core Belief ┐
Peripheral Belief ┘             │
                                ├ Primary Belief
Peripheral Belief ┐             │
Peripheral Belief ├ Core Belief ┘
```

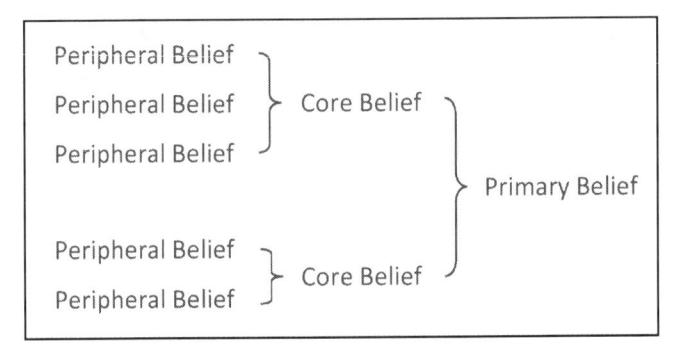

Figure 19: Finding Your Primary Belief

Core beliefs are reasonably easy to identify because they underlie the things we tell ourselves all the time. Once we have identified a core belief or two, it usually isn't too difficult to work out what primary belief underlies them. Why not try it for yourself?

Dysfunctional, habitual and reactive behavioural patterns are great starting points for self-inquiry. We can inquire into the beliefs that may drive these behaviours and what we gain from them. For example:

- Behaviour: I talk too much.
- Peripheral Belief: I won't be noticed if I stop talking.
- Peripheral Belief: If I am not noticed, I might not exist.
- Peripheral Belief: I will cease to exist if I am not noticed.
- Core Belief: I am invisible.
- Core Belief: I must be noticed in order to exist.
- Primary Belief: I am unworthy of existing.

It is important not to judge our false beliefs, and more importantly, not judge ourselves for having them. Judgement comes from the ego (super-ego actually) and we are trying to dis-identify with that.

Once we have identified our primary belief we can simply stop believing it. But this isn't always easy because we identify our self with our primary belief – it defines us; it is our identity. To dis-identify from a primary belief we have to shift our perspective and change the way we see things. It is a bit like waking up from a dream. When we are immersed in a dream it feels very real, and our fears feel very real. In a bad dream we truly believe that our life is at risk, but when we wake up and see it from a different perspective we realise that we were never in any real danger – so it is safe to release our false beliefs.

Primary beliefs are linked to our enneatype (personality type), which in turn is linked to our skandhas. The enneagram is a useful tool for helping us to identify our personality type, our ego strategies and our underlying false beliefs. I recommend reading about the enneagram, the nine enneatypes and the 27 subtypes. Please refer to the Bibliography on Page 243 for further details.

Neutralising False Beliefs

A false, distorted or limiting belief (a belief that no longer serves us) cannot be neutralised without first making it conscious. A conscious false belief will not be acted upon so readily because its falseness is now apparent – this was not the case when the false belief was subconscious. The more conscious we become, the more false beliefs we will identify and release.

Understanding an issue from a purely cognitive perspective may not change anything because we are not embodying the new belief or understanding. To truly impact our life our new understanding needs to filter down from our mind into our body, where it can actually bring about a positive change in our behaviour. This can be facilitated by holding the new belief/understanding/wisdom/concept in mind whilst simultaneously maintaining a sense of body-presence. This forms a connection between the two which facilitates the embodiment process. The same process can be used to embody an essential quality (see section 5 of this chapter).

When you become aware of a belief that no longer serves you, try the following:

1. Write down the false or limiting belief. If it is a long sentence, condense it into a few words that embody the essence of the belief, e.g. "not good enough" or "must be perfect".

2. Write down the opposite of the false or limiting belief. If it is a long sentence, condense it into a few words that embody the essence of the opposite belief, e.g. "good enough" or "imperfection is ok".

3. Enter into a state of presence (full body awareness).

4. Hold the false belief in mind for 30 seconds, without any judgement or agenda (whilst maintaining presence throughout your body).

5. Hold the opposite belief in mind for 30 secs, without any judgement or agenda (whilst maintaining presence throughout your body).

6. Hold both beliefs in mind simultaneously, without any judgement or agenda, until the beliefs neutralise each other.

Dis-identification vs Dissociation

Dis-identification is healthy because it frees our soul from identification with self-images from the past (exiles, holes and ego structures). Dissociation is unhealthy because it distances us from our parts (exiles, holes and ego structures) and it distances us from life. Dis-identification is a natural result of self-inquiry into the nature of the ego. Exploring our false beliefs, concepts, attitudes and strategies is an inherent part of the process of dis-identification.

One of the main objectives of personal self-inquiry is to dis-identify from our conditioned behaviours, reactive emotions and false beliefs – the biggest of which is that we are our ego-self. The aim of transpersonal self-inquiry (described in Chapter 6) is to become more identified with our true-Self and our essential qualities. This enables us to consciously respond to life authentically and appropriately in the present moment, instead of subconsciously reacting to life with generic automated behaviours from our past.

Other Types of Self-Inquiry

Personal self-inquiry is not just about bringing false, distorted and limiting beliefs to light. It can also be used to discover the roots of our emotional and physical issues too:

- **Emotional Patterns**: If, for example, arrogant behaviour in other people triggers us in some way, there is a good chance that we are repressing arrogance our self. Their arrogance resonates with our repressed arrogance and we get annoyed because we don't want to face it. The old saying "what you see in others is a reflection of yourself" is very true. These uncomfortable moments are perfect opportunities to inquire within and perhaps discover what we are hiding and why. If arrogance doesn't push our buttons there will probably be other behaviours that do. Here are a few common examples: people who talk too much, people who never take things seriously, people who fidget constantly, people who know-it-all, people who tell us what to do, people who don't listen, people who take advantage, people who walk all over us or others, etc... These behaviours are our strategies for coping with life without our essential qualities. Arrogance, for example, is a cluster of coping structures that are attempting to compensate for a lack of essential confidence, strength and wisdom. When we remember that these coping strategies and structures were initially created when we were very young children, it is difficult not to feel compassion for ourselves and others. Note: To discover when an issue first arose, you can ask yourself "what age was I when this originated?" and trust the first number that pops into your head. Then contemplate what happened in your life around that age and see if any of it relates to the issue you are inquiring into.

- **Physical Pain**: Give yourself the space to feel the pain fully, without any resistance, judgement or trying to stop it. Break down the onset of the pain into subtle stages so that you understand and feel every aspect, element and quality of the pain. Allow yourself to fully embody the pain – let the pain become you and you become the pain. Be with the pain in presence and pure awareness for as long as you can. The sustained presence may help to heal or reduce the pain, and the pure awareness may provide some insight into its cause. Exploring the physical component of the pain can bring up related psychological components (which are often the root cause of physical pain). Apparently 60-80% of physical pain has no physical cause, in which case the cause is almost certainly psychological. Healing the psychological component will generally heal or reduce the physical component of the pain.

2. Body Awareness (Feeling and Healing with Presence)

During our childhood, the authentic aspects of our consciousness that should have been activated by positive life experiences got shutdown (and exiled) by negative life experiences. It is the ego's job to get us through life without feeling the pain and distress of these negative experiences. Personal development goes directly against this objective because it requires us to feel into our old hurts and inquire into our false beliefs. It is about reconnecting with the parts of ourselves that we have repressed and exiled from conscious awareness. It is sometimes called "shadow work" because it deals with the parts of us that live in the shadows of our consciousness (our subconscious).

Feeling and healing with presence is a relatively new approach to psychological healing and spiritual growth. Instead of focussing on the symptoms (as a regular doctor or psychologist might) we focus on the root cause. It involves tuning into our body and fully feeling the sensations, blockages and structures that make their presence felt. Because they are making themselves felt we can infer that they are ready to be healed and reintegrated. Simply staying with the body sensations (and emotions) and feeling them fully (with loving presence) gently reintegrates the part back into the wholeness of our being.

We can identify which areas of the body hold psychological material (e.g. exiles, holes and ego structures) by the sensations we can feel in our body (e.g. pressure, tightness, blockages, magnetic repulsion, stickiness, membranes, hollowness, rigidity, pain, energetic sensations, etc.). The more "handles" (sensations, feelings, emotions, thoughts, beliefs, etc.) we can get on a part the more fully we can feel it and the easier we can heal it. Our role is simply to keep our presence and awareness on these "handles" and feel them as fully as possible, and to keep our awareness pure – i.e. not have any agenda or desire to fix or change anything. Then the healing and reintegration will occur naturally in their own time.

Feel It To Heal It

This body-centred approach is a very simple yet effective way of working with emotional parts, e.g. exiles and distracting ego structures.

1. **Connect with Presence**: Before you begin, take a few really deep breaths and centre yourself. Connect with your soul by closing your eyes, spreading your awareness throughout your entire body (e.g. by expanding it from the feet up) and feeling your soul's presence.

2. **Open Invitation:** Gently invite your wounded parts, conditioned behaviours, reactive emotions and distorted beliefs to show themselves. Reassure them that it is safe to come out. Let them know that you would really like to get to know them and that they don't have to be alone or afraid anymore. Invite them to tell you or show you their story.

3. **Pure Awareness:** Pay attention to whatever arises, then move your awareness/presence into it. Really feel it and intimately merge with it so there is no separation. You and the feeling are one, but in a non-identified way; i.e. you feel it completely but you are not overwhelmed by it. Maintaining pure awareness enables your sense of identity to remain distinct from the feeling whilst still feeling it fully. It is a pure and intimate connection but it is still objective.

4. **Healing with Loving Presence**: Acknowledge the part, reassure it, be with it, hold it, comfort it, accept it and love it. Loving presence really helps to heal your relationship with the part. You were too afraid to fully feel its pain all those years ago because your young and undeveloped consciousness didn't have the capacity. Now, as an adult you easily have the capacity to feel pain and distress. The only thing that might stop you from maintaining an intimate connection is if you become over-identified with the traumatised part and allow its fear to overwhelm you. Establishing a deep connection with your soul's presence before you begin reduces the chances of emotional flooding, but it does still happen sometimes.

5. **Reintegration**: Allow your soul's presence to dissolve into the part, and allow the part to dissolve into your presence. The exiled piece of soul will reunite with the rest of your soul, and the mental, emotional and energetic components will dissolve and reunite with their respective subtle bodies. Note: Inviting in essential qualities such as love, joy and strength deepen our connection with our soul and increase its healing and reintegrative effect.

The fear, trauma, confusion and distress that are carried by an exiled part can be reactivated when doing inner work. If we focus our awareness solely on the area of emotional distress, it can sometimes feel as if the localised distress is overwhelming our entire being. This can be quite frightening but it can easily be overcome by spreading our awareness throughout our entire body. Widening our focus in this way puts the scale of the emotion into perspective, i.e. it helps us to realise that only a small part of us is affected. Slow deep breathing is also helpful because it dissipates the build-up of emotional energy.

Feeling into Holes and the Void

Discovering a "hole" in our being (a "missing" piece of our soul) can be frightening because it can feel like we are standing on the edge of a precipice, looking down into a bottomless pit, entering an endless void, or even facing total annihilation. But the fear is imaginary because the "hole" isn't actually a hole; it is our soul. The soul is simultaneously wholeness and nothingness, fullness and emptiness, oneness and void. This may sound like a paradox but the following analogy might help: A fish doesn't notice the water it lives in (until it is removed from it), so the sea seems to be full from one perspective and empty from another. It is the same with the soul – it can feel like fullness-wholeness-completeness but it can also feel like emptiness-spaciousness-void. In addition to this, the soul's emptiness can be perceived from two different perspectives:

- **Full Emptiness**: When soul is aware of its own presence there is no sense of deficiency or lack. The emptiness feels full, complete and whole.

- **Deficient Emptiness (a hole)**: The soul is far subtler than the mind so the mind cannot directly perceive it. Hence the soul appears to be absent/missing/emptiness/void from the mind's perspective. We feel fearful when we encounter this kind of emptiness because it feels like our (false) sense of self is facing annihilation, but it is actually facing the subtle purity of our soul.

When we stop defending against feeling a hole or void and actually allow ourselves to feel it fully, we discover that it doesn't feel like a deficiency at all – it feels like spaciousness, which is actually very pleasant. When we allow this spaciousness to "be" (i.e. accept its existence and feel it without any resistance) we re-discover the "missing" piece of soul and realise that it has been there all along.

3. Healing and Reintegration

Section 1 was about using the pure awareness aspect of the soul for self-inquiry. Section 2 was about using the presence aspect of the soul for body-centred feeling and healing. This section integrates and expands upon the previous two sections.

Effective healing and reintegration requires our Self/soul's presence to intimately connect with the exile, hole or ego structure. Put simply, it requires taking the "healer" (Self/soul) to the "patient" (the exile, hole or ego structure). However, we generally avoid our psychological material because it feels painful or uncomfortable, and we generally avoid our soul because it is not our usual sense of self. So we need to practise connecting with them both if our self-healing work is to be effective:

- Our psychological wounds are always present but we repress them and distract ourselves so that we don't have to feel them. Personal self-inquiry and body awareness (both previously described in this chapter) are effective methods of identifying and connecting with our psychological wounds.

- Our soul is also always present but it is often obscured by the activities of the mind, emotions and body. When we stop "doing" and start "being" we will soon become our soul's presence.

It is the presence of the Self/soul that brings about healing and reintegration. The Self/soul doesn't have to "do" anything – its intimate presence is all that is required. Psychological healing isn't like healing a physical wound; it is more like healing a wounded relationship – the relationship between the soul and the part (exile, hole or ego structure):

- **Exiles**: Every exiled part is animated by a piece of soul that has forgotten it is soul. The piece of soul feels like it is wounded and traumatised because it is identified with the exiled part, but soul cannot actually be wounded. The soul's presence helps the piece of soul to awaken from its misidentification with the exiled part, at which point its lack of wounding is immediately apparent and it reunites with the rest of the soul. Without the piece of soul to hold it together, the mental, emotional and energetic aspects of the exiled part soon dissolve and reintegrate with their respective subtle bodies.

- **Holes**: Every hole is a piece of soul that has forgotten it even exists, because it is identified with a perceived lack. The Self/soul's presence helps the "lost" piece of soul to awaken from this misconception, at which point its wholeness immediately becomes apparent and its "lost" essential quality is immediately found.

- **Ego Structures**: Every ego structure is animated by a piece of soul that has forgotten it is soul. The piece of soul is identified with the ego structure so it is restricted by the ego structure's programming. The Self/soul's presence helps the piece of soul to awaken from this misidentification and reunite with the rest of the soul. Without the piece of soul to hold it together, the mental, emotional and energetic aspects of the ego structure soon dissolve and reintegrate with their respective subtle bodies.

In all three cases nothing actually needed to be healed. Psychological healing is simply about helping these misidentified pieces of our soul to remember who they truly are. When they remember that they are soul, they naturally reintegrate with the rest of our soul. The more parts we reintegrate, the more we awaken to wholeness.

The Basic Healing and Reintegration Process

Important Note: It would be unwise to begin any kind of personal development work with the intention of "fixing" things that are "wrong" with us. Our intention should be focused on developing our true-Self's clear perception and clear expression, rather than fixing our ego-self. Always focus on the positive; not the negative. Because focussing on the negative brings more of the negative, and focussing on the positive brings more of the positive. It is the ego that wants things to be fixed, and starting any kind of inner work from the position of the ego is destined for failure and disappointment. Inner work must be initiated by the Self/soul, because they have the essential qualities that this work requires: patience, acceptance, compassion, love, curiosity, intuition, etc.

4. Personal Development

There are two starting points for inner work:

1. **A Specific Issue**: If you have a specific issue in mind that you want to work on, recall a time when the issue arose and notice what arises within you (e.g. body sensations, emotions, thoughts, memories, beliefs). If you choose to work on a general issue such as anxiety, it helps to narrow things down and work on one aspect at a time; e.g. performance anxiety or anxiety when talking to your boss. This is because a general issue such as anxiety is actually a cluster of many inter-related exiles, holes and ego structures, so it is best to work on them one at a time.

2. **No Specific Issue**: If you don't have a specific issue in mind, simply sense into your body and notice whatever is arising in the present moment.

The "Feel It To Heal It" technique described in section 2 forms the basis of many of the healing and reintegration techniques in this book. I won't repeat the steps again because they can be found on page 133, but I will briefly describe some additional elements that can be incorporated into the process to widen its scope and increase its effectiveness. Note: The processes described in this chapter are really just to introduce you to the basic processes of self-inquiry, healing and reintegration – the full range of therapeutic techniques are described in the next chapter.

- If you sense an abstract part: Sense its location, shape, size, colour, texture, emotional tone, state of mind, etc. The more "handles" you can get on it, the deeper the connection and the deeper the healing.

- If you sense a child-like part: Sense his/her age and emotional state. Does he/she have a job to do? Is he/she friendly or hostile? Where does he/she live? Does he/she have anything to say to you? The more you get to know him/her the better your chances of healing the relationship and reintegrating the part. Note: Dialoguing with child-like parts is described more fully in the next chapter.

- If more than one part is vying for your attention, choose one and feel into it as fully as you can, with pure awareness and intimate presence (while still maintaining presence throughout your body).

- Let go of any agendas to change your experience or fix the issue. Just be with your experience fully.

- If memories or thoughts arise, contemplate them for a while to see if any further insights come, but don't get drawn into too much thinking or analysis – stay with the body sensations and emotions.

- If emotions arise, feel them as fully as you can without becoming overwhelmed by them. Maintaining presence throughout your body should reduce or prevent overwhelming emotions.

- Try dialoguing with the part – Does it have anything to say to you? Does it have a story to tell? Is there anything it wants to show you? Is there anything it needs to do to help release its pain?

- You might encounter layered parts, e.g. confusion at the surface, then anger, with fear at the core. Just stay with each one and they will shift naturally (the core emotion will probably take the longest).

- If things don't seem to be shifting, stay with it and increase your focus on the body sensations and emotions to feel them as fully as you can. Trust that the healing and reintegration will occur naturally in its own time, and remember that your (ego's) interference will block this natural process.

- You may feel a little delicate or spaced out after doing deep psychological work. This is quite normal. Just take it easy for a couple of hours to give your system time to assimilate the changes.

- Working with a partner to "hold the space" and support you while you explore and reintegrate your psyche greatly increases the depth and effectiveness of the work.

Overcoming Obstacles and Resistance

It can be difficult to get close enough to an exiled part to feel it fully and heal the relationship because protective and distracting ego structures often prevent us from doing so (that is their job after all). These ego structures won't relinquish their roles until the exiled part is no longer a threat (or no longer needs protecting), but we can't help the exiled part until the ego structure backs down. At times like these our internal system seems to be in stalemate but a useful insight I learned from Dr

4. Personal Development

Richard Schwartz, the creator of Internal Family Systems (IFS), can help us to negotiate our way out of this deadlock.

Most of our protective and distracting ego structures were originally created when we were very young (at the same time that the associated exile was created). So these ego structures were created from very young consciousness and are still composed of young consciousness because they have been isolated from life so have never grown up. This has two important ramifications:

1. The ego structures are not aware that many years have passed, so they don't know that we have grown up into a capable adult. They still believe that we are young, vulnerable and incapable of facing the distress that they are protecting us from.

2. Like well-behaved children they diligently keep doing what they were originally told/programmed to do, without question.

The first point contains the key to overcoming the second. Protective and distracting ego structures can often be circumvented by simply informing them that we are no longer a helpless little child and that we have grown up into a mature and capable adult. This revelation usually allows us access to the protected exile, which we can then heal and reintegrate with the presence and pure awareness of our Self/soul. If the protector part comes onto the scene again, reassure it, then kindly ask it to step aside so that you can continue helping the exiled part.

Protective and distracting ego structures were originally created to protect our young ego-self from becoming overwhelmed by the exiled part's distress and confusion. But ego structures can be augmented later in life with older more-developed consciousness. These older ego structures sometimes develop sympathy for the exiled part and can even become protective of it. So the ego structure's role can change from protecting our young ego-self from being overwhelmed to protecting a young exiled part from the general hostility of the egoic environment. If you encounter a caring ego structure in your work, use the same basic approach (education and negotiation) but allow the protective part to keep an eye on the exile while you are with it.

Stages of Reintegration

To reintegrate an exiled part (which we would initially refer to as "it"), we first have to form a relationship with it (at which point we would refer to it as "you"), then we can welcome it back into our being (at which point we would refer to our integrated being as "I"):

- **Third Person Relationship (It):** The exiled part is totally separate from us. We don't even know the part so we refer to it in the third person; e.g. it is in my belly.

- **Second Person Relationship (You):** We get to know the part and form a relationship with it. When we are dialoguing with the part we refer to it in the second person; e.g. you seem very sad.

- **First Person Relationship (I):** The part no longer exists as a separate unit because it has been reintegrated into our being. We refer to our self in the first person; e.g. I feel whole again.

When the exiled part has been healed and reintegrated, the protective ego structure usually dissolves or disappears. If it doesn't, the exile may not be completely healed, or the protector may be protecting another exile. These are both avenues for further exploration. A more detailed practical description of this approach is given in the next chapter.

Deeper Layers

After healing and reintegrating a part, we may get a sense that it is not 100% complete or that a trace of it remains. This does not necessarily mean that the work is incomplete – it is likely to be one of the following:

- A few hours may be required for the reintegration to complete.

- It may take a day or two for our system to return to equilibrium after such deep inner work.

- We are already starting to sense another related part in the same area of the body.

When we clear one part it usually isn't too long before another comes out of hiding. It can be seconds, minutes, hours, days or weeks – it all depends on how fast our system is able to process and how our psychological material is organised. This work can feel like a rollercoaster ride because we can be on a high after clearing one part but then start to feel down when another part reveals itself. During these lows, we may think that we are not making any progress at all, or are even regressing. But we only have to look back on how we were a few months or years ago to realise how far we have come. We should actually be grateful that the next issue is revealing itself because it means we can start working on it and take another step towards freedom and wholeness. Once we get a handle on the issue we can inquire into it, feel into it, heal it and reintegrate it. This work is about peeling off the layers of the ego to reveal more of our true nature and eventually realise our true-Self.

4. Conscious Living (in the present moment)

The soul is like a seedling – it requires the water of Life to grow and to blossom, but most people's relationships with Life are semi-conscious. If we don't consciously engage with Life we will make little progress and remain passive victims of Life's circumstances.

The ego is a tangled mess of distorted beliefs, critical thoughts, reactive emotions and conditioned behaviours. It is not a particularly pleasant place to be, which is why we generally avoid feeling our "stuff". The ego-self usually tries to distance itself from anything uncomfortable so we never fully experience life. Our soul requires direct conscious experience for optimal growth, but the ego's avoidance strategies prevent this. If we are fully present (here and now) our soul can experience life directly and fully, but if we are not present (i.e. identified with the mind, emotions or body) our soul can only experience life indirectly. And an indirect experience of life is only a partial experience of life. Living life fully means living consciously – with pure awareness and presence.

There are two sides to living consciously and they both connect us with our Self and with Life:

- **Perception**: Conscious perception (seeing, hearing, feeling, etc.) enables us to experience life more directly, objectively and fully, because our perceptions are not so distorted by ego structures.
- **Expression**: Conscious expression includes thinking, speaking and doing things as consciously as possible. It puts our Self back in

control and gradually dissolves the subconscious beliefs, emotions and behaviours that have kept us living on autopilot.

"Doing" doesn't stop us from "being" (because "being" always is), but doing often lessens our awareness of being, in which case it lessens our experience of life. When we are busy doing, we typically have less awareness in the present moment, so we experience less and develop less. But if we can "do" with presence (i.e. "be" and "do" at the same time), we have the best of both worlds. This is what conscious living is all about.

Conscious living is about waking up from the trance of our ego structures and enabling our Self to become the conscious director of our life. Our subconscious beliefs, reactive emotions and conditioned behaviours will continue to run our lives until we make them conscious:

- **Thoughts & Beliefs**: Conscious living involves constant awareness to spot negative thoughts and false beliefs so that we can stop buying into them and stop subconsciously reinforcing them. Once we have consciously identified a false belief it is less likely to fuel the negative thoughts, reactive emotions and conditioned behaviours that keep us suffering unnecessarily. It also provides us with subject matter for our self-inquiries.

- **Emotions**: Conscious living involves constant awareness to catch reactive emotions before they take hold of us. I am not talking about suppressing our emotions; I am talking about not expressing them (i.e. feeling their energy but not acting them out). Acting out our emotions discharges them, which stops us from really feeling them and understanding them. This, in turn, prevents us from discovering the root cause of each reactive emotion and healing it.

- **Behaviours**: Conscious living involves constant awareness to notice when we succumb to conditioned and compulsive behaviours. Consciously identifying previously subconscious impulses and behaviours disempowers them to some extent, and it provides us with subject matter for our self-inquiries.

Conscious living is also known as mindfulness. It involves observing the mind; not the thoughts. The mind is like an over-eager pet dog – It brings us things to get our attention, but we generally give our attention to the things it brings us (thoughts), rather than to the mind itself. So the mind keeps bringing us thoughts because it sees that we are interested in them. And if we tell the mind to go away it will come straight back with something else to show us. If we really want the mind to calm down (and stop showing us unwanted thoughts), we need to stop paying attention to the thoughts and give our attention to the mind. The mind is keen to serve us and just wants to be noticed and appreciated, but we keep ignoring it and telling it off. The same basic principle also applies to the heart and the body.

Conscious Awareness

Conscious awareness is observing the mind without getting caught up in thoughts, it is observing the heart without getting caught up in emotions and it is observing the body without getting caught up in sensations. It gives us the power to notice our thoughts, emotions and behaviours without identifying with them or defining ourselves by them. We don't need to hold onto our identities, roles, limitations, stories, beliefs, emotions or feelings to be that which we truly are. In fact, to be that which we truly are, we need to let go of all the stuff that keeps us from realising our true nature.

The ego typically identifies with thoughts and emotions on a conceptual level whilst remaining disconnected from them on a visceral level. Basically it clings to thoughts and emotions, but avoids feeling them fully. Expressing emotions (i.e. acting them out) is one way to avoid feeling them fully (because it dissipates the emotional energy) and repressing them is another way. Conscious awareness enables us to do away with these ego strategies and simply allow our thoughts, emotions and body sensations to be:

- **Thoughts**: When thoughts arise, notice them but do not engage with them.

- **Emotions**: When emotions arise, notice them and feel them fully, but do not get caught up in them.

- **Sensations**: When sensations arise, notice them and feel them fully, but not to the exclusion of everything else.

When we widen our focus and expand our awareness throughout our body, we discover a fuller, deeper and more direct experience of the present moment. This gives us the perspective we need to dis-identify from the ego-self, and the space we need to re-align with our true-Self. Conscious awareness helps to free us from the bondage of our critical thinking, reactive emotions and conditioned behaviours. It gives us the opportunity to respond appropriately rather than react automatically.

Once we have achieved conscious awareness, it can be difficult to stay with it. The most common difficulty is inadvertently moving from directly experiencing awareness to thinking about awareness, and subsequently getting caught up in a running commentary or critical thoughts about our (now indirect) experiences. When we notice this happening we simply need to shift our awareness back to our body; to our physical experience of the present moment. The worst thing we can do is to judge or criticise ourselves because this keeps us in the mind – away from the direct experience of presence.

Other common difficulties include trying to change an experience that we have judged to be unpleasant (e.g. I must stop getting stressed), or trying to fix an issue that we have judged as problematic (e.g. it is wrong to get angry). This only occurs if the preceding thinking, commentating and judging steps have gone unnoticed due to a lack of conscious awareness. We can easily slip from Directly Experiencing > Thinking > Commentating > Judging > Changing or Fixing, but the more we practise conscious awareness the quicker and easier we can identify and interrupt this subconscious chain of events.

When we are feeling a powerful "negative" emotion such as anger or anxiety, we must be careful not to become overwhelmed by it or act it out. This can be done by expanding our awareness to include our entire body (not just the area where the emotion is centred). This gives us enough space to feel the emotion fully without it filling our entire field of awareness and overwhelming us.

Some people subconsciously keep their centre of awareness outside of their body because it is an effective way of avoiding the painful emotions that are held within the body. Being "out of body" keeps them detached from their pain but the lack of psychological grounding can cause them to become psychologically unstable. If their consciousness is absent, it is not present, and without presence they are unable to face their issues, let alone heal and reintegrate them. Such people should practice body awareness (sensing their entire body) as often as possible. In fact, that advice applies to everyone – we will all benefit from this simple practice.

Conscious Screening

Many of our thoughts and emotions originate from ego structures and exiled parts, so they are basically the thoughts and emotions of a young child. Sometimes a young child will talk nonsense, sometimes they will exaggerate or bend the truth and sometimes they will deliberately lie – yet most of us believe our thoughts without question.

We can't directly stop thoughts from arising but we can decide whether to believe them and buy into them, or simply notice them and let them go. Conscious screening involves selecting the thoughts that are positive, meaningful, useful and appropriate, and disregarding those that are negative, trivial, unhelpful or inappropriate.

If we don't consciously dismiss negative thoughts they will be absorbed and programmed into our subconscious mind where they will adversely affect our beliefs, emotions and behaviours. But we should not try to push negative thoughts away because "what we resist persists". Engaging with a thought in any way (e.g. judgement, resistance or attachment) prolongs its existence and tells the mind that we are interested in that type of thought. If we simply acknowledge a thought it will naturally dissolve because it will have served its purpose (i.e. delivered its message).

Acknowledging a thought does not mean that we believe it and buy into it – we are simply noticing it without any judgement, resistance or attachment. We can acknowledge a thought and simultaneously dis-identify with it by silently saying "that is not me". Once we stop identifying with thoughts; once thoughts are depersonalised they lose their value, which makes it easier for us to stop believing them. If we no longer value our thoughts our mind will create fewer thoughts because it will not waste time and effort creating unwanted thoughts. The same basic principle can also be applied to reactive emotions and conditioned behaviours.

Conscious Acceptance

Our beliefs about how life "should be" cause us a lot of unhappiness because the external world rarely lives up to our expectations. We create an ideal model (in our minds) of how we think life should be. When the outside world matches our ideal we are happy, and when it doesn't we become sad or angry. It is incredibly naive to believe that we can make the external world (and everyone in it) comply with our ever-changing wants and desires. The simple solution is to not have any expectations – just see what actually happens and then see how we actually feel about it. This is living life in the moment; this is living an authentic life.

In the present moment we can choose to accept our situation; trusting that life will provide us with the exact experiences our soul needs for its continued development. Or we can choose to resist our situation and resist life. The first option brings a huge sense of peace and freedom because it takes all the pressure off our shoulders, but the second option results in tension and suffering. Life carries on regardless whether we accept it or resist it, but it is a whole lot easier when we accept it.

Resisting a situation that we have no control over is pretty futile. The following points serve as useful reminders for conscious living:

- **Don't Resist**: Accept life without resistance:
    - **Outer Life**: Accept what you cannot change, and change what you cannot accept.
    - **Inner Life**: Feel everything and resist nothing.
- **Don't React**: With present moment awareness we can notice what we are experiencing, be with it, develop understanding, and then respond appropriately (instead of automatically reacting).
- **Don't Judge**: Classifying our experiences as good or bad takes us away from the immediate and direct experience. It takes us away from the real world into our virtual-reality world, it takes us away from the here and now, and it takes us from presence to absence. If we decide that our experience is bad, our focus moves from directly experiencing to trying to change our experience for the better. If we decide that our experience is good our focus moves from directly

experiencing to trying to ensure that we don't lose the experience. Additionally, mental judgements often give rise to an emotional reaction which takes us even further from the present moment.

- **Let Go**: Drop the delusion of being in control and get comfortable with not being in control. Be open to anything and be comfortable with everything.
- **Attitude of Gratitude**: Be thankful for everything – even the "bad" stuff – because every experience is an opportunity for our soul to grow.

Conscious Awakening

We started living in our virtual inner worlds when we were very young children. At that time we didn't have all the psychological faculties to cope with the complexity, confusion and distress that we sometimes encountered in the real world, but as adults we no longer need this protective psychological buffer.

Many of our thoughts, emotions and behaviours are concerned with maintaining our virtual inner-world and our virtual-self. We are subconsciously wasting lots of vital energy on maintaining beliefs and behaviours that no longer serve us and create a lot of unnecessary suffering. All this energy that is being wasted on subconscious ego maintenance could be put to better use. The following practices can help us to increase our degree of conscious awareness, gradually awaken from our virtual inner world, and discover the fullness of conscious living:

- **Body Awareness**: Focussing on the body is the simplest way to become mindful of our present moment experience. Spreading our awareness from our head into the rest of our body allows us to experience the world more directly than we normally do through our inner mental model. It allows our senses to interact with the world more deeply and more authentically so we get a clearer and truer perception of reality. It helps us to see through and overcome the distortions that our ego-self projects onto the outer-world.
- **Open Focus**: The mind is usually narrowly focussed, on the one thought or emotion that is foremost right now. This makes it seem very important and very personal because it fills our entire (narrow)

field of consciousness. Soul consciousness is different; it is naturally open focused. The simple act of opening and widening our field of consciousness brings us into alignment with our soul and lessens our identification with our thoughts and emotions (because it puts them into perspective).

- **Heads Up**: Many of us walk through life with our heads down (literally and metaphorically). This fear-based approach to life keeps us feeling safe. The less direct interaction we have with the "dangerous" external world, the safer we will be. So we keep our heads down, but in doing so we miss out on a myriad of engaging life experiences. It also makes us feel isolated and alone, which further compounds our fears. The simple act of walking through life with our head held up straight not only allows us to take in more of life, it aligns us with the fullness of life, our true nature and our place in the world.

- **Stepping Out**: Periodically stepping out of our comfort zone disempowers our ego structures. It shows them that our life isn't going to fall apart if we try something new or make a fool of ourselves. Growth involves moving forward into new experiences with openness and courage. Protection involves retreating into the safety of known experiences and closing down. We cannot do them both at once (moving forwards and moving backwards). Most of us spend about 95% of our time in protection mode, so we grow very little.

- **Avoid Nothing**: Avoidance and resistance reinforce our ego and our identification with it. We have to face up to our unresolved and repressed issues if we want to be free of them. We have to develop the courage to inquire into the things that push our buttons, and feel into the things that are frightening and painful. When we feel ourselves becoming upset or angry we don't need to automatically blame the other person. We can make the most of the situation (opportunity) by looking inside to understand why their behaviour triggered us.

- **Live Life Fully**: Experience the fullness of life and everything it sends our way. Don't cling to the "good" feelings and avoid the "bad" because when we drop the ego's limited perspective we discover that it's all good. Everything happens for a reason, and that reason is the development of our consciousness.

- **Love Life**: Fear shuts us down and prevents us from moving forwards, but love opens us up and enables us to grow. It can be love for another person, love of an activity, love of life – any kind of love will do. Loving something is the most complete way of demonstrating our acceptance of it.

- **Be Authentic**: Authenticity is bearing our soul; speaking and acting from the heart of our being. It is bringing our inside outside, so that other people can see us exactly as we are. It is a soul to soul connection that allows others to deeply and compassionately understand us. It is having the courage to be "undefended" and it is allowing others to see our divinity and our faults.

- **Be Here Now**: The most important place on our journey of awakening isn't our destination; it is right here and now. Because this is the only time and place that we can truly, fully and directly experience life (and consequently grow from our experiences). So appreciate the present moment, no matter what is happening.

Conscious Presence

When we are consciously present our sense of self moves away from our ego-self and towards our true-Self. The more we practice conscious presence the more permanent the shift becomes. Conscious presence is conscious awareness (of our entire being and our local environment) combined with presence (the palpable presence of our soul throughout our body). This simple practice is incredibly beneficial for psychological and spiritual development, but it can be difficult to sustain all the time, especially if we live busy lives.

The following "Five Point Check-In" is a short period of intense conscious presence that attempts to make up for some of the time when we are not consciously present. The more we practise it the greater the effect, but even a few minutes a day is beneficial. It can be done before we get up and go to sleep or whenever we get a few minutes alone.

1. **Thoughts**: Notice them but don't analyse them, judge them or buy into them.
2. **Emotions**: Feel them but don't get caught up in them. Focus on the bodily sensations rather than the mental story that may be attached to them.
3. **Body Sensations**: Quickly scan your body for tension, blockages and other sensations. Feel them fully while maintaining awareness of your entire body.
4. **Breathing**: Breathe slowly and deeply into any tense or blocked areas. Imagine the in-breath is flowing to the core of the tension or blockage and allow it to gently release a little on each out-breath.
5. **Expanded Awareness**: Move your awareness to your heart, then expand it throughout your entire body, finally expand it a little more out into your aura, and reside in "what is".

If you identify an issue that requires more attention: stay with it (if time permits) or return to it later. If there is too much going on, just focus on one thing at a time and give it your full attention.

It doesn't matter if you can't get a handle on anything specific. The simple act of holding your presence and awareness in your body will help to loosen your ego structures and develop your connection with your true-Self.

5. Embodying Essential Qualities (Expressing Self)

Embodying (positive) essential qualities is just as important as clearing (negative) ego structures. From the personal development perspective, these are the two aspects of the two-fold path:

1. **Qualitative Development** involves developing authentic personal qualities (e.g. compassion, joy and inner strength) by embodying our soul's essential qualities. It is "waking up" to our true nature and expressing it more.

2. Quantitative Development involves freeing up more of our soul's consciousness by reintegrating exiles, holes and ego structures. It is "growing up" psychologically and becoming more authentic.

Prior to enlightenment the soul's consciousness is passive – its perceptive aspect (presence + awareness) is usable, but its expressive aspect (essential qualities) cannot be utilised directly, which is why essential qualities have to be transposed into the personality to become usable personal qualities.

- **Awakening** is a gradual process. The soul's perceptive aspects (presence & awareness) are gradually awakened through conscious living and the reintegration of exiles, holes and ego structures. The soul essence that was previously mis-identified with these "parts" awakens and is liberated. The soul's expressive aspects (essential qualities) are re-discovered through the liberation of mis-identified soul essence, and are developed and refined by actively expressing their corresponding personal qualities in our daily lives.

- **Enlightenment** is an instant process. It occurs when the Self ascends from the head centre (mental body) to permanently centre itself in the soul (causal body). From here we can directly and objectively perceive reality because we have transcended the mind's virtual-reality overlay. We can also directly utilise and develop our soul's essential qualities, so they no longer need to be transposed into personal qualities.

Lost Essential Qualities

Essential qualities are naturally transposed into usable personal qualities at the appropriate stage of our personality's development. But when an essential quality is seemingly "lost" (as a result of psychological distress, trauma or confusion), this natural transposition process cannot occur, which leaves a "hole" in our being. So our immature and inexperienced ego-self had to <u>think</u> of a way to manage without the personal quality, and this mind-created strategy was formed into a coping ego structure. The younger we were, the less mental capacity we had, so our ego's strategy was driven more by instinct and emotion than rational thought. This explains why our ego structures are often primitive, emotional, irrational, inappropriate and reactive.

Under-Developed Personal Qualities

Personal qualities gradually unfold over the course of several years, mainly during our childhood. If the unfoldment of a particular personal quality is interrupted by psychological distress at the very start of the transposition process we will lose sight of the essential quality and the personal quality is unable to develop (leaving a "hole"). But more often than not the transposition process begins and is interrupted later on by psychological distress. This results in a partially-developed personal quality. When this occurs, a coping ego structure may need to be created to supplement the under-developed personal quality. Because coping structures are not as sophisticated or refined as authentic personal qualities, they distort the personal quality that they are supplementing. The following example describes the differences between an authentic personal quality (compassion) and partially-developed compassion that has been supplemented and distorted by two different ego structures (sympathy and empathy):

- **Compassion** is an authentic personal quality that establishes an intimate soul-like connection with another person. It allows us to feel the other person's emotions without becoming identified with them (so the same emotions are not triggered in us). Compassion enables us to be with the other person emotionally and support them psychologically.

- **Sympathy** is the overly-detached ego-version of compassion that establishes an unemotional connection with another person. It allows us to understand the other person's emotions from a mental perspective but it prevents us from actually feeling them. Sympathy enables us to support the other person psychologically, but our lack of emotional understanding can limit the value of our support.

- **Empathy** is the overly-attached ego-version of compassion that establishes an overly-emotional connection with another person. It allows us to deeply feel the other person's emotions, to the extent that we identify with them as if they were our own (which triggers the same emotions in us). Empathy enables us to be with the other person emotionally, but it limits the effectiveness of our support because we are as emotional as they are.

Someone who is going through a difficult time needs compassion, not sympathy or empathy. They need our presence to help them through a period when theirs is lacking (because it is identified with emotions). They don't need us to cry with them (empathy) or be strong for them (sympathy) – they just need us to be there with them fully.

Reactivating Lost Qualities

"Lost" essential qualities were never actually missing; we just lost sight of them. They can be rediscovered through self-inquiry or meditation, typically by feeling into a "hole". Once an essential quality has been rediscovered the natural transposition process will automatically resume, but we will probably need to assist the process because we are no longer at the ideal age. The challenges we faced as young children, e.g. learning to walk, exerting our will and becoming independent, were ideally suited to developing our personal qualities. The challenges we face as adults are not usually so ideal, so we may have to assist the process in other ways.

Personal qualities are developed by directing Self-conscious attention towards the essential quality. This can be done by consciously meditating on the quality or by consciously embodying and expressing the quality (see below for further details). Over time, the personal quality will develop to the point where the coping structure becomes obsolete. The structure will then dissolve and the constituent elements will be reintegrated into their respective subtle bodies.

A: Embodying an Essential Quality

Embodying or "being" an essential quality requires presence and conscious awareness. "Being" brings the soul and the personality into perfect union so that the essential quality can be transposed into a personal quality. It takes time for an essential quality to permeate down from the soul and become established in the personality. So we must persistently keep "being" the essential quality and keep expressing the essential quality. We must engage our soul's conscious presence and every aspect of our personality (mind, heart and body) to fully embody a new quality. We must think, feel and act differently in order to "be" different. It is common sense really: If we want to be more loving, we must actually "be" more loving – there is no point just wishing we were.

As Ghandi said – "You must be the change you wish to see in the world". With practise, a temporary trait will become a permanent state.

Note: Doing loving things (e.g. kind, caring and romantic) is not the same as "being" love. Presence is what differentiates being from doing. If the soul is not "present" the quality cannot be transposed or developed. So we must be consciously present when expressing essential qualities such as love. Expressing love can include "doing" loving things, but only if the "doing" is done with conscious presence.

B: Meditating on an Essential Quality

Essential qualities can also be embodied by meditating on them. The experience of meditating on an essential quality is slightly different to actually "being" the quality, but the two approaches complement each other perfectly. Meditation helps us to really connect with the essential quality and realise that it has always been within us, and "being" the quality helps us to embody it in a way that meditation alone cannot.

The following method for meditating on an essential quality is adapted from the "Feel It To Heal It" technique (which was described earlier in this chapter):

1. **Connect with Presence**: Before you begin, take a few really deep breaths and centre yourself. Connect with your soul by closing your eyes, spreading your awareness throughout your entire body and feeling your soul's presence.

2. **Open Invitation:** Gently invite in your desired essential quality (e.g. love, joy, compassion, curiosity, humour, patience, serenity, etc.). Or ask: Is joy present? Is love present? And wait for the quality to reveal itself.

3. **Pure Awareness:** Pay attention to whatever arises, then move your presence/awareness into it. Really feel it and intimately merge with it. Any psychological material that has blocked your perception or expression of the quality may begin to gradually dissolve.

4. **Loving Presence**: Fear previously stopped us from embodying the quality. Loving presence helps us to overcome that fear and embody the essential quality.

5. **Embodiment**: Allow your soul's presence to dissolve into the quality and allow the quality to dissolve into your presence. You become the quality, and the quality becomes you.

Developing Essential Qualities

The following essential/personal qualities are particularly useful for psycho-spiritual development (and life in general), so actively developing these authentic qualities is highly recommended: Love, Joy, Compassion, Curiosity, Courage, Trust, Strength, Stillness, Will, Enthusiasm, Wonder, Peace, Patience, Value and Clarity.

The more we embody and express an authentic personal quality, the more the corresponding essential quality in our soul is developed and refined. This is just one of the ways that the personality helps the soul to develop and evolve.

Chapter 5: **Self-Help Techniques**

Introduction

The personality and the ego are tools that our Self/soul uses to develop our consciousness. So focussing solely on personal development is of limited benefit, because it is concerned with developing the tool rather than developing consciousness. Never-the-less, it is important to clear all the old psychological material that holds us back and prevents us from being all that we are. This chapter builds on the last by providing a range of simple self-help techniques that can facilitate psychological healing and personal development.

Effective development requires us to maintain conscious awareness (to spot the signs and clues) and do the inner work (to create opportunities for healing and reintegration to occur). Inner work should be done from the perspective of the Self/soul, without any agenda or expectation as to what will happen or when. We can set our intention at the start, but we should then let it go and allow "what will be" to unfold naturally. Trying to "fix" psychological issues or speed up our development shows that we are ego-identified, because we are actively trying to change "what is". Inner work is not effective if it is ego-driven; it has to be Self-driven, because it is our Self/soul's presence that makes everything happen.

The ego formed over the course of many years, primarily at a time when our consciousness was immature, inexperienced and undeveloped. The really deep parts of the ego formed before we could even speak (pre-verbal), so getting a handle on our psychological material is not always easy. Inquiring, discovering, connecting, healing and reintegrating take time. The techniques described in this book are effective and efficient, but even so, there are no quick fixes. Decades of psychological material cannot be processed and reintegrated in a matter of weeks. Inner work takes time, and if you are not in it for the long-haul you may as well forget it.

Inner work is about creating opportunities for healing, reintegration and growth to occur. We cannot make it happen, and if we try too hard we will not succeed. We have to learn to stop striving, resisting and controlling. When we simply allow things to "be" we can clearly and directly perceive the ripples of life experience that flow though our field of consciousness. This fuller, clearer and direct experience allows our healing and our evolution to progress at their optimal rates, which paradoxically are much faster than when our ego tries to expedite the process. In this case, less really is more.

Disclaimer: The information, practices and techniques described in this book are not intended or implied to be a substitute for professional medical or psychological advice. The information, practices and techniques described in this book are not intended for self-diagnosis or self-treatment, and should not be used to diagnose or treat mental health problems. Please consult a qualified health care professional about any medical or psychological issues. The author is not qualified to give medical or psychological advice, so please do not ask. The information, practices and techniques described in this book are for educational purposes only. If you decide to utilise any of the information, practices or techniques described in this book, you do so at your own discretion. The author is not responsible for any adverse effects or consequences resulting from the use of any of the information, practices or techniques described in this book. If any adverse effects are encountered, stop immediately and seek professional advice.

1. Presence Techniques

If we don't consciously and fully experience our physical, emotional and mental responses to life (as they occur in the present moment), our resistance causes them to become stuck (until such time as we are willing to consciously and fully experience them). This aspect of the inner work involves consciously and fully feeling these psychological blockages to "metabolise" them with the presence of our soul.

5. Self-Help Techniques

Presence techniques are useful for healing issues without us having to fully understand them. Connecting with the body sensations as deeply as possible (from the inside) is the key to this approach, because the body and the soul are the only two aspects of our being that are anchored in the present (here and now). Intimately sensing the affected part of our body with our Self's pure awareness intensifies our soul's presence and the healing effect. There are two important factors to remember when using presence techniques:

- Don't try to visualise structures or blockages dissolving because you may be deluding yourself that it is healed when it isn't. Trust your felt sense over your imagined sense and you will know when it has dissolved. If you see images in your mind's eye, that's fine, they will probably give you more insight – just don't try to change them – be a passive observer.

- Don't try to "fix" anything, because that means you are seeing it as a problem (and consequently rejecting it). You need to fully accept it, love it, embrace it and become one with it, because without being one with it how are you ever going to reintegrate it?

The healing and reintegrative power of presence techniques is greatly increased by the loving presence of other people. Their presence combines with our presence to produce a much more powerful field of healing presence. They don't have to do anything except remain in loving presence (this is sometimes called "holding the space").

1a – Feel It To Heal It (as previously described in Chapter 4)

This body-centred approach is a very simple yet effective way of working with emotional parts, e.g. exiles and distracting ego structures.

1. **Connect with Presence**: Before you begin, take a few really deep breaths and centre yourself. Connect with your soul by closing your eyes, spreading your awareness throughout your entire body (e.g. by expanding it from the feet up) and feeling your soul's presence.

2. **Open Invitation:** Gently invite your wounded parts, conditioned behaviours, reactive emotions and distorted beliefs to show themselves. Reassure them that it is safe to come out. Let them

know that you would really like to get to know them and that they don't have to be alone or afraid anymore. Invite them to tell you or show you their story.

3. **Pure Awareness:** Pay attention to whatever arises, then move your awareness/presence into it. Really feel it and intimately merge with it so there is no separation. You and the feeling are one, but in a non-identified way; i.e. you feel it completely but you are not overwhelmed by it. Maintaining pure awareness enables your sense of identity to remain distinct from the feeling whilst still feeling it fully. It is a pure and intimate connection but it is still objective.

4. **Healing with Loving Presence**: Acknowledge the part, reassure it, be with it, hold it, comfort it, accept it and love it. Loving presence really helps to heal your relationship with the part. You were too afraid to fully feel its pain all those years ago because your young and undeveloped consciousness didn't have the capacity. Now, as an adult you easily have the capacity to feel pain and distress.

5. **Reintegration**: Allow your soul's presence to dissolve into the part, and allow the part to dissolve into your presence. The exiled piece of soul will reunite with the rest of your soul, and the mental, emotional and energetic components will dissolve and reunite with their respective subtle bodies. Note: Inviting in essential qualities such as love, joy and strength deepen our connection with our soul and increase its healing and reintegrative effect.

The fear, trauma, confusion and distress that are carried by an exiled part can become reactivated when doing inner work. If we focus our awareness solely on the area of emotional distress, it can sometimes feel as if the localised distress is overwhelming our entire being. This can be frightening, but it can be easily overcome by spreading our awareness throughout our entire body. Widening our focus in this way puts the scale of the emotion into perspective, i.e. it helps us to realise that only a small part of us is affected. Slow, deep breathing is also helpful because it dissipates the emotional energy.

5. Self-Help Techniques

1b – Soul Child Reintegration

The Feel It To Heal It technique can be adapted to work with a repressed soul child (see Chapter 2). Frustration is the key to discovering a soul child – typically mental frustration in the forehead and/or frustration in the throat that inhibits clear expression. It can be detected by simply holding our awareness in these areas (one at a time) and waiting for frustration to reveal itself (or not). Thinking about people or situations that frustrate us can help us to connect with our repressed frustration. Once we have connected with it (and maybe even expressed a little to deepen the connection), it is just a matter of feeling it fully with loving presence. When the frustration has been fully felt it will give way to reveal the young, pure and innocent soul consciousness. We simply need to stay with this while it reintegrates back into the oneness of our soul.

Sometimes our inner work will intuitively bring us to a soul child, but we won't immediately know that we are dealing with a soul child. Our initial contact will be with the repressing ego structure (that encases the soul child), so its false quality (e.g. hatred or seriousness) will be the first thing that we sense. When we feel deeply into the false quality (with our soul's presence) the ego structure will dissolve to reveal the radiant soul child that was encased inside. We simply need to stay with the soul child while it reintegrates back into the oneness of our soul.

1c – Heal It As We Feel It

The Feel It To Heal It technique can be used in real time as issues arise in our everyday lives. Life is a series of experiences that trigger all sorts of things within us, and every experience is an opportunity for us to grow (or heal, which results in growth). Everything in life is a blessing, even if it doesn't feel like it is from the ego's perspective. In every moment we have the choice to live from our ego or live from our soul. We can either react and blame the other person (which strengthens our ego), or we can proactively feel into it and heal it while it is "up" (which dissolves the ego structure and frees the soul essence).

1d – Connect & Release Technique

This is another variation of the Feel It To Heal It technique. It is a simple and effortless technique to release unwanted issues and behavioural patterns by connecting with them fully.

1. **Select**: Select a specific issue to work on. Note: If you want to work on a general issue such as anxiety, it often helps to narrow things down and work on one aspect at a time; e.g. anxiety when talking to your boss, anxiety at the dentist, anxiety when going out, etc... This is because a general issue such as anxiety is usually a cluster of many related issues, so it is best to focus on them one at a time.

2. **Activate**: Think about the issue or recall a recent situation when the issue arose and notice what sensations get triggered in your body. Note: You can rate the intensity of the sensations on a scale from 0-10 before and after the exercise, so that you can gauge your progress.

3. **Presence**: Take a few really deep breaths and centre yourself. Connect with your Self/soul by closing your eyes, spreading your awareness throughout your entire body and feeling your soul's presence.

4. **Connect**: Focus your attention on <u>one</u> of the body sensations and feel it as fully as you can. Move your awareness/presence into it and intimately connect with it. Explore it from various perspectives to get as many handles on it as possible. For example: feel into its core; feel its periphery; expand to feel it all at once; what shape is it?; does it have an emotional tone?; does it have a colour or a texture?

5. **Accept**: Accept the body sensation and allow it to be, without resistance or judgment. It is just a feeling in your body; it cannot harm you. It is just a message to make you aware that a piece of your consciousness is trapped and wants to be released. You didn't want to feel it when you were younger, which is why it was exiled. So really accepting it and allowing it now will begin to heal the relationship.

6. **Love It**: Love the body sensation. This proves beyond all doubt that you fully accept it and welcome it back into the wholeness of your being.

7. **Release**: Let go of the body sensation, since it has served its purpose. You have got the message, so you no longer need to feel it. Allow it to dissolve and reintegrate with your subtle bodies.

8. **Invite**: Invite in an essential quality (such as love, joy, strength or peace) to support the reintegration process.

9. **Next**: Move onto the next body sensation (if any remain) and repeat until they are all released.

1e – Expanded Awareness Technique

Most of our awareness is focussed in our head or our heart, so our perceptions are primarily coloured by thoughts or emotions. If we defocus our awareness (from our head or heart) and spread it throughout our entire body, we gain a fuller perception of reality (because our awareness is wide open), and a clearer perception of reality (because it is not so distorted by thoughts or emotions). This expanded state feels "silent" because our awareness is not focussed in our head, it feels "still" because our awareness is not focussed in our heart, and it feels "grounded" because our awareness embodies our entire physical body. We can even go a stage further and spread our awareness slightly beyond our physical body; as if our consciousness was radiating from us like an aura. This opens us up and brings us out of our virtual inner world into the real world. It enables us to experience life more fully and clearly, and it deepens our connection with our Self/soul.

1f – Body Scan Technique

This technique involves systematically scanning our body to identify psychological material (e.g. exiles, holes and ego structures). Once identified, each one can be healed and reintegrated using one of the previously described Presence Techniques or one of the Dialogue Techniques described in the next section.

1. **Presence**: Take a few really deep breaths and centre yourself. Connect with your Self/soul by closing your eyes, spreading your

awareness throughout your entire body and feeling your soul's presence.

2. **Scan**: Slowly scan your body from head to toe to sense any areas that feel blocked, heavy, sticky, cold, uncomfortable, irritated or somehow out of balance.

3. **Feel It To Heal it**: Use the Feel It To Heal It or Connect & Release technique to heal and reintegrate each blockage.

When a blockage has been cleared the area feels open and clear. But after a while we may start to feel that the blockage has returned. This does not mean that our previous work has come undone – it means that we are feeling a deeper layer of the same issue (or a new but closely related issue). Some ego structures build up like the layers of an onion as we grow older. When we clear the outer layer it feels like the blockage is gone but after some time (hours, days, weeks or months) our awareness deepens and we become aware of a deeper layer that needs to be processed. This may occur numerous times as we work our way down through the layers to get to the core of our issues.

There are usually a few areas of our body that our awareness/presence cannot sense into – it is as if our soul is not present in these areas. These blocked or restricted-access areas usually contain a mass of unresolved psychological material (e.g. exiles, holes and ego structures). The big blockages often have many layers, and the parts may have complex co-dependent relationships, so they can take many months or years to process fully.

Another obstacle that we may encounter is magnetic repulsion. It feels like a magnetic force is pushing our awareness away from a specific area, and it means that a protective ego structure is trying to keep us away from an exile or hole. We can use a Presence Technique to stay with the sensation, or we can use a Dialogue Technique (described in the next section) to learn more about it and maybe even gain access.

1g – Body Focus Exercise

This simple but effective exercise involves holding our presence and pure awareness in different parts of our body for a few minutes at a time. Most of our unresolved psychological material is located along our midline, which runs from the top of the head to the perineum (between the genitals and anus). So focusing our presence and awareness on areas along the midline are most likely to bear fruit: e.g. crown, forehead, behind eyes, jaw, throat, upper chest, sternum, diaphragm, solar plexus, navel, pelvis, genitals, perineum, spine and coccyx (tail bone).

1. **Presence**: Take a few really deep breaths and centre yourself. Connect with your Self/soul by closing your eyes, spreading your awareness throughout your entire body and feeling your soul's presence.
2. **Select**: Select an area of your body and focus your presence and awareness there (while still maintaining presence and awareness throughout the rest of your body).
3. **Feel It**: Feel into the area and any sensations or emotions that may arise.
4. **Heal It**: Stay with it, unite with it and allow it to reintegrate. Don't try to fix it or make anything happen – just maintain presence and pure awareness.
5. **Move on**: When it feels complete, move your awareness to another area of the body.

1h – Dissolving Pain Exercise

Pain is a message from a part of our being (body, heart or mind) informing us that something is wrong. If we try to resist or ignore the pain it will persist until we fully take notice. Our typical psychological response to pain is to distract ourselves from it, or to focus in on it to the exclusion of everything else. Both are forms of resistance, and neither really hears the message that the pain is trying to deliver. The best response to pain is actually a combination of the two: i.e. make the pain the centre of our awareness but keep our peripheral awareness widely focussed on the rest of our body. This way we can feel the pain fully without it overwhelming us because it is not the only thing that we are focussed on. Here are the basic steps:

1. **Presence**: Take a few deep breaths and centre yourself. Connect with your Self/soul by closing your eyes, spreading your awareness throughout your entire body and feeling your soul's presence.
2. **Focus**: Sense the precise location of the pain and centre your presence and awareness in the very core of pain (while still maintaining presence and awareness throughout the rest of your body).
3. **Feel**: Fully feel the core of the pain and the periphery of the pain. Immerse yourself totally in the pain.
4. **Surrender**: Don't resist it or try to make it go away. Embrace it, be one with it, accept it and surrender to it.
5. **Release**: Allow the pain to dissolve and diffuse – just relax and let it go (if/when it is ready to).

Do not do this exercise expecting to get rid of the pain (this is an ego agenda); do it with the intention of healing and reintegrating your consciousness (this is your soul's desire). The soul is the healer, so how can we expect to heal the issue if we are operating from the ego? The more ego that is present the less soul is present.

Our attitude must be one of total acceptance. If the pain dissolves we must accept that, and if the pain remains we must accept that. The pain will only go when it has taught us all it can. Personal self-inquiry or insight meditation can help us to understand the pain, its root cause and its reason for being. Bear in mind that some pain is karmic and may never leave us, and we must accept that too.

2. Dialogue Techniques

2a – Talking To Parts: Introduction

This dialogue technique involves talking to "parts" of our ego (e.g. exiles and ego structures) to help them release the fears and distorted beliefs that have burdened them since their creation. We are not trying to change the past; the past has already happened and cannot be changed, but we can help them to change their perception of the past. We can then invite them to join us in the present and re-integrate with the wholeness of our being.

5. Self-Help Techniques

The goal of this work is usually to make contact with an exiled part (wounded inner child), then heal our relationship with it and reintegrate it back into our being. But exiles are usually protected by guarding or distracting ego structures, and these have to be circumvented before we can get to the exile/wounded inner child. Other guarding, distracting or coping ego structures in the vicinity may also interfere with the process. They usually interfere (e.g. distract us, trigger us or blank our mind) at the start of the process while we are trying to understand the territory or negotiate with a protective ego structure.

All the dialogue is internal, so don't necessarily expect to hear clear voices responding to your communication. It does sometimes happen but you will probably just receive subtle impressions. You already know both points of view because the part you are talking to is a part of you. Listen to the first thing that pops into your head – if there is no immediate response stay calm and present. Don't try to make anything happen and don't try to think of an answer. Just stay open and receptive and the insight will come.

The following four sections describe the four main stages of the process – (1) Preparation, (2) Negotiating with a protector part, (3) Healing and reintegrating an exiled part (wounded inner child), and (4) Closure.

Talking To Parts: Stage 1 – Preparation

The Talking To Parts process is part self-inquiry and part body-centred healing (both of which were described in Chapter 4), and the information provided here supplements that information. Some elements of the process were inspired by the Internal Family Systems (IFS) model created by Dr Richard Schwartz. Please refer to *www.selfleadership.org* for further details.

As previously mentioned, there are two starting points for any kind of inner work:

1. **Specific Issue**: If you have a specific issue in mind that you want to work on, recall a time when the issue arose and notice what arises within you (e.g. body sensations, emotions, thoughts, memories, beliefs).

2. **No Specific Issue**: If you don't have a specific issue in mind, simply sense into your body and notice whatever is arising in the present moment.

Once you have identified a part to work with, close your eyes and go within to feel how it affects your body, emotions and mind. Observe whatever arises with "new eyes" and feel it with a "new body", without any expectation, belief or agenda.

Even though this is not a presence technique, the soul's presence is still essential to the process because it is presence that heals the relationship between the exiled part (misidentified piece of soul) and the rest of the soul. This enables the misidentified/exiled piece of soul to reintegrate with the rest of the soul. If the Self/soul is not present the process simply cannot work. Checking how we feel towards the exiled part is a good way of determining how much Self/soul is present:

- **Positive**: If you feel compassionate, loving and accepting towards the part, your consciousness is primarily operating through the soul, so there is a good chance the process will be effective.
- **Negative**: If you feel judgemental, irritated or resentful towards the part your consciousness is primarily operating through the ego. Your consciousness is blended with another part (exile, hole or ego structure), which is inhibiting your soul's presence.
- **Neutral**: If you feel indifferent towards the part your consciousness is operating partly through the soul and partly through another part (exile, hole or ego structure), so your soul's presence is partially inhibited.

If you are feeling negative or neutral towards the part you want to work with, the following steps can be taken to separate from the part that is inhibiting your soul's presence, and thus increase your soul's presence:

1. **Presence**: Spread your awareness throughout your entire body to increase your felt sense of presence.
2. **Acknowledge**: Acknowledge the inhibiting part that you are blended with and thank him/her for doing his/her job so well; i.e. protecting you from potentially painful psychological material.

3. **Reassure**: Reassure the inhibiting part that you are a mature, capable and loving soul who is here to help relieve suffering and ease burdens.

4. **Move Aside**: Kindly ask the inhibiting part to move aside while you talk to this other part, and invite him/her to keep an eye on what you are doing.

5. **Help Later**: You can also ask him/her if he/she would like you to come back and help him/her after you have finished helping this other part. If he/she says yes, please don't forget to come back and help him/her later.

Note: "he/she" and "him/her" don't read very well, so I will mainly just use the masculine terms from now on, but the parts may be masculine or feminine. Generally, men have masculine parts and women have feminine parts, but there are always exceptions.

Once your soul is sufficiently present, check how you feel towards the original part. If you still feel neutral or negative, repeat the process as many times as necessary until all the distracting parts have moved aside and given your soul some space to be present. When you feel positive towards the part, gently move your conscious presence nearer to the exiled part and see if there is any further resistance or interference:

- **No Resistance**: If there is no further resistance or interference you will start to sense the exiled part's fear and/or confusion. You can now move onto Stage 3 (skipping Stage 2).

- **More Resistance**: If you sense further resistance or interference you are probably encountering another protective part (a guarding or distracting ego structure). Before you can get closer to the exiled part you will need to convince the protective part(s) to allow you free access. This is described in Stage 2.

Talking to Parts: Stage 2 – Negotiating with a Protector Part (if req'd)

This stage isn't necessary if the protective part(s) that you (may have) encountered in Stage 1 have already moved aside and granted you access to the exiled part. Sometimes the soul's loving presence alone is enough to gain their trust, but if not the following steps will help.

Protective parts (guarding or distracting ego structures) are composed of young consciousness, and they usually believe that we are still the same age that they are. They won't let us through because they still believe we are a vulnerable young child that needs protecting from the pain, trauma and confusion that are locked up inside the exiled part. They need to be re-educated about how much more grown-up, capable and mature we are now, and that we can help them and the exiles to release their burdens and come back into the unity of our being. The basic process is outlined below:

1. **Presence**: Ensure your soul's presence and awareness can still be felt throughout your entire body.

2. **Acknowledge**: Greet the protective part and thank him for doing his job so well (i.e. preventing access to the exiled part). Communicate using simple language as if you were talking to a child. If you visualise yourself talking to a part, you must do so from the first person perspective, as if you are looking out of your own eyes with the part directly in front of you.

3. **Befriend**: Get to know the protective part and make friends with him. Take things slowly; be honest, sincere and genuinely interested in what he has to show or tell you. Express compassion when appropriate to demonstrate that you care. When a trusting and caring relationship has been developed, reassure the part that you are here to help.

4. **Understand**: Ask the following questions to ascertain the part's purpose, beliefs, motivation and origin: What is your job (e.g. to guard or to distract)? Why do you do it? What are you protecting? What are you protecting it from? What happened to make you first start doing this? Do you still need to do it – Why? Would you like a break from it? You will probably find that the protector part has some misconceptions that need re-framing; e.g. that you are no longer a vulnerable child that needs protecting.

5. **Educate**: Let the protector part know that you are now a grown-up. Tell him how old you are and what your life is like now. Re-frame any misconceptions, especially concerning danger, e.g. that you are

no longer being beaten by your father. Remember to communicate using simple language that a child can understand.

6. **Negotiate**: Reassure the protector part that you are only here to help. Say that in order to help him (the protector part) you first need to help the frightened little boy/girl (the exiled part). Say that you just want to make friends with the little boy/girl and help ease their suffering, then he (the protector part) will also be free. Ask if it would be ok for you to talk to the little boy/girl (the exiled part). Don't push too hard or too fast and never try to make him do anything before he is ready.

7. **Move Aside**: When you have permission to talk to the exiled part, gently ask the protector part to move aside. Invite him to keep an eye on what you are doing then continue with Stage 3.

Note: If the protector part comes onto the scene again in Stage 3, kindly ask him to move aside so that you can continue helping the exiled part. Let him know that you will come back and see how he is doing after you have helped the exiled part.

Talking to Parts: Stage 3 – Healing and Reintegrating an Exiled Part

Exiled parts are wounded and isolated parts of our consciousness – they need to be seen, heard, felt, acknowledged, befriended, loved, healed and reintegrated back into the wholeness of our being. All of this can be done with presence – simply being with the exiled part as fully as we can. The basic process is outlined below:

1. **Presence**: Ensure your soul's presence and awareness can still be felt throughout your entire body.

2. **Acknowledge**: Softly say "Hello" and ask if you can come a little closer because you would really like to be friends with him. If you visualise yourself talking to the exiled part/child, you must do it from the first person perspective, as if you are looking out of your own eyes with the part/child directly in front of you. Note: Some exiled parts make a big emotional scene when they are first discovered. This is due to the overwhelming relief of finally being found, the fear that they may never get this chance again, and the associated pressure to make the most of this opportunity.

3. **Approach**: If you get permission, move in slowly and respectfully; if not, try to develop a friendship then ask again. When approaching an exiled part you may sense his fear, pain, sadness, relief or happiness. But some exiled parts are indifferent because they have been alone for so long, and some are resentful because they were abandoned.

4. **Compassion**: An exiled part is a fragile little child that needs to be treated with loving compassion. Express genuine interest, gradually develop a bond and let him know that you really feel for him.

5. **Befriend**: Get to know him a little – ask him how old he is and how things are for him. Reciprocate by telling him your age, a bit about yourself and the good things in your life. After you have made friends he will probably start moving closer to you. If you get the sense that he wants to be picked up and cuddled, do so. Hold him close to your heart and feel the loving connection as strongly as you can.

6. **Fears:** Once you have developed a loving and trusting bond, gently ask him: What are you afraid of? If he is afraid for himself then he is definitely an exile, but if he is afraid for another part then he is a protector; in which case return to Step 4 of Stage 2.

7. **Understand**: Continue the gentle questioning to ascertain his origin and hopes for the future: What happened around the time that you were first left alone? How was that for you? Would you like to let go of that pain? What would you like to do afterwards? Would you like to come with me?

8. **Educate**: If he has any misconceptions or unrealistic beliefs, these need to be re-framed; e.g. "It is my fault that daddy left", "I should have done more" or "I deserved it". Help him to understand that he was not responsible for anything – it was not his fault.

9. **Reassure**: Nourish and nurture him by making him feel wanted and special. Tell him things like "I am so glad I have found you again" and "Thank you for being in my life". These kind words give him what he has been longing for all these years – to be welcomed back into our life and being.

10. **Release**: The simple act of being there for him (presence) is often enough to de-traumatise and unburden the child-part, but he may still be holding onto some hurt. If so, ask him how he would like to release it. It could be released by telling someone off, shouting at them, giving them a shove or kicking them in the shins (in your imagination). Or it could be released symbolically, e.g. by letting the wind blow away all his hurt, or washing away all his pain in the sea.

11. **Anything Else**: Ask him: Is there anything else you want to release or anything else you want to tell me? Respond with loving support and repeat the previous steps until everything has been resolved.

12. **Essential Qualities**: Invite in any positive qualities that the child may need to help him cope better in the future (e.g. courage, strength, wisdom and joy). The positive qualities help to fill the hole where the hurt and trauma once were.

13. **Reintegration**: Allow your soul's presence to dissolve into the child-part, and allow the child-part to dissolve into you. The exiled piece of soul within the child-part reunites with the rest of your soul, and the mental, emotional and energetic components dissolve and reunite with their respective subtle bodies. You may feel the child merge with you and begin to grow up within you – reviewing your life from the child's age to your present age can aid this process. Note: Reintegration sometimes occurs spontaneously (you will just know it has happened), in which case this step will not be required.

Stage 4 – Closure

1. **Protector Dissolution**: When the exiled part has been healed and reintegrated, the protector part will often dissolve spontaneously, because he is no longer required. But check to see if he is still there, and if so, ask him if he would like to release his burden, and help him to do so. If he is protecting another exiled part, ask if you can go and help that part – then return to the start of Stage 3.

2. **Other Parts**: Before you bring the session to a close, remember to check in with any other parts that you said you would at the start of the process. You can offer to help them now or arrange to meet with them another time.

The entire process can take an hour or two to complete, depending on how it goes. It is much easier if a compassionate friend guides you through the process by following the instructions above. The added benefit is that their soul's presence supplements yours to make the process more efficient and effective.

2b – Changing Chairs Technique

The Talking To Parts process is perfect for dialoguing with exiled parts and protector parts, but it is not really designed for dialoguing with coping ego structures (including the super-ego / inner critic). A more mature approach is required for talking to coping structures, because they are usually more grown up than exiles and protectors. Coping structures often adapt and develop as we grow older and change our approach to life, but this doesn't happen so much if we live our lives on autopilot. A degree of conscious living is required to update our coping structures. The coping structures that grow up don't cause much trouble because they are sensible and mature; it is the ones that don't grow up that can be problematic. When we live our lives on autopilot, our coping structures don't develop and we are stuck with the same old conditioned behaviours, reactive emotions and rigid beliefs for the rest of our lives. This explains why many adults often behave like kids or teenagers. The only way to change this state of affairs is though conscious inner work.

The Changing Chairs Technique is a simple yet effective way of dialoguing with a coping ego structure (including the super-ego / inner critic). It involves physically moving to a different chair when speaking from different parts of ourselves (e.g. ego-self and super-ego). This helps us to embody each part so that we can understand each part's perspective more clearly, and it helps us to separate from that part when we move to another chair and embody another part. The purpose of the exercise is to develop understanding and build bridges between the two parts to create harmony and integration. The added benefit is that subsequent inner work is usually easier and more effective due to the increased inner harmony that this process develops. The basic steps are outlined below:

1. **Two Chairs**: Place two chairs about 1m (3 feet) apart, facing each other, and sit in one of them.
2. **Presence**: Centre yourself and connect with your soul's presence.

3. **Yourself**: As yourself (ego-self), say what you need to say to the other part (e.g. inner-critic). You can ask it a question, such as "Why are you so critical of me when I make a mistake?", or you can vent your anger and frustration towards it. Just express whatever feels right for you.

4. **Other Part**: When you are done, move to the opposite chair and respond from the other part's perspective. Again, just say whatever comes naturally to you. This part is a part of you so you can speak authentically from its perspective.

5. **Switch**: Switch chairs and respond. Repeat as required.

6. **Resolution**: It is not about one side winning and the other losing; it is about both sides sharing their views to develop mutual respect and understanding. It is about reconciling differences and agreeing on a resolution or compromise that will enable both parties to peacefully co-exist.

7. **Third Chair** (optional): If the two sides cannot resolve the issue you can bring in a third chair (to represent your true-Self) from where you can mediate the peace talks.

Note: The process can also be done standing up, by just taking a couple of steps forward and turning around to face the place where you were originally standing.

2c – Peace Talk Technique

This technique helps us to become more tolerant and accepting of people who irritate us, by working on the part of us that gets irritated. It doesn't involve talking to the other person because our irritation has nothing to do with them – it is all us. The person who irritates us represents the part of us (ego structure) that carries the same trait. Our imaginary dialogue with the irritating person is actually a dialogue with a part of our self. We disowned and repressed that part because we didn't like its behaviour, which is why the other person's behaviour bugs us so much. Healing the relationship with our repressed part has the added benefit of improving our relationship with the (previously) irritating person. The process is quite similar to the Changing Chairs Technique so it can also be done using two facing chairs:

1. **Presence**: Centre yourself and connect with your soul's presence.
2. **Tell Them What**: Imagine that you are having a conversation with the person who bugs you and tell them what it is about their behaviour that irritates you. You can do this in your head, out loud, or in writing.
3. **Other Person/Part**: Then imagine you are the other person and respond on their behalf. Allow it to be authentic, so don't worry about expressing anger, frustration, sadness, disappointment, etc.
4. **Ask Them Why**: Then return to being yourself and ask the other person/part why they behave that way, or what drove them to behave that way?
5. **Switch**: Switch positions and respond. Repeat as required.
6. **Peace**: Mutual compassion slowly develops as both sides begin to understand each other. The tension and irritation give way to peace and acceptance.

You will know if your "peace talk" has been successful because the other person won't bug you so much. They will not have changed; they will still exhibit the same behaviour, but your attitude towards that behaviour will have changed. If it doesn't work completely the first time, study the person's behaviour to gain more insight into the issue and why it affects you; then repeat the exercise.

3. Inquiry Techniques

Our conditioned behaviours, reactive emotions and distorted beliefs will continue to shape our lives until we bring them into the llght of our conscious awareness. We can do this by looking for clues in our daily lives and inquiring into them to deepen our understanding. Inquiry techniques are useful for healing and reintegrating exiled parts and ego structures (protective and coping structures).

3a – Mirror Technique

The Mirror Technique uses other people as mirrors to identify our own subconscious patterns because it is always easier to see issues in other people than it is to see them in ourselves. If we identify a behavioural trait that irritates us or pushes our buttons, we can be fairly sure that a part of us has the same trait. We repressed that part of us because we didn't like the trait, which is why we don't like it when other people exhibit the same trait. Examples may include: bossiness, sarcasm, greed, not listening, talking too much, never serious, too serious, taking advantage, know-it-all, etc. Even situations where we think we have the moral high ground (e.g. people pushing in, being rude, or cutting us up on the road) are perfect for this technique. Their behaviour may be unsocial or impolite but that is not our concern. We need to focus on why it bugs us. Some people are not bothered by it, so why are we? The fact that we get emotionally triggered means there is almost certainly a distorted belief somewhere inside of us that triggers our emotional reaction.

The Mirror Technique uses self-inquiry to identify the reactive pattern and presence to connect with, heal and reintegrate the repressed part of us. Here is an overview of the process:

1. **Presence**: Centre yourself and connect with your soul's presence.

2. **Identify**: Contemplate your family, friends, colleagues and people on the TV. Identify any of their behaviours or attitudes that disturb you, irritate you, anger you, bug you or push your buttons. Then select one to work on.

3. **Inquire**: Ask yourself what it is about their behaviour or attitude that bothers you, and inquire into the possibility that you have that trait within you:

    a. Look for signs of the trait within you.

    b. Recall situations when you may have exhibited the trait.

    c. Discover if there are any false or distorted beliefs that might make you express that trait or try to repress that trait.

4. **Awareness**: Once you have acquired all the insight you can from your self-inquiry, hold all the elements in your awareness and notice any body sensations, emotions, thoughts or images that arise.

5. **Connect**: Focus your attention on <u>one</u> of the body sensations and feel it as fully as you can. Move your awareness/presence into it and

intimately connect with it. Explore it from various perspectives to get as many handles on it as possible. For example: feel into its core; feel its periphery; expand to feel it all at once; what shape is it?; does it have an emotional tone?; does it have a colour or a texture?

6. **Accept**: Accept the body sensation and allow it to be, without resistance or judgment. It is just a feeling in your body; it cannot harm you. It is just a message to make you aware that a piece of your consciousness is repressed and wants to be released. You didn't want to feel it when you were younger, which is why you repressed it. So really accepting it and allowing it now will start to heal the relationship with this repressed part.

7. **Love It**: Love the part. This proves beyond all doubt that you fully accept it and welcome it back into the wholeness of your being.

8. **Release**: Let go of the body sensation since it has served its purpose (connected you with the repressed part). You have got the message, so you no longer need to feel it. Allow it to dissolve and reintegrate into your subtle bodies.

9. **Invite**: Invite in an essential quality (such as love, joy, strength or peace) to support the reintegration process.

10. **Next**: Move onto the next body sensation (if any remain) and repeat the process until they are all released.

3b – Reversing Behaviours

This quick and easy technique helps us to understand (and perhaps neutralise) habitual actions and behaviours; e.g. bouncing our leg whist sitting or licking our lips before speaking. We normally perform these habitual actions without conscious awareness, so we can gain insight into them by reversing them in one of the following ways:

- Instead of doing it without conscious awareness, do it deliberately with a lot of conscious awareness.
- Instead of doing it at normal speed, do it in ultra-slow motion.
- Instead of actually doing it, just imagine that you are doing it.

I know it sounds strange but it works because it connects us with the issue in a really conscious way. Once we have gained some insight into the subconscious behaviour we can use one of the presence or dialogue techniques to process it.

3c – Reversing Negative Thoughts

When a negative thought arises (e.g. I am useless), ask yourself the following questions:

1. Can I be 100% certain it is true? Don't just listen to your mind's immediate reaction; take the time to feel how your soul responds.

2. What would my life be like if I didn't believe this thought?

3. What is the opposite of this thought? There may be a few options (e.g. I am not useless, I am good enough, It is ok for me to be useless), so take your time to choose the one that is right for you.

4. Say the opposite thought in your mind while exhaling slowly. Allow it to sink into your body and enjoy "feeling" it as you repeat this step for a minute or two. Really embody your new belief until you are at one with it.

Note: This technique was inspired by Byron Katie's "The Work" – please visit *www.thework.com* for further information.

4. Visualisation Techniques

4a – Empowered Time Travel Into The Past

We cannot change our past but we can change our disempowering beliefs and behaviours that are associated with our past. We don't have to carry the psychological burden of our past for the rest of our lives. This technique involves going back to a difficult time in our childhood to support our inner child with our adult capabilities and qualities. Here is an outline of the process:

1. **Recall**: Recall a difficult or distressing scene from your childhood. Visualise the scene and notice what is happening, what is being said, the vibe, how you feel, etc. Make it as vivid as possible without it becoming overwhelming.

2. **Strengths**: Think of the strengths and qualities you have now (as an adult) that you could have used back then when you were a child, e.g. confidence, will-power, intelligence and resilience.

3. **Support**: Feel all of those positive qualities within you, then imagine your adult-self stepping into the scene to support your child-self. You can either:

    - Imagine your adult-self (with all your strengths and qualities) stepping into your child-self, with the two of you merging to become one.

    - Or you can imagine your adult-self standing behind your child-self with your hands on their shoulder's to let them know that you are there to help, support and look after them.

4. **Replay**: Then allow the scene to play out again, knowing that your child-self has all the support they need and all your adult strengths and qualities to draw upon. The scene will probably play out quite differently now that your child-self has become empowered. There will probably be less fear and confusion now that the balance of power has shifted in favour of the child.

5. **Repeat**: Allow the scene to play out a few times, until you are happy with it (as happy as you can be). Really sense how different the scene feels and how different the child feels.

6. **Present**: When it is complete, gently bring your awareness back to the present and notice how you feel now; knowing that you have just travelled back in time to support your inner child.

4b – Empowered Time Travel Into The Future

The same technique can be used to travel into the future to empower yourself for a future event that you are worried about:

1. **Imagine**: Begin by imagining how the scene might play out if your insecurities, fears and anxieties become activated.

2. **Strengths**: Think of all the strengths, qualities and resources that you have when you are calm, confident and in control, then feel them all within you.

3. **Support**: Step into the future scene, merge with your future-self, and allow your positive qualities to empower your future-self.

4. **Replay**: Allow the scene to play out again, knowing that your future-self has all your positive resources to draw upon. Really sense how different the scene feels and how different your future-self feels.

5. **Repeat**: Allow the scene to play out a few times, until you are happy with it. Note: Don't try to envisage a positive outcome for the scene (e.g. getting the job), just focus on handling yourself positively. The scene is likely to involve other people so the outcome will never be completely in your control, so don't concern yourself with it. Just focus on doing the best you can – that alone is a positive outcome.

6. **Rehearse**: Rehearse the positive scene again just before the actual event. When the time comes you will be empowered with all the inner resources you need.

Note: These visualisation techniques aren't really a substitute for self-inquiry and presence-based healing and reintegration, but they can be helpful none-the-less.

The Therapeutic Relationship

After reading about all these different therapeutic techniques you may be wondering how you are ever going to remember all the steps, particularly when you are caught up in difficult or distressing emotions. The answer is to work with another person and support each other's healing journeys. You help to facilitate their process and they help to facilitate yours.

Therapeutic techniques and self-inquiry are much more effective when they are facilitated by another person who is present, compassionate and caring, because:

1. The subject can be 100% present instead of being 50% present and 50% facilitator.

2. The facilitator's presence helps to create a safe space that enables the subject to open up.

3. The combined presence of the facilitator and the subject is greater than the sum of their individual presences.

Empathic Resonance

It was unempathic (out-of-tune) childhood relationships with our parents that invalidated our true sense of Self and resulted in parts of our consciousness being repressed or exiled. So it follows that an attuned empathic relationship can help to heal and re-integrate these repressed and exiled parts of our being. It is tremendously healing to be "held" in a safe and nurturing space, and to be seen as we truly are, without any preconceptions or agendas. It is tremendously healing to finally get what was missing back then.

The empathic relationship doesn't have to be with a trained therapist. In fact many therapists have an agenda – they want to "fix" you and they want to do it their way. Approaching a vulnerable child-part with the intent of fixing it or healing it (treating it as a faulty object) is setting up the same inappropriate type of relationship that caused it to become distressed and exiled in the first place. Remember: we don't actually have to heal the child-part (because he isn't actually wounded); we just need to heal our relationship with him so that he can remember who he really is (i.e. our soul).

A vulnerable child-part will only emerge in a safe, empathic, accepting, honouring and nurturing environment, so the facilitator must be able to create such a space. The facilitator must be present, compassionate, gentle, calm, caring, supportive, a good listener, non-judgmental, and most importantly, be there just for you. Incidentally, if you are looking for a therapist with these qualities, I would suggest looking for one who is trained in the Diamond Approach, Hakomi, Internal Family Systems or Psychosynthesis. Failing that, a therapist from a humanistic or person-centred background should have the required qualities.

Therapeutic techniques are not the be-all and end-all of inner work; they are merely tools that we can utilise along the way. As Carl Jung said, "Learn your techniques well, but be prepared to drop them when you touch the human soul."

Chapter 6: **Spiritual Development**

Introduction

Spiritual or transpersonal development means "waking up" spiritually, i.e. raising our level of consciousness (to connect with our true-Self) and widening our breadth of consciousness (to experience life more fully). It involves re-connecting with, knowing and ultimately realising the true-Self. It is not about transcending the world; it is about bringing higher levels of consciousness down into our being and expressing them in our daily lives. It is about being here as fully as we can and experiencing all of life. There is nothing we can actually "do" to spiritually evolve because it is the result of not doing, undoing or being. Simply "being" is at the core of every authentic spiritual practice, including meditation, mindfulness and prayer.

There are four main elements to spiritual development:

1. **Meditation** is about presence not absence; it is about being fully present in our bodies. It is not about escapism or transcendence. Transcendent states may arise and the boundaries of our physical body may feel indistinct but we should remain 100% present.

2. **Living Presence** is bringing the presence that we discover during meditation into the rest of our lives. It is closely connected to the personal development practices of Conscious Living and Embodying Essential Qualities.

3. **Prayer**: If conventional prayer is asking for something from God, authentic prayer is giving something to God. Giving our presence and awareness to God/Life/Universe to help create "what is".

4. **Spiritual Self-Inquiry** is getting to know our true-Self. It is not a path that leads us anywhere – it is a path that stops us in our tracks so that we can rediscover who we really are.

Spiritual development and personal development are distinct but not separate – there is considerable overlap and integration. Developing and embodying the spiritual aspect of our being (soul) helps to develop our personal aspects, and developing and integrating the personal aspects of our being (mind, heart and body) helps to develop our spiritual aspect. Both approaches synergistically combine to help us to become more authentic and help our consciousness to evolve.

The Infinity of Self

We would generally describe a glass that is half filled with water as being half full, half empty, or perhaps both; but none of these descriptions are completely true. The "empty" part of the glass is actually full of air but because we cannot see the air we see empty space. It is the same with our ego and our soul – the ego cannot perceive the subtleness of the soul (the Self's primary field of consciousness), so it sees empty space. Just as the air is not confined to the glass (it is connected with all the air in the atmosphere), our Self's consciousness is not confined to our being – it is connected with all the consciousness in the universe. When we are attuned with Self, our awareness naturally shifts to this higher subtler perspective.

Here are a couple of quick and easy methods for connecting with Self:

- Close your eyes and turn your attention inwards, spread your awareness throughout your entire body and feel the palpable presence of your Self/soul. When you have a strong felt sense of presence, expand your awareness beyond the limits of your physical body. You may notice that the boundary of your physical body begins to feel indistinct – this demonstrates that your consciousness is more attuned to your soul than your body.

- Ask yourself the following question: "Without using my thoughts, memories, emotions, perceptions or associations, what am I?" Like a Zen kōan, this question confuses the mind and stops it in its tracks, which results in a direct sense of Self.

6. Spiritual Development

The Light of Awareness

In *"A Return to Love"*, Marianne Williamson wrote: "Our deepest fear is not that we are inadequate. Our deepest fear is that we are powerful beyond measure. It is our light, not our darkness that most frightens us... We are all meant to shine, as children do... And as we let our own light shine, we unconsciously give other people permission to do the same. As we are liberated from our own fear, our presence automatically liberates others."

The ego's awareness is like a flashlight that is focussed into a small spot. Its field of perception is very limited but it can be very focussed, so it often puts too much importance on what it perceives, which causes us to over-identify with the object of our perception (thought, emotion, sensation, etc.). For example, when we are expecting an injection in our arm, all of our awareness is focussed on the point where the needle pierces our skin, so all we consciously experience at that time is the pain in our arm. The pain fills our field of awareness, so the pain feels intense. If, on the other hand, our awareness was spread throughout our entire body, like a wide-focussed floodlight, the area of pain would only occupy a small part of our field of awareness, so the pain would feel less intense. The same principle applies when our awareness is focussed somewhere else and we accidentally injure our self – we often don't immediately know that we are hurt.

Spreading our awareness throughout our body emulates the all-encompassing nature of our soul, which aligns our consciousness with our soul. Maintaining our conscious awareness on the soul (causal body) during meditation, prayer, self-inquiry or life helps to entrain our other subtle bodies (mental, emotional and energy) with the essential qualities of the soul. By embodying our inherent divinity we are literally bringing heaven down to Earth. By focusing on the background awareness instead of the objects within our awareness (thoughts, emotions, sensations) we can sense the subtle peace, bliss and joy that is our soul.

1. Meditation

An Introduction to Meditation

Meditation used to be an esoteric practice for spiritual growth, but in recent years it has entered the mainstream and has become diluted, distorted and sometimes overcomplicated. It is now commonly used for stress relief and relaxation and is being promoted as a way to bypass life's difficulties. It is being used to relieve the symptoms of an ego-driven life, but it was originally intended to be a way of dis-identifying with the ego-self and developing a deeper connection with our true-Self. Meditation is not supposed to give us a break from our troubles; it is supposed to help us connect with the root causes of our troubles, whilst simultaneously dis-identifying from the belief that we are our troubles (e.g. I am angry, anxious or depressed). Basically, meditation helps us to experience the infinite nature of Self and the ephemeral nature of ego.

So what exactly is meditation? Meditation is practising presence; it is practicing present-moment awareness; it is experiencing what is arising without any judgement or agenda. It is as simple as that. Hundreds of books have been written on how to meditate but they are largely unnecessary because meditation is not something that we "do" – meditation is pure "being". All it requires of us is to stop doing everything and just experience what is occurring, within us and perhaps without. It is that simple, but it is not that easy.

Undoing decades of conditioning is not easy. Stopping the mind from analysing and judging is not easy. Stopping the emotions from reacting to our thoughts is not easy. Stopping the body from becoming tense or restless is not easy. The good news is that we don't have to do any of that – we can just let it all be.

Perhaps the biggest misunderstanding about meditation is that we have to be mentally, emotionally and physically calm. This is not true, and trying to achieve it can be incredibly difficult and can result in a lot of unnecessary frustration and suffering. Striving to achieve inner peace by attempting to control the mind, heart and body can actually take us further away from our goal. Meditation is all about letting things be. If we stop resisting the mind, heart and body they will quiet down naturally – not through our efforts, but through our non-effort. Meditation is not

6. Spiritual Development

about being calm or blissed out; it is about being present and aware. Calmness and bliss are not the goal, but they are often pleasant by-products.

It is the nature of the mind to think thoughts, form associations and make judgements – they are its purpose for being. Yet some people on the spiritual path try to quiet the mind, repress the mind, or stop the mind in the hope that it will allow them to become more "spiritual". Actually, the problem does not lie with the mind at all (which is just doing what it is supposed to do); the "problem" is with our awareness. We do not need to train our minds to become quieter; we need to train our awareness to be less affected by and less identified with the contents of mind. The same applies to our emotions and desires. The mind must be allowed to think, the heart must be allowed to emote and the body must be allowed to act. Trying to repress them is almost impossible, but noticing them with conscious awareness and feeling them with conscious presence stops them from getting out of control. The spiritual path is not really about our physical, emotional and mental bodies; it is primarily about developing and refining our soul (causal body).

Meditation is about observing, feeling and welcoming whatever arises, even if what arises is resistance, boredom, restlessness, mind-chatter, critical thoughts or all of the above. If these things come up we simply notice them and feel them without any agenda (to stop them) or judgement (about them or about ourselves). Distracting thoughts and emotions are not enemies that must be vanquished; they are teachers that we can learn from. Everything that arises is an experience through which our consciousness can grow and evolve; even if, on the face of it, it seems unpleasant. But that is just the ego's subjective view – the Self is completely objective so it doesn't judge these things as good or bad. The Self isn't interested in controlling or changing things. The Self just wants to experience all that life has to offer, "good" and "bad", and experience it fully. Meditation is practicing being our Self.

Meditation involves observing with an open mind and feeling with an open heart; without thinking, analysing, judging or trying to change anything. Meditation is noticing "what is" and surrendering to "what is". Surrendering does not mean a passive detached "whatever" attitude. It means active and engaged presence. It means being with it fully.

Meditation is open-focused presence; not mindless absence. It is not about escapism or being in a spaced-out trance; it is about being present (here and now), more than we are normally. Presence is our natural state of being but we have forgotten this because we are too busy thinking, reacting and doing – we have forgotten how to just be. Meditation helps us to return to our natural state; it trains us to simply be.

Just stop for a few moments and simply be. In this still quiet space, our false sense of self falls away and all of our troubles fall away. There is no suffering – there is only "what is". Meditation involves practicing this state of being so that it becomes second nature; so that it becomes our default state of being. Meditation is practicing "being" – anything more complicated than that is not meditation.

Many so-called meditations give the meditator (the ego-self) a task to do, such as counting the breath or repeating a mantra. These practices aren't actually meditation; they are a type of mindfulness. Meditation is about "being", not "doing". It is about identifying with the true-Self, not the ego-self. Meditation is the practice of consciously "being", so it doesn't require any "doing". These other practices are fine; there is nothing wrong with them, but they will not help us to discover our true-Self.

Meditation isn't a means of achieving anything; it is merely a way of realising presence and pure awareness. Meditation involves noticing that pure awareness is present, feeling that presence, and being that presence. With meditation there is no goal, so there is no expectation. If you expect to become enlightened by meditating an hour a day for 20 years you will probably be disappointed, because fixation on an ego goal is never going to lead you to your true-Self.

Meditation is not about trying to achieve pure awareness, nor is it about practicing presence and pure awareness (although it does involve this). Meditation, in its purest sense, is simply being presence and awareness. It is about experientially knowing that our true nature is presence and pure awareness. It is about "being" who we are as much as possible and "doing" as little as possible. So please don't try to manipulate your experience in any way – just be with "what is".

I am going to build on the glass half full analogy to describe what makes an effective meditation: A glass (our awareness) that is half full of water (mind, emotions and body) is also half full of air (soul). The contents of the glass remain the same whether the water is still or unsettled, so meditating to still the psyche (mind, emotions and body) is of little benefit. The real benefit of meditation comes from raising our awareness from the everyday level of the psyche to the higher/subtler level of the soul (i.e. aligning with Self). Admittedly this is easier when the psyche is still, but it is by no means essential. It doesn't really matter if our mind, emotions and body are all restless. If we sit in pure awareness and simply notice the turmoil within us, without trying to change it, we will benefit from the meditation. All meditation is beneficial and effective, whether it feels like it or not. If we meditate without any agenda, expectation or judgement we will reap the benefits whether we know it or not.

The Difference Between Meditation and Mindfulness

Mindfulness and meditation are highly beneficial practices: mindfulness for personal development and meditation for spiritual / transpersonal development. The main difference between these two practices is where our attention is focused:

- **Meditation**: During meditation our attention is primarily on the pure background awareness of our soul (the cinema screen).
- **Mindfulness**: During mindfulness our attention is primarily on the content of our mind (the moving pictures on the cinema screen).

One of the goals of mindfulness is to clear and calm the mind. This is not a goal of meditation because meditation has no goals. However, by not focusing on the content of our minds we are no longer encouraging the mind to keep bringing us more content – so meditation does indirectly result in a clearer and calmer mind.

The Benefits of Meditation

Meditation has been the central practice of almost every spiritual and religious tradition for thousands of years and will quite rightly continue to be so for millennia to come. Regular meditation will enrich your life, develop your consciousness and cultivate qualities that will benefit you now and in the future. Some of the direct and indirect benefits of meditation are listed in Figure 20:

Direct Benefits (spiritual development)	Indirect Benefits (personal development)
Facilitates spiritual/transpersonal development.	Facilitates psychological healing and reintegration.
Develops "mind" qualities such as creativity, intuition and wisdom.	Calms the body and mind, and improves the clarity of thought.
Develops "heart" qualities such as compassion, courage and joy.	Increases feelings of peace, happiness and contentment.
Develops "body" qualities such as will, resilience and presence.	Reduces stress, anxiety, depression and anger.
Systematically activates higher levels of consciousness.	Increases efficiency and productivity in our daily lives.
Increases presence and purifies awareness.	Reduces automatic ego reactions and conditioned behaviours.
Develops a deeper understanding of Self and the nature of reality.	Can reduce our biological age by 5-10 years (i.e. health benefits).

Figure 20: The Benefits of Meditation

The presence, pure awareness and essential qualities that we cultivate in our meditation practice gradually percolate through into our daily lives. Being present and surrendering to "what is" is a lifelong practice – both in meditation and in life.

Posture & Timing

Meditation is a spiritual practice, so physical posture is of secondary importance. The only things that really matter about meditation posture are comfort, stability and not falling asleep. Here are a few suggestions:

- **Seated**: Sit on a straight-backed chair, with your hips slightly higher than your knees (so as not to strain your back), and your back not leaning against the chair back (to stop you from getting sleepy).
- **Cross-legged or kneeling**: on a zafu, cushion or folded blanket on the floor.

6. Spiritual Development

- **Standing**: with feet shoulder-width apart and knees very slightly bent (but not locked).
- **Lying**: on a rug or yoga mat on the floor (not a bed or sofa because you will get sleepy). Small cushions can be used under your head and/or knees if that is more comfortable.

Relax any areas of tension, tightness or clenching in your body. A quick scan of your body from top to bottom can help you to identify areas of tension. Tension is common in the brow, jaw, tongue, shoulders and buttocks. Keeping your chin tucked in slightly helps to ensure the spine remains erect, which reduces back strain. Your eyes can be kept fully-closed, half-closed or open, depending on your preference and the type of meditation.

Whatever posture you choose to adopt, if you encounter any physical pain, please change your position. You don't want to hurt yourself or be distracted from your practice. Some mild discomfort or numbness may be experienced. If it is not too distracting it can be used as the object of the meditation, i.e. move your awareness into the area of discomfort and feel it as fully as you can. Don't just notice it from your head (that will make it feel worse); actually move your presence and awareness into the area so that you become one with it.

Meditate for an allotted time period, and ensure that you will not be disturbed for that time period. Start with 10 minutes and increase it by 5 minutes a month until you reach 30 or 60 minutes. Don't use an ordinary alarm clock or a kitchen timer because they are too harsh to end the meditation. Suggested options include:

- Buy a dedicated meditation timer or interval timer.
- Set a vibrating timer on your smartphone or tablet.
- Download a meditation timer app onto your smartphone or tablet.
- Place a clock in front of you. Use your judgement to estimate how much time you have been meditating. Gently open your eyes and check the clock when you think the time is up. If not, close your eyes and continue meditating.

When the time is up, ease yourself out of the meditation by expanding your awareness out into the room before gently opening your eyes. Take in the room with all of your senses while still maintaining your body awareness. Carry this living presence into the rest of your day.

Difficulties & Distractions

Don't get frustrated by distractions, because the attention you give them will actually reinforce them and make them more difficult to overcome – just let them "be" and they will eventually fade away. Don't beat yourself up for getting distracted because that will take you back to your ego (or super-ego) and away from your soul. The following pointers will help your meditations to flow more smoothly; with fewer difficulties and distractions:

- **Before You Begin**: Ask if there are any parts (e.g. exiles or ego structures) that want to be seen or heard before you begin. If so, invite them to share their concerns. Listen to them compassionately and reassure them as best you can. Tell them that you are only going to meditate – you are not trying to stir anything up – you just want to meditate to develop your consciousness. Ask them to give you some space so that you can sit quietly and just "be". Let them know that they are welcome to keep an eye on things, but you would appreciate it if they did not interfere or try to distract you.

- **During The Meditation**: If a distraction arises during a meditation and you get a sense that it is being caused by a part (e.g. exile or ego structure), ask it to share its concerns with you. Listen to it, reassure it and ask it to give you some space while you finish your meditation. You can also ask it if it would like to talk to you again after the meditation (or at a convenient time) so that you can get to know it better and welcome it back into your life. If you make an agreement like this, please stick to it because developing trust is an essential element of the healing and reintegration process.

- **Persistent Thoughts & Emotions**: If you notice a persistent thought, emotion or body sensation, stay with it, experience it as fully as you can and see if it has anything to show you. This could be a perfect opportunity for doing a self-inquiry (see Section 1 of Chapter 4).

- **Distracting Thoughts**: Meditation involves noticing "what is" without resisting it, so don't try to stop your thoughts (it won't work anyway). If your thoughts are active, that is perfectly fine – just notice them. The very act of noticing them may quiet them down, but it may not. It doesn't matter either way; so drop the belief that you need a quiet mind and accept "what is". The next point may also help with this.

- **Mind Chatter**: Imagine that your field of awareness is the size of a football stadium. Mind chatter is the equivalent of a small radio playing in a far corner of the stadium. It seems loud and distracting when you focus your awareness directly on the radio, but if you de-focus your awareness and spread it out to fill the entire stadium you will barely notice it. So spread your awareness throughout your body (and beyond) to reduce the significance of mind chatter.

- **Can't Concentrate**: Drop the belief that meditation requires a focussed, still and quiet mind. This is a judgement and a false belief; both of which come from the ego. Meditation is about transcending the ego and connecting with your soul's presence and pure awareness. Just say the word "presence" when you notice that you've lost concentration. Then expand your awareness to feel your entire body (with presence) and continue the meditation.

- **Boredom**: If you meditate dutifully and mechanically you are bound to get bored sometimes because you are in the wrong state of mind. Meditation should be done with a sense of aliveness and innocence because you are connecting with something truly authentic and wondrous. Boredom is a consequence of the ego's expectations – if you don't have any expectations or agenda you have no idea what will happen next. You will be completely open to anything, and that is what meditation is all about. It is about moving from the closed, predictable, rigidity of the ego to the openness, aliveness and wonderment of the soul.

- **Unsettled**: If you feel unsettled, it means you are not in harmony with "what is"; it means you are resisting "what is". If you can accept "what is" you will feel settled again.

- **Sleepiness**: If you feel tired or sleepy before meditating, don't meditate – wait until you are more alert. If you become sleepy during a meditation, the usual advice is to stand up and continue meditating and/or keep your eyes half open. But you can actually use the sleepy symptoms (heavy eyes, detached consciousness, etc.) as the focus of your meditation. If you stay with these sensations and feel them fully, your meditation may become more focused and you may become more alert.

- **Restlessness**: A restless mind and/or body doesn't have to affect your meditation. You can just "be", no matter what is going on, internally or externally. The purpose of meditation is to dissociate from the content of your awareness and associate with "being" that awareness. However, it can help to do 5-10 minutes of moderate exercise about 30 minutes before your meditation to burn off any excess energy.

- **Itches**: If you become aware of an itch, just noticing it in your mind will probably drive you crazy. The itch will intensify and before long you will just <u>have</u> to scratch it. But if you move your awareness into the area of the itch and feel it fully, you will probably find that you are better able to tolerate it. By fully feeling the itch you will not be mentally judging it as a source of irritation – you will just be noticing a body sensation without any resistance, which makes it easier to tolerate. Your soul's presence may soothe the itch and allow it to fade away. But if it doesn't, just give it a good scratch, because itches fall into the category of "change what you cannot accept" not "accept what you cannot change".

- **Pain & Discomfort**: The above principles also apply to physical pain and discomfort. The pain might simply be telling you to change your body position to a more comfortable one. If this is the case, listen to it and do something about it. But if the discomfort is tolerable, feel into it as fully as possible – move your awareness to the location of the pain, merge with it and engage with it. It is just a part of you that wants some attention. If it doesn't calm down, inquire into the pain to find out what it is trying to tell you. Mild discomforts can often be eased by spreading your awareness throughout your entire body, which will take your focus off the discomfort.

- **Energy Blockages**: You may become aware of some subtle sensations (e.g. dense, cold, uneasy, irritated, sticky, clogged, tight or heavy) in certain areas your body. These blockages are the energetic components of ego structures, exiles and holes. If you notice such a blockage, move your awareness into it, feel it fully and cultivate loving acceptance. Try to get a sense of what it is about, but do not resist it, try to change it or want it gone. Alternatively, if you don't want to turn your meditation into a healing session or a self-inquiry, you can simply notice the blockage and continue with your meditation.

- **Blissful States**: Not all distractions are unpleasant. If you experience a blissful state or a spiritual phenomenon whilst meditating, enjoy it by all means, but don't cling to it. Simply notice it, feel it and allow it to be, then allow it pass.

- **After the Meditation**: If the meditation didn't go as well as you would have liked, don't be too hard on yourself – that will just take you further away from where you want to be. Drop the false beliefs that meditation must be peaceful and that you must do it perfectly. Drop all your agendas (inner peace, healing, psychic powers, enlightenment, etc.) and just allow yourself to "be". There is no right or wrong; there is only "what is".

- **No Improvement**: If your meditations aren't "improving", even after several weeks, don't worry – they are still having a beneficial effect. Just accept that this is the way things are for now and know that things will "improve" in good time. Sometimes you just need to demonstrate your determination and resolve to stick at it. The path of awakening is not easy, and these early challenges separate the wheat from the chaff. Your Self will not allow you to enter the path unless you are truly prepared to follow through.

- **The Best Advice**: The next time you sit down to meditate, don't <u>try</u> to be calm and still; simply ask yourself "Is stillness here now?" Then allow yourself to feel the answer – don't go looking for it with the mind – feel it in your body. You will probably discover that the inherent stillness of your soul will reveal itself naturally. You can do the same for peace, happiness, fulfilment, etc. You don't need to go looking for these things because they are already present – you are them. Tuning into your body disengages the meditator (the ego-self) and allows you to feel the presence of these qualities within you.

Some steadfast meditators may not agree with my suggestions about allowing a meditation to become a self-inquiry or a healing session. But if the opportunity is there to discover more of ourselves, or heal and reintegrate a part of our consciousness, we should probably not ignore it. Life provides us with all the opportunities we need to develop our consciousness, and all the clues to discover what is holding us back, but it is up to us to decide whether we want to take those opportunities or not.

Two Types of Meditation

There are two main types of meditation:

- **Form or Object Meditation**: It involves concentrating on an "object", e.g. the breath, the body, an essential quality, a candle flame, a mandala (image) or a chant. This type of meditation trains the mind. It requires the mind to concentrate on one thing to the exclusion of everything else. Concentrating on the object of our meditation means there is little room in the mind for anything else. Strictly speaking, form meditation is not true meditation because it focusses on the content, not the underlying awareness – so in that respect it is more like mindfulness.

- **Formless or Objectless Meditation**: With no "object" to focus on, our attention shifts to the underlying pure awareness that is our Self/soul. Not "doing" but simply "being" enables us to experience our true-nature. We may experience a refreshingly cool and clear sense of spaciousness, or a warm and loving sense of unity, or perhaps a deep sense of peace and well-being. In this highly receptive state of pure awareness we may also receive insight, intuition or inspiration. Formless meditation is true meditation.

It is useful to include both types of meditation in our daily practice. In fact, form meditation is the ideal practice to lead us into formless meditation. The following meditation incorporates both types – form and formless:

6. Spiritual Development

Basic Meditation

1. Get comfortable, close your eyes (or half close them) and centre yourself.

2. Take three slow deep breaths to release any stress and muscle tension. Fill your lungs completely by pushing your belly and chest out, then gently exhale.

3. Expand your awareness to encompass your entire body. Notice any tension, tightness or clenching and relax as much as you can.

4. With your awareness still in your body, turn your attention to your breath. Feel the rise and fall of your ribcage. Feel the coolness of the air flowing into your nostrils and the warmth of the air flowing out. (FORM)

5. If your mind is restless or if you want to develop your concentration, try counting your breath for a few minutes. Silently count (inhale-exhale) 1, (inhale-exhale) 2, (inhale-exhale) 3, (inhale-exhale) 4, (inhale-exhale) 5, (inhale-exhale) 6, (inhale-exhale) 7, (inhale-exhale) 8, (inhale-exhale) 9, (inhale-exhale) 10. Then return to 1 and repeat for as many cycles as you wish. If you lose concentration or get distracted just return to the practice and start counting from 1 again. (FORM)

6. Return your attention to simply watching the breath for a few minutes (i.e. stop counting). Allow your breathing to occur naturally, without trying to control it or change it. Notice if it feels steady or uneven – it doesn't matter either way, it just helps to keep you focussed and present. (FORM)

7. Release your focus from the breath and check that you are still aware of your entire body. If not, expand your awareness to encompass your entire body. Feel the palpable presence of your soul in your body. (FORM to FORMLESS)

8. Expand your field of awareness slightly beyond your body (into your aura). The body is no longer the object of your awareness; you are simply "being". Stay with this for as long as you like. (FORMLESS)

9. Optional – At this point you can incorporate additional elements into your meditation, for example:

   a. Meditate on an essential quality to help embody it.

   b. Contemplate a question or concept to develop insight.

   c. Scan your body for energetic blockages and feel into them with presence.

   d. Inquire into a psychological issue.

   e. Contemplate the true nature of Self.

10. When you are finished, slowly open your eyes and incorporate the room/environment into your field of awareness. Give yourself time to adjust from a purely internal focus to an integrated internal and external focus.

Centres of Consciousness

In the last chapter I briefly explained how we could meditate on an essential quality to help embody it (i.e. transpose into a usable personal quality). Similar results can be achieved by meditating on the centres of consciousness, but rather than developing one specific quality, this method is more general and helps us to develop and embody a group of essential qualities. It simply requires holding our presence and awareness in one of the main centres of conscious and just "being" there (without trying to change anything or make anything happen):

1. **Belly Centre**: Located about 7cm (3") below the navel and 5cm (2") inside. Meditating with our awareness in the belly centre feels grounded, stable, serene and assured. It helps us to develop the qualities of will, resilience, confidence, patience, presence, etc. and helps to heal anxiety and anger. The meditation can be enhanced by imagining and feeling the Earth inside of our belly.

2. **Heart Centre**: Located behind the centre of the breastbone. Meditating with our awareness in the heart centre feels like an "inner smile" – warm, soft, light and happy. It helps us to develop the qualities of love, peace, joy, openness, etc. and helps to heal depression, shame and grief. The meditation can be enhanced by imagining and feeling the warm golden Sun inside of our chest.

3. **Head Centre**: Located between the temples. Meditating with our awareness in the head centre feels cool, clear, open and insightful. It helps us to develop the qualities of clarity, creativity, insight, intuition, etc. and helps to heal criticality, frustration and hatred. The meditation can be enhanced by imagining and sensing the clear open sky inside of our head.

4. **Soul Centre**: Located about 15cm (6") above the top of the head. Meditating with our awareness in the soul centre feels expansive, transcendent, wholeness, oneness, etc. It helps us to develop a deeper connection with our soul. The meditation can be enhanced by imagining and sensing the vast emptiness of space pervading our entire being.

The first three centres of consciousness are where the soul connects with the centres of the physical-energy body, emotional body and mental body respectively. If you have difficulty finding or holding your awareness in one of these centres, it probably means that you have a lot of psychological material (exiles, holes and ego structures) in that area. This is particularly common with the belly centre because it is usually where we stuff our repressed emotions. If you can't actually feel the centre, imagine that you can because it will give you a point to focus on, rather than just holding your awareness in a general area. It can take many years to fully develop this centre and its associated qualities, but the rewards are incredible.

Meditating in the soul centre is not advisable for beginners, because very little progress will be made until the three lower centres have been developed. The logical approach is to work our way up the centres of consciousness, but we should allow our intuition to guide us each time we meditate.

2. Living Presence

The transpersonal states that are sometimes achieved in meditation are all well and good but they are of little use in our daily lives. Just connecting with our soul is not enough because the soul is only one dimension of our being. We are multi-dimensional beings (Self, soul, mind, heart, energy and body) and our evolution is not complete until all these aspects of our being have been refined by our Self/soul's presence.

So our meditative practice must be expanded into a "living presence" that will permeate every aspect of our being and every aspect of our lives. Words cannot adequately describe the quality of presence, because the experience is not verbal or mental. Presence transcends the mind, heart and body, yet it includes and pervades them all:

- The mind-quality of presence feels cool, clear, fresh, calm, still and expansive.
- The heart-quality of presence feels soft, warm, intimate, joyous, loving and nebulous.
- The body-quality of presence feels grounded, stable, present (here and now) and has a real "I am" quality.

Presence has a palpable feeling – it feels like a subtle energetic swelling or literal presence within the body. It has a sense of fullness, like our soul is expanding and trying to express itself; which is precisely what spiritual development is all about. Presence requires our awareness to be present spatially (here) and temporally (now). It requires us to "be" – right here and now. But we have forgotten how to "be" because we have spent decades "doing". Living presence is "doing" whilst "being" – it is about practicing presence in our daily lives. Every moment of life is an invitation to be present but 99% of the time we let this opportunity pass us by.

Practicing Presence

The introduction to Chapter 4 described how to discover and practice presence (refer to page 120 if you need reminding). Being "present" means being here (in this space) and now (at this time), but not every aspect of our being is capable of being present:

- **Mind**: The mind finds it difficult to be present because it has difficulty being still. It is constantly on the look-out for stimulation and if it can't find it in the present, it will dwell on the past, worry about the future, or create a fantasy to escape to.
- **Heart**: Emotions can be stimulated by thoughts about the past, present or future. The heart can't tell the difference, so it doesn't really know what presence is, or what here and now are.

- **Body**: The body is always present because it can only ever be here and now. Wherever it goes is always here, and whenever it does it is always now.

- **Self/soul**: The soul is always present because it can only experience life right here and now. The soul can be aware of the past, present or future, but that awareness is happening right here and now.

So the body and the soul share a common trait – presence. The body is a short-cut to the soul's presence, which is why maintaining our awareness throughout our physical body helps us to stay present. When we are not present our Self/soul is absent so our ego is in control.

Conscious Awareness

The soul is sometimes described as a "shape-shifter" because it shapes and moulds itself to intimately merge with the "objects" of our experience (sensations, emotions, thoughts and direct perceptions). The soul can experience life directly by merging with a person or object, or it can experience life indirectly by merging with our mental, emotional and physical bodies and experiencing life through their perceptions.

Direct experience is only possible with conscious awareness, and indirect experience is more efficient with conscious awareness. But the ego's conditioned reactions inhibit our conscious awareness and keep us on autopilot. Conscious awareness requires the presence of Self/soul, as opposed to ego-identified soul. The soul still learns and grows through its ego experiences because a large part of the soul is one with the ego. Ego identification allows the soul to learn and evolve in ways that wouldn't otherwise be possible, but there comes a time for the soul to gradually awaken from its ego-misidentification, and this awakening process is facilitated by conscious awareness and presence.

Living Presence = Conscious Awareness + Presence

Living presence is conscious awareness and presence in union. Presence boosts the power and effectiveness of conscious awareness, and helps our awareness to stay fully present (i.e. here and now). Living presence puts the Self back in the driving seat and relegates the ego to the passenger seat:

- When we are neither present nor aware (i.e. "out of body") our Self is almost totally absent so our ego is in complete control.
- When we are present but not aware (i.e. just in our body) our Self is only partly-present so our ego is largely in control.
- When we are aware but not present (i.e. just in our head) our Self is only partly-present so our ego is largely in control.
- The Self is only in complete control when we are both present and aware.

So how do we practice living presence? It is very simple – just maintain conscious awareness and body awareness (presence) at the same time. Body awareness develops the connection with our soul's presence and conscious awareness develops the connection with our Self/soul's pure awareness. Living presence also helps our soul's essential qualities to become embodied into every aspect of our being, so it really is a very effective spiritual practice.

It is relatively easy to stay present and aware when we are peaceful, relaxed and still, but we should not restrict our practice to these times. To live with presence we need to bring presence and awareness into every aspect of our lives. We need to challenge ourselves by trying to stay present and aware during more testing times. For example, it can be very beneficial to practice living presence when you are feeling angry or anxious. Begin by focusing on the main bodily sensations, and breathe slowly and deeply into this area. Then as you begin to relax, expand the focus of your awareness throughout your entire body. At this point you are no longer identified with the anger (I am angry); you are identified with presence (I am presence). You are simply aware of your experience of anger (I am living presence noticing the sensations of anger).

3. Prayer

Who or What is God?

The Self is a point of consciousness that is connected with all other points of consciousness, and it is a field of consciousness that is connected with all other fields of consciousness. From that perspective there is only one Self and there is only one consciousness, which is commonly called God,

6. Spiritual Development

Universal Consciousness, the Universe or Life. Perhaps the simplest way of conceiving God is "nature on a universal scale".

I was driving behind a really slow car one afternoon and was getting a bit frustrated with the old man behind the wheel. Then I thought to myself: Would I be frustrated if God was driving that car? No, of course not! Then I realised that God was driving that car, because God/Life/Universe is everything and everyone. I was getting a direct message from God telling me to be patient and accept "what is". Life becomes so simple when we remember that everyone is an aspect of God and everything is a message from God. We are literally being spoon fed by Life, and it can direct our lives far better than the ego can.

Life, the universe and everything are actively working for our awakening – that is why it all exists. The universe exists and operates specifically for the development of our (and everyone else's) consciousness. The universe does this by challenging our false beliefs, emotional reactions and conditioned behaviours. It pushes our buttons to show us what we need to work on, and it challenges us to overcome our perceived deficiencies. It uses suffering to show us where we are going "wrong" and it rewards us when we get things "right" (although not always immediately). The universe also inspires us to expand our awareness and experience new things. Whatever Life sends our way is "meant to be" – so why do we feel the need to pray for things to be different?

No matter what we think we want, all we ultimately want are peace, happiness and contentment. We already have these qualities in abundance because they are our true nature; we have just lost sight of them. So we don't really need to pray for anything; except perhaps to be able to see more clearly who we really are and what we already have.

Creative Power

The true-Self, being an integral part of God/Life/Universe, has creative powers that enable it to manifest change in our lives. So if we pray from our true-Self there is a reasonable chance it will happen; provided it does not interfere with the divine plan (for the unfolding of the Life and the development of consciousness). However, most of us can't pray from our true-Self 100% because our exiles, holes and ego structures influence everything we do. Also, the true-Self doesn't need to pray (in the conventional sense) because it is already perfect, complete, blissful and immortal, so it wants for nothing and it trusts God/Life/Universe completely.

The ego-self is a part of the true-Self but it has forgotten that, so it cannot utilise the true-Self's creative power. This is why the ego-self has to resort to asking for help. Conventional prayer is like asking the government to help us out with a personal problem. We are just one voice in a million, and they can't give everyone what they want, so the chances of anything significant happening are pretty slim. Authentic prayer is like being a member of the government – we have much more influence from being on the inside, so we can actually make things happen, but only if they are aligned with government policies (the divine plan). The differences between conventional prayer and authentic prayer are described below.

Conventional Prayer

Conventional prayer is asking an external god for something in our (or somebody else's) life to change. This mode of prayer has a number of shortcomings:

1. **External God**: Asking an external god may feel empowering, but it is actually disempowering because it separates us from the creative power of God/Life/Universe (which we are a part of).

2. **Rejecting What Is**: Conventional prayer is rejecting "what is". It is saying "I am not happy with what God is doing". It demonstrates our lack of trust in God and the divine plan.

3. **Suffering**: Conventional prayer creates "distance" between how things are now (in the present) and how we want things to be (in the future). We are basically telling ourselves that we cannot be happy or contented until we get what we want.

4. **Lack**: When we ask for something, there is an underlying belief that we do not have enough. If we are focused on that lack, we will probably get more lack (i.e. nothing).

5. **Karmic Price**: The universe gives us everything we NEED (for the development of our consciousness), but we have to pay for everything we WANT (to satisfy our ego's short-sighted, fear-based and sometimes selfish desires).
6. **Powerless**: The ego is not fully integrated with God/Life/Universe, so it has very little power or influence.
7. **Misaligned**: The ego's prayers are quite likely to conflict with the divine plan and/or our life plan.
8. **Ignorant**: The ego doesn't know what's best for its own life, so we should think twice before asking for changes in other people's lives (no matter how good-intentioned they may be).

That being said, God/Life/Universe does sometimes give us what we want; not always in the way we may have hoped, but in the way that is best for our development. But rather than asking an external god to make things better, we can use conventional prayer to ask our true-Self (the god within) to show us how to make things better (i.e. reintegrate, evolve and awaken). Seeking insight and inspiration from our true-Self is the ideal use of conventional prayer. We can then use authentic prayer to actively bring it into being.

Authentic Prayer

If conventional prayer is asking for something from God, authentic prayer is giving something to God – giving our conscious presence to God/Life/Universe. Authentic prayer is a communion between our Self and the one SELF (God/Life/Universe). It is not an outward expression; it is an inner connection, with the infinite power of God/Life/Universe that is inherent within us all. Authentic prayer is giving our presence and awareness to God to help create "what is" and then giving thanks for "what is" (irrespective of whether it is "good" or "bad" from our own personal perspective). It does not involve asking for anything, because "what is" is already perfect and more perfection is continually unfolding. Authentic prayer is actively being the change that we want, right here and now. The universe is one integrated system, so whatever we embody affects everyone and everything. Authentic prayer isn't something that we "do"; it is a subtle process that engages different qualities of "being".

Here is an outline of the authentic prayer process:

1. **Soul Connection:** Take a few deep breaths to centre yourself, then connect with your soul by closing your eyes and spreading your awareness throughout your entire body.
2. **Pure Awareness**: Enter into an open and receptive state of pure awareness.
3. **Presence**: Feel your soul's presence throughout your body (and slightly beyond).
4. **Being**: "Be" the change that you want (e.g. peace). Feel it and embody it.
5. **Energy**: A heart-felt prayer creates a lot of spiritual energy that can be used to empower the process.
6. **Communion:** Feel the connection with God/Life/Universe and allow your embodied quality/energy to infuse the oneness.
7. **Gratitude**: Appreciate the perfection of "what is", give thanks to God/Life/Universe, and trust that everything is exactly how it needs to be.

4. Spiritual Self-Inquiry

Self-inquiry is not a path that leads us anywhere – it is a path that stops us in our tracks so that we can rediscover who we really are. We may conceptually know that we are our true-Self, but Self-realisation cannot occur until we experientially know it. It doesn't necessarily take years of spiritual practice to realise our true-Self; we may just need to overcome our habitual fixation on our thoughts and emotions, because this is what keeps us identified with our false concept of self (ego-self). Self-inquiry is not about stopping thoughts and emotions; it is about dis-identifying from them; it is about becoming that which is beyond thinking, feeling and doing.

We create internal representations of everything and everyone we encounter in life, including ourselves. The ego-self is an internal mental representation of who we think we are. The ego-self interacts with the other "objects" within our inner virtual world, and these mental and emotional interactions reinforce our false concept of self. Without the reinforcement from these internal interactions our ego-self would soon dissolve.

If we stop being fixated by internal "objects" (concepts, thoughts and emotions) there will be nothing for our ego-self to interact with. Without "objects" to relate to our concept of self cannot exist, so there can be no ego-self. This principle is the key to spiritual Self-inquiry. By clearing our mind of "objects" our false concept of self dissolves, which allows our more of our true-Self to be revealed and eventually realised. Spiritual Self-inquiry is essentially reversing the process of ego creation that occurred when we were 6-8 months old.

When we focus on thoughts and emotions we identify with them; e.g. "I am confused" or "I am happy". It is these "I" thoughts that reinforce our false concept of self and keep us from realising our true-Self. Our concept of self is a Self-limiting belief. When we focus on thoughts about "I" we reinforce our concept of self (ego-self), but when we focus on the feeling of actually being "I" we directly experience our true-Self. If we can sustain this direct experience of "I", the ego-self will gradually dissolve and Self-realisation will occur.

In many ways spiritual Self-inquiry is very similar to meditation, but they have different objectives:

- **Meditation**: utilises Presence to help develop Pure Awareness (the perceptive quality of Self/soul).
- **Spiritual Self-Inquiry**: utilises Pure Awareness to help develop Presence (the felt sense of Self/soul/unity).

The two practices complement each other very well because the pure awareness that we develop in meditation aids Self-inquiry, and the presence that we develop in spiritual Self-inquiry aids meditation.

There are two different types of spiritual Self-inquiry: Discriminative and Experiential. Both types are valuable and complement each other:

A. Discriminative Self-Inquiry

Discriminative Self-inquiry is about distinguishing Self from "not self" (e.g. ego-self, self-image, body, emotions, thoughts, concepts, beliefs, etc.). It is about releasing the things that block our experience of the true-Self. It is primarily a mind-based exercise that helps us to see through our conditioned thoughts, emotions and behaviours, but it deeply relies on the soul's awareness and presence to keep us from identifying with these "objects". If a thought does not serve us, we can release it. If, for example, our super-ego is telling us "I am worthless", we don't have to oppose it; we can just recognise that it is just a thought and know that it has no more validity than the thought "I am worthy". Every time we oppose a negative thought we inadvertently strengthen it, but every time we release a negative thought it loses some of its power. Discriminative Self-inquiry is not about opposing anything or accepting everything; it is about questioning the validity of our experiences and letting go of anything that is invalid. There is no need for any further analysis or judgement because such actions would perpetuate the drama and reinforce the ego.

The mind is just a series of thoughts; none of which are us – even the ones that are about us. Discriminative Self-inquiry is about questioning and transcending our beliefs, concepts and assumptions associated with "I" and "I am"; e.g. "I am Lee", "I am this body", "I am a human being", "I am consciousness" and even "I am Self". These are all mental concepts; they are not who we truly are. Who we truly are can only be felt; it must be directly experienced.

Every thought and emotion, even the trivial and neutral ones, can be inquired into using this simple process:

1. **Awareness**: Present moment awareness is required to notice your thoughts and emotions as they arise.

2. **Presence**: Presence boosts the power and effectiveness of your conscious awareness and helps you to stay fully present in the here and now.

3. **Contemplate**: Contemplate a thought or emotion – either one that is arising now, one that caught your attention earlier, or one that regularly affects you.

4. **Inquiry**: Is the thought or emotion valid and does it currently serve you? If it is invalid or unhelpful, know that you can release it.

5. **Release It**: Let it go and stop believing it. Releasing does not mean rejecting – there should be no judgement or resentment. The release must come from stillness and acceptance, which is why the soul's presence and awareness are so vital for this process. Every time we release an invalid thought or emotion it loses some of its power, so the more times we release it, the weaker it becomes. Note: If the same thought or emotion keeps arising, it might be worth inquiring into the reason behind it and then healing and reintegrating it (see Chapter 4).

Discriminative Self-inquiry differs from personal self-inquiry (see Chapter 4) because it is not about discovering the roots of the false-self; it is about releasing the things that block our experience of the true-Self. Discriminative Self-inquiry is not about understanding why we think and behave in ways that block Self-realisation; it is about identifying those things and not doing them anymore. Both types of self-inquiry (personal and spiritual) are equally useful and both are important for balanced psycho-spiritual development.

B. Experiential Self-Inquiry

Experiential Self-Inquiry is a soul-based practice that helps us to directly experience the true nature of our Self and its intimate union with "all that is". It is an incredibly direct method of Self-inquiry that simply involves asking "Who am I?" and feeling for the answer. When we ask the question "Who am I?" and let go into pure awareness, the answer will be there, not as an intellectual idea, but as a felt sense of presence.

The mind will want to answer: "I am [Name]", "I am this human being", "I am consciousness", etc. These mental answers can be inquired into (with personal self-inquiry) or released (with discriminative self-inquiry) until all subjectivity dissolves leaving only the direct experience of beingness. The key is to go beyond the mind to the unconditioned pure awareness of the Self/soul. The purer our awareness the purer our perception of Self becomes, and the deeper our presence the deeper our experience of Self becomes.

The inquiry "Who am I?" diminishes the conceptual "I" to reveal the true "I". Self-realisation is not attained by being aware of an "I", but by actually being the "I". Our usual way of experiencing something is to be aware of the "object" of experience. Self-inquiry is the opposite of this – It involves experiencing the "subject", not the "object". It involves being the experiencer instead of merely being aware of the experience. It involves contemplating and sensing the true nature of Self to bring about a direct experience of Self. With practice the experience becomes easier, deeper and steadier, and can ultimately result in Self-realisation:

1. **Presence & Awareness**: Enter into a body-centred state of presence and pure awareness.

2. **Inquiry**: Silently ask yourself one of the following questions (just once – do not keep repeating it like a mantra):

   - Who am I?
   - Where (in my body) am I?
   - Who is it that is thinking about this?
   - Who is it that is feeling this emotion/sensation?
   - From where does this sense of "I" arise?

3. **Feel**: Don't think about the question and try to answer it with the mind; simply contemplate it and feel for the answer.

4. **Experience**: Sense the presence of the experiencer and stay with that. Don't think or do anything else; just be with the experience of the experiencer – just "be" the experiencer. If thoughts or emotions arise: notice them and release them, ideally while still remaining in true nature. Note: If the same thought or emotion keeps arising it might be worth inquiring into the reason behind it and then healing and reintegrating it (see Chapter 4).

The deeper we sense, the less we find. Our concept of "who we think we are" falls away to reveal nothing but true nature (presence, pure awareness and essential qualities), which is "who we really are". When we look to see who is having this experience, we don't find anyone. There is barely any identity; only pure consciousness. The experience can be described as timeless, expansive, blissful, presence and pure awareness, but during the experience there is no experiencer – the experiencing is just happening. Without an object to focus on our awareness has no centre. Without a focal point of consciousness there is no "I" to have the experience. Self is simultaneously nothing and everything. Realising this truth means letting go of every concept and belief we have about who we are, and releasing every mental and emotional habit that sustains our (false) concept of self, because it is these things that keep us from knowing who we really are.

Chapter 7: **Awakening, Realisation & Enlightenment**

Introduction

Ego is our misidentification with our conceptual self (our mental concept of who we are). Our idea of who we are is just a thought, which is obviously not who we really are.

Our true-Self is more than just a thought-form and has an enduring existence. This chapter describes our true-Self's developmental journey of awakening, including Self-realisation and enlightenment. So what are the basic differences between these often misused terms?

- **Awakening**: is the gradual unfolding of human consciousness – it is like gradually turning up a dimmer switch where more of our true nature gradually emerges and expresses itself in our daily lives. Our soul's essential qualities are developed and refined by actively expressing them. Our awareness is purified by conscious living, meditation and processing the ego structures that keep us in a semi-conscious, semi-autonomous state. Awakening is the result of both of these factors – actively processing the ego structures that hold us back AND actively developing the essential qualities that carry us forward.

- **Self-Realisation**: is the result of seeing through our conceptual misidentification with ego and realising our true identity. It is sometimes referred to as a "sudden awakening" as our experiential perspective instantly shifts from our false/ego self to our true-Self. Self-realisation results a fundamental shift in our conscious perspective the moment we awaken from our misidentification of being the ego-self to experientially realise the fullness of our true nature and the integrated wholeness of reality. Self-realisation results in non-dualistic perception, which is described later in the chapter. It can only occur when sufficient ego structures have been dissolved to allow the Self to dis-identify from the ego and realise its true nature.

- **Enlightenment**: is a term that is often used interchangeably with Self-realisation, but it is not quite that simple. Self-realisation is realising the true-Self. Enlightenment is the true-Self ascending from the personality (specifically the mental body/conceptual mind) to the soul (causal body/abstract mind). Enlightenment and Self-realisation almost always occur simultaneously because it is almost impossible for the true-Self to be realised while our consciousness is centred in the conceptual mind. This is because the mind conceptualises everything, including ourself. So when our true-Self transcends the conceptual mind we are instantly liberated from our misidentification with our false/conceptual/ego-self and we immediately realise our true-Self. The true-Self is so subtle compared to the relative grossness of the ego-self that many newly enlightened people believe they have no-self. Enlightenment cannot be undone, although prior to enlightenment, grace may give us temporary tastes of what is to come. Usually it is just one aspect of the full enlightenment experience, e.g. a sense of loving unity and connectedness with everything or the silent stillness and emptiness of the no-self/true-Self experience.

We were all born Self-realised (not enlightened) but we lost sight of our true-Self when our mind developed sufficiently and our false/conceptual/ego-self formed. Since then we have developed all sorts of psychological strategies to protect our ego-self. But the moment we transcend the conceptual mind (at enlightenment) our misidentification is so obvious that we instantly disidentify from our false-self and realise the truth of who we are, and always have been.

7. Awakening, Realisation & Enlightenment

The main differences between regular and enlightened people are summarised in Figure 21 below:

	Regular Person	Enlightened Person
The Self	The Self is centred in the belly (energy body), heart (emotional body) or head (mental body), not the soul (causal body), so it cannot directly utilise the soul's essential qualities.	The Self is centred in the soul (causal body) so it can directly utilise the soul's essential qualities.
Essential Qualities	Essential qualities are passive so they have to be transposed into personal qualities to become usable. Ego structures are created to stand in for personal qualities that are not transposed fully or correctly.	Essential qualities become active, so they can now be used directly. Some ego-structures remain, but they can now be metabolised more easily because we are less identified with them.
Pure Awareness	Pure awareness increases as the soul evolves and gradually dis-identifies from ego, so we gradually become more awakened.	Enlightenment only becomes possible* when pure-awareness is greater than 50% (i.e. ego-identification is <50%). Pure awareness increases to 100% during the enlightened stage.
Causal Body (The Soul)	Only about 5% of the causal body incarnates. The other 95% that remains on the causal plane is often referred to as the "higher self" or oversoul.	The two parts of the causal body permanently merge at enlightenment. So an enlightened person has access to the entire soul (including all of their past life memories).
Perception	Dualistic Perception: Objects appear to be separate and unconnected.	Non-dualistic perception: Objects still appear to be separate, but the underlying connection that unifies everything can now be sensed.

Figure 21: Differences between regular and enlightened people

* Note: Self-realisation and enlightenment rarely occur the moment pure awareness reaches 50%, because the soul's identification with core ego structures is stronger than usual. It therefore takes more work to dis-identify from our core ego structures because they have been our home for decades. If Self-realisation occurs before 50% it will probably only be temporary and partial because the influence of the remaining ego structures is too great, so re-identification with the ego-self is inevitable.

What Is Achievable?

What is actually possible for the average spiritual seeker to achieve in this lifetime?

- **Enlightenment** in this lifetime is unlikely for most people because it requires such a highly developed consciousness that very few have yet attained. Even though enlightenment is an instant event, a lot of inner work needs to be done (over many lifetimes) to raise our consciousness to the level where enlightenment becomes possible. But the work we put in now will pay great dividends in the future, so please don't be disheartened.

- **Re-enlightenment** is relatively easy for people who have already attained enlightenment in a previous lifetime. It usually happens spontaneously in the late teens or early twenties. Those who have experienced this may give the impression that enlightenment does not require working on ourselves, but unfortunately that is not the case.

- **Awakening**: We all have the potential to become more awakened in this lifetime. It simply involves working on ourselves to purify and develop our consciousness.

Consciousness has an inherent drive to experience, grow and evolve. So consciousness will develop with or without our conscious effort, but it will develop very slowly without our conscious involvement. Development occurs at the optimal rate when we do our best without any expectation; when we tap into our natural drive to evolve, without getting caught up in the ego's striving and struggling.

The Journey of Awakening

The Self gradually awakens to higher levels of consciousness during our evolutionary journey through the human kingdom. The entire journey takes thousands of lifetimes but it can be broken down into 5 distinct stages, each of which gives our Self a different perspective from which we can experience, learn and grow. These different perspectives are literally different positions within our being; i.e. the belly centre/physical body, the heart centre/emotional body, the head centre/mental body and the soul centre/causal body. The Self experiences and learns all it can from each perspective before moving up to experience and learn from a new and higher perspective:

1. **Primitive Stage**: The Self is centred in the belly centre and most of our experiential growth comes through our identification with the physical senses. About 60% of people are currently at this level.

2. **Civilised Stage**: The Self is centred in the heart centre and most of our experiential growth comes through our identification with lower emotions. About 25% of people are currently at this level.

3. **Developed Stage**: The Self is centred in the heart centre and most of our experiential growth comes through our identification with higher emotions. About 15% of people are currently at this level.

4. **Humanistic Stage**: The Self is centred in the head centre and most of our experiential growth comes through our identification with thoughts. Less than 1% of people are currently at this level.

5. **Enlightened Stage**: The Self is centred in the soul centre and most of our experiential growth comes through pure awareness, i.e. no identification. The Self fully awakens to its true nature and transcends its identification with the personality. About 1 in a million people are currently at this level.

Note: All aspects of our being (body, heart, mind and soul) are utilised during all five stages of development, but each developmental stage has its primary focus. Fuller descriptions of the levels of consciousness can be found in Chapter 8 of my first book, *The Science of Spirituality*.

The Self's journey of awakening is depicted in Figure 22. In the Bible, this journey of awakening to higher levels of consciousness is described as climbing Jacob's ladder. Origen (an early Christian theologian) used similar terminology when he described how the soul climbs a ladder by developing virtues (essential qualities).

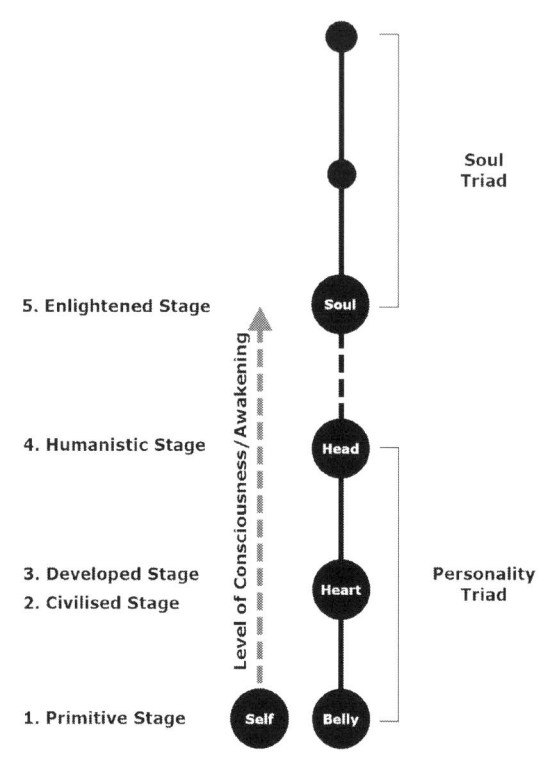

Figure 22: The Journey of Awakening

Figure 23 depicts the same information in a slightly different way. The diagonal dotted line represents the Self's journey of awakening through the 5 stages of development (horizontal axis). The black circles show which centre of consciousness the Self is centred in on each stage of the journey. The vertical axis shows the type of consciousness the Self primarily uses during each stage of the journey. For example: during the civilised stage our Self primarily uses the heart and the lower emotions to develop our consciousness (as shown by the small black arrows).

7. Awakening, Realisation & Enlightenment

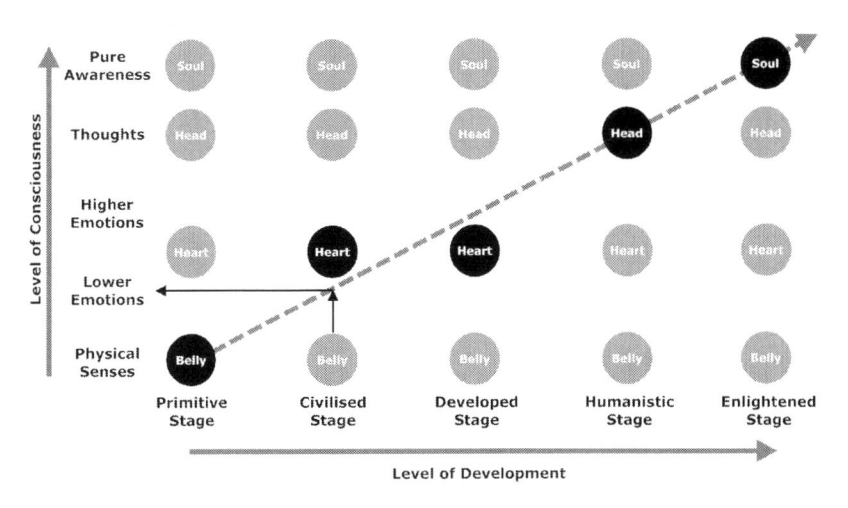

Figure 23: The Development of Consciousness

The same journey of awakening occurs on a smaller scale in each lifetime, during our childhood. As we grow up our consciousness climbs to the same level that we attained in our last lifetime. This ensures that our spiritual development can continue at the same level we left off. As stated in Chapter 3, our skandhas are also reactivated during childhood to create an ego that broadly resembles our ego from our last lifetime. This ensures our psychological development continues where it left off.

Self-Realisation

Most people are suffering from mistaken identity – taking ourselves to be someone we are not. The goal of psycho-spiritual development is to correct this mistaken identity; not to strengthen or improve our false identity. The self that we think we are does not exist; it is a figment of our imagination. The self that we think we are cannot awaken – we have to awaken from that false-self in order to realise our true-Self. When this occurs, we realise that we have been our true-Self all along, but had simply forgotten.

The Labyrinth

Our inner journey takes us through the labyrinth of our ego structures to discover our true-Self (at the core of our being). A labyrinth differs from a maze in that it only has one path which leads to the centre, so the path is already mapped out for us – all we have to do is walk it. If we stop resisting and controlling, the flow of life will naturally carry us to our destination. Some parts of the journey will be tough and others will be wonderful, but they will all be experiential opportunities for the reintegration, development and liberation of our consciousness.

Figure 24: The Labyrinth – Symbolic Images of the Ego Super-Structure

The most effective way of journeying through the labyrinth of our ego structures is to do so with conscious awareness and presence, because then we can process the psychological material (i.e. dissolve the ego structures and reintegrate our consciousness) as we encounter it. Then, when we finally reach the core of our being and realise our true-Self, we can be confident that we will not relapse back into ego-identification because the ego will have largely been dissolved.

Seeking Self-realisation before we are ready is unwise and will ultimately be unsuccessful because we are seeking freedom from something (the ego-self) that we still require for our development. However, our conditioning can cause us to remain misidentified with the ego-self for longer than is absolutely necessary. So here a few simple things that we can do to loosen our identification with our ego-self (in addition to the methods and techniques previously described in this book):

- **Challenge your thoughts**: Don't automatically assume that just because you thought it, you have to believe it and buy into it. Most thoughts are unnecessary hindrances that don't serve at all. When you notice such thoughts, silently say to yourself "that's not me".

- **Don't take things personally**: Our psychological patterns are simply being activated by someone else's patterns. Our patterns feel personal but they are actually generic. So it's not personal - it is just reactivity.
- **Forgive everyone and everything**: You can't change what has happened so why hold onto the personal feeling of victimhood?
- **Be selfless**: Put other people needs ahead of your own and dedicate part of your life to serving or helping others.
- **Be authentic**: Don't put on different personas at different times.
- **Have fewer preferences, opinions and beliefs**; especially about things that don't really matter.
- **Change the question**: Don't ask "How can I become Self-realised?" Ask "What am I doing that is keeping me from being Self-realised?"

The Path to Self-Realisation

In early childhood, if something authentic (e.g. an essential quality or our true-Self) is not acknowledged and mirrored back to us by our parents, we assume it is unimportant so we repress it and develop ego structures to help us cope without it. Psycho-spiritual development is about reversing that process – removing the blockages, bringing things into the light and turning the repression into expression. Self-realisation only becomes possible when sufficient psychological "undoing" has been completed – when our conditioning has been neutralised and our awareness has been purified (i.e. dis-identified from ego).

Even though Self-realisation is an instant event, there are several stages leading up to it that can be used to gauge our progress and guide us on to the next stage of our journey:

- **Stage 1** involves becoming aware of our thoughts, emotions and sensations.
- **Stage 2** involves becoming aware of thoughts, emotions and sensations as if they are not ours and not us.
- **Stage 3** involves becoming aware that we are the awareness that is noticing these things.

- **Stage 4** involves developing a felt sense that we are this awareness.
- **Stage 5** involves experientially knowing and feeling that we are awareness.
- **Stage 6** involves experientially knowing and feeling that Awareness (God/Life/Universe) is being us.

In a meditation (superconscious) we might be able to reach stage 3 or 4, but in our everyday lives (waking consciousness) we may still be at stage 1 or 2. This is quite normal, but we can bring these higher states of consciousness into our everyday lives through Conscious Living (see Chapter 4) and Living Presence (see Chapter 6). When we reach stage 3 or 4 in our meditation practice we can start practicing spiritual Self-inquiry (see Chapter 6); prior to that it is more beneficial to practice personal self-inquiry (see Chapter 4).

Non-Duality

Self-realisation results in non-dualistic perception – a direct and intimate unity with everything we encounter. But what does it really mean and how does it work?

- **Dualistic Perception**: The true-Self has forgotten who it really is and believes it is the false-self (a conceptual self-image). The false-self stands between the true-Self and objective reality (as depicted in Figure 25). The false-self perceives the object, and the true-Self perceives itself as the false-self perceiving the object, so there is no direct perception. There is separation between the true-Self and the object – hence duality. Note: The false-self doesn't actually do any perceiving (because It Is Just a thought-form); it is more like a lens that the image passes through (and often gets distorted) on its way to being perceived by the true-Self.

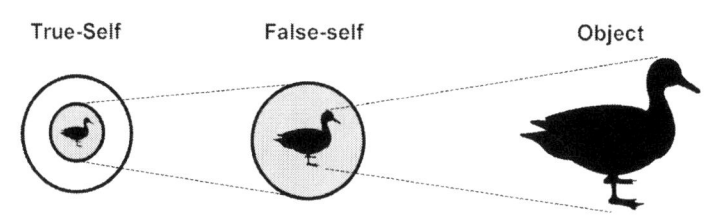

Figure 25: Dualistic Perception

- **Non-Dualistic Perception**: With the false-self no longer present, the true-Self can perceive the object directly. Nothing stands between the true-Self and objective reality (as depicted in Figure 26), so there is direct perception. There is nothing between the true-Self and the object, so the true-Self can intimately merge with the object to directly perceive every attribute– hence unity (or non-duality).

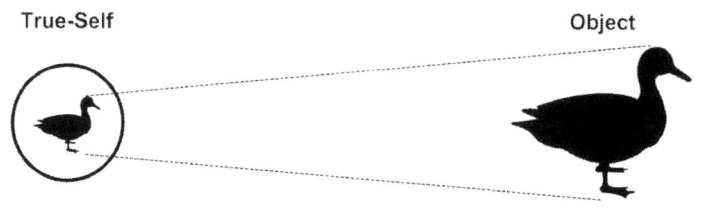

Figure 26: Non-Dualistic Perception

Separation and duality are learning experiments. The Self becomes identified with the ego-self in order to experience duality – to experience life from a different, separate, non-unified perspective. Then when we have learnt all we can from separation and duality we will naturally return to unity and non-duality (i.e. Self-realisation).

The Mechanics of Self-Realisation

Figure 27 shows the relationships between the authentic personality, the true-Self, the false-self and the ego-personality. The numbered blocks at the bottom of the diagram correspond to the following numbered points:

1. Collectively, the mind, heart and body constitute the authentic personality.

2. The true-Self is the core of the authentic personality (prior to enlightenment).

3. But the true-Self has lost sight of its true nature and believes it is the false-self.

4. The false-self is the core of the ego personality.

Awakening to Wholeness

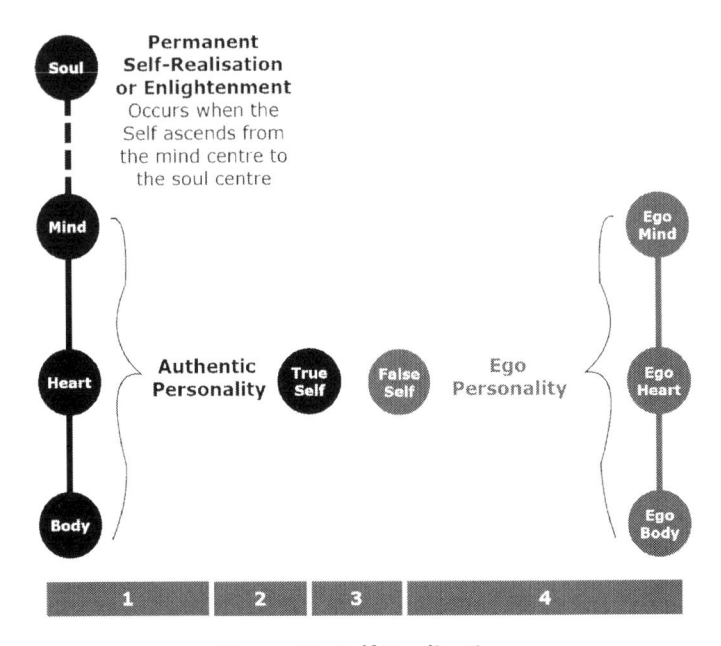

Figure 27: Self-Realisation

The more ego structures we dissolve, the more authentic consciousness is liberated. This gradually shifts the balance of power from the false-self and the ego-personality to the true-Self and the authentic personality. Self-realisation becomes possible when the balance of power has shifted in favour of the true-Self and authentic personality.

Four Aspects of Self-Realisation

There are 4 aspects of Self-realisation, all of which are realised simultaneously at enlightenment, but we may temporarily experience one or more aspect prior to enlightenment:

1. **Body**: The "will" dimension of Self is realised. This is experienced as profound sense of embodied beingness, steadfastness, empowerment, confidence and well-being.

2. **Heart**: the "love" dimension of the Self is realised. This is experienced as a wide-open heart and an intimate and loving sense of unity and connectedness with everything.

3. **Mind**: The "knowing" dimension of the Self is realised. This is experienced as brilliant illumination in the head, and a knowingness and acceptance that everything is perfect, whole and complete exactly as it is.
4. **Soul**: The soul dimension is realised. This is experiences as the silence, stillness and emptiness of the no-ego-self/true-Self.

Enlightenment

Enlightenment occurs when the Self transcends the personality to centre itself in the soul, at which time the Self instantly and fully realises itself (whether it was partially realised before or not). Enlightenment is full and permanent Self-realisation. It is waking up to a new and higher level of reality which allows us to see things from a completely different perspective. This new perspective is difficult to describe because it transcends (yet includes) the conceptual mind. At enlightenment we realise that pretty much everything we ever believed was true; isn't. And pretty much everything we ever thought was important; isn't. Consequently, it can take weeks, months or years to become fully accustomed to this new state of being.

The Personality

Immediately prior to enlightenment, the Self is centred in the mind (the highest aspect of the personality triad – mind, heart and body). At the moment of enlightenment, the Self transcends the personality and centres itself in the soul. In transcending the personality our consciousness becomes more transpersonal (i.e. not limited to the personal). The Self must transcend the personality to complete the final stage of human evolution, namely to dissolve the remaining ego structures and perfect the personality. Just as we cannot demolish a building while we are still inside it, the last of our ego structures cannot be dissolved while our Self is centred in the personality. After enlightenment, the personality remains an important aspect of our being but we are no longer identified with it. The mind, emotions and body are simply tools that we can utilise in our daily lives. Tools that we can continue to utilise for the development of our consciousness, but in a different way now.

The Soul (Causal Body)

Only a small part (typically about 5%) of our soul essence incarnates for each lifetime. We incarnate with the soul essence (essential qualities) that will best facilitate the successful completion of our life-plan; i.e. the development of whichever aspect of our consciousness we are working on:

- The "lesser" causal body (the 5% of the soul that incarnates) develops essential qualities through our personal life experiences. It is the "silent witness" that sees, hears, feels, experiences and records every aspect of our lives. At the end of the lifetime the soul essence that incarnated should be more developed and more refined than it was at the start of the lifetime, assuming we led a productive life.

- The "greater" causal body (the 95% of the soul that doesn't incarnate) is the permanent storehouse of all of our life experiences across all of our lifetimes. It is not fully active while we are "in the flesh" prior to enlightenment because the Self is not centred in the greater causal body; it is centred in the personality.

At the moment of enlightenment, the Self rises up from the personality to permanently centre itself in the greater causal body, and the lesser causal body permanently reunites with the greater causal body. So not only do we realise our true-Self, we also realise the totality of our being.

The reasons that only part of the soul incarnates are as follows:

- It is a safety net in case our life doesn't go to plan. If our soul regresses (instead of evolving) due to lots of negative choices and experiences, it minimises the "damage" because only a small part of our soul is affected; not all of it. Basically, we cannot be trusted with our entire soul until we have demonstrated our spiritual maturity (i.e. attained enlightenment).

- Not being able to remember much about our past lives enables us to more fully focus on this lifetime. It is only when we have access to our entire soul (causal body) that we are able to remember many of our past lives in reasonable detail.

- Not having access to all of our essential qualities in each lifetime enables us to focus on specific aspects of our development. For example, if we want to focus on developing courage we may bring very little courage with us and choose a fearful life. This will compel us to develop the courage we need to cope with life. Initially it will be "false" courage (i.e. ego-driven coping strategies), but eventually our true courage will begin to emerge. All essential qualities exist within our soul as potential and our life experiences facilitate their unfolding, development and refinement.

The Causal Lotus

The causal lotus is the "organ" of enlightenment. It is called the causal lotus because it is located at the centre of the greater causal body and its shape resembles a lotus flower. It is composed of four interlocking centres of consciousness (chakras), each of which is composed of 3 "petals":

1. The 3 **Knowledge Petals** connect the soul to the head centre (mental body).
2. The 3 **Unity Petals** connect the soul to the heart centre (emotional body).
3. The 3 **Will Petals** connect the soul to the belly centre (physical-energy body).
4. The 3 **Central Petals** are the primary centre of consciousness within the greater causal body (soul).

The 9 outer petals (3 x Knowledge petals, 3 x Unity petals and 3 x Will petals) connect the soul to the mind, heart and body centres and the 7 major chakras, as shown in Figure 28. Enlightenment occurs when all 3 sets of outer petals (knowledge, unity and will) are fully open. This allows the Self to pass through into the centre (central petals) of the causal lotus – this is known as the "jewel in the lotus".

Awakening to Wholeness

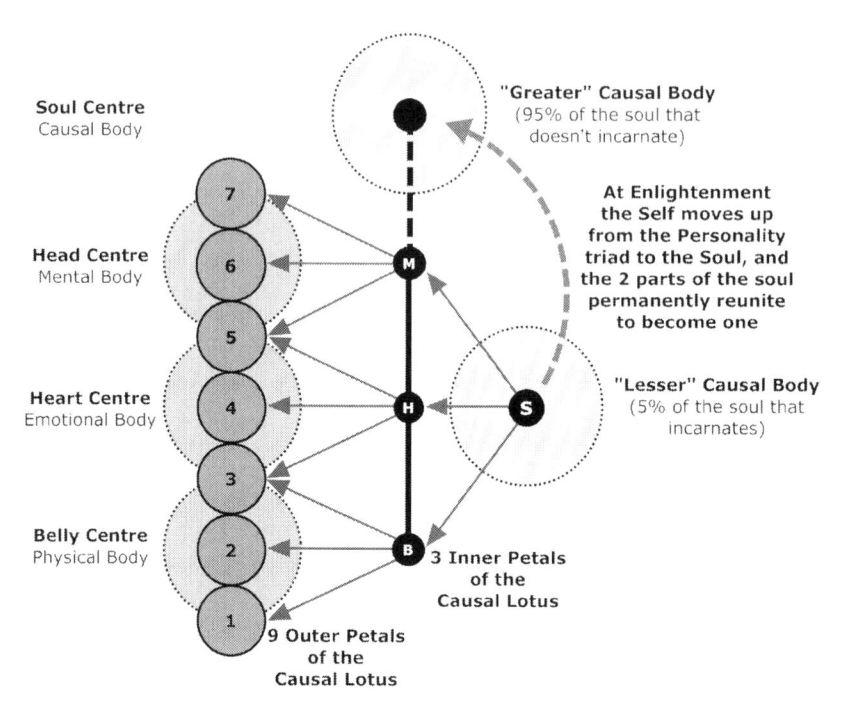

Figure 28: Enlightenment

Life After Enlightenment

Many of the things that I am about to describe are often experienced for short periods of time prior to Enlightenment, as we are given glimpses of what our lives could be like:

- Most people think that enlightenment will be something different and amazing (e.g. peace, bliss and unity), but we are already these things – they are our true nature. When we rediscover our true nature we realise that these qualities have been present all along, we just didn't notice them. So yes, enlightenment is very different in one respect, but it is also very normal and familiar.

- Our new sense of Self is far subtler than our old (false) sense of self, so much so that we may initially believe that we have no self.

- We discover new ways of being, knowing, loving and doing.

7. Awakening, Realisation & Enlightenment

- Finding and realising our life's purpose becomes less important as our concept of a personal self fades away.
- "I am" becomes "I am everything", but it also becomes "I am not" as the duality of being and non-being dissolves.
- Without a false-self to defend and bolster we can relax into our being, which results in a relaxed confidence and a general sense that everything is ok.
- The entire personality relaxes under the direction of the true-Self (i.e. without interference from the ego-self). The need to plan our lives and control everything falls away – without our old fear-based strategies we can relax and just allow life to unfold.
- A sense of direct knowing arises, which means we no longer need anyone else to validate our experiences, beliefs or sense of self.
- Our sense of Self is inherent – it is no longer derived from our thoughts, emotions or body, or feedback we receive from others.
- The mind becomes quieter and stiller. The constant labelling, narration and projection stop, and our personal story no longer seems important.
- The emotions become purer, more authentic and less reactive. The heart opens up and personal, clingy love transforms into impersonal, indiscriminate, unconditional love that is more intimate than anything we have felt before.
- The body relaxes and becomes more sensitive. Even the ordinary things in life take on a new depth and can become extraordinary. It is like seeing the world through new eyes – everything seems so fresh, new, beautiful, exciting, curious and satisfying.
- We realise that we are Life (Consciousness, God, Nature, Universe, Source, etc.) dressed up as a human being, and so is everyone and everything else. There is only one consciousness and Life is playing all the roles. But like a molecule of water in the ocean, each of us is an individual _and_ a unified part of the whole.

- We realise the inherent perfection in all things and know that everything is perfect just as it is.

Common Misconceptions After Enlightenment

Henry Laurency wrote, in The Knowledge of Life Part 5, "The evolutionary way of man consists of a series of 'awakenings' and at these he is seized with the desire to throw 'overboard' all that he has acquired so far... This only shows how far he has still to go before he becomes one with all." This section explains a couple of the common misconceptions:

- **There is no individual Self**: Some say that there is no individual Self and that there is only oneness. By definition there can be only one oneness (i.e. the entire universe), so if an enlightened person was that oneness they would be the entire universe and would have detailed awareness of everything that is occurring within the entire universe. But they don't; they only have detailed awareness of the part of the universe that is around them. So there is a centre of consciousness after enlightenment, but it is extraordinarily subtler than the previous false sense of self was – hence the misunderstanding.

- **(No individual Self means) we have no free will**: Learning from our own decisions is an essential aspect of human development. It is true that ultimately everything is controlled by Life/Universe/God, but we are part of that universal consciousness. Gradually letting go of our individual will and becoming more aligned with universal will is an important aspect of our journey, but at no point do we have to completely give up our individual will. We remain an individual while our consciousness expands into the universal oneness.

Common Difficulties After Enlightenment

The profound shift in our identity that accompanies enlightenment can give rise to some psychological difficulties:

- **Integration Time**: It is quite normal to be a little "spaced out" after completing any healing and reintegration work, as our psychological circuitry re-wires itself. After enlightenment the changes are much more significant and can have far greater and longer-lasting effects

- **Lack of Motivation**: After enlightenment our ego's false-will may no longer be accessible, so unless we have already activated our essential-will (an essential quality) we may be left with little will or motivation. Without anything to motivate us we may not want to do anything, which could cause our entire life to fall apart. It won't matter much to us, but it will affect those around us. It can take months or years to actively develop sufficient essential-will to enable us to properly function in the world again.

- **Remaining Ego Structures**: We can't completely demolish our home (ego) while we are still living in it (prior to enlightenment). So after enlightenment, when our Self has moved out of the ego, we must finish dissolving any remaining ego structures to refine our personality and complete the final stage of development through the human kingdom. Until we do this, the remaining ego structures will still activate and impact our life.

Generally, the more ego structures (false qualities) that remain at the time of enlightenment the more difficulties will be encountered. So it is advisable to do the inner work first and allow enlightenment to occur naturally, when we are truly ready.

Beyond Enlightenment

The central petals of the causal lotus don't open fully until the end of the enlightened stage, at which time the Self rises up to the next level and we transcend the human kingdom (although we remain in our human body). There are 49 major levels of consciousness and enlightenment is the transition from level 3 to level 4. The Absolute Self is not realised until the very end of our journey, when we realise that we are God, Source, the Absolute, the Universe, or whatever term you feel comfortable using. We are the path to the Absolute, and Life is the force that guides us home. The more we trust in Life and trust in our Self, the sooner we will awaken to this truth. The process of enlightenment and beyond is described in much more detail in my first book, *The Science of Spirituality*.

The Development of Consciousness

Enlightenment is attained through presence, awareness and authenticity, but there is nothing I can say and nothing you can do to actually make it happen. Nothing can make enlightenment happen, but it is a forgone conclusion for everybody, once we reach the required level of consciousness. Eventually it will happen to everyone, no matter what. Once we accept that enlightenment is a foregone conclusion we can relax into our being and allow it to happen in its own time. Enlightenment will only happen when we have gotten all we can from being un-enlightened; and striving for enlightenment clearly demonstrates that we are not there yet. So what can we do to facilitate the development of our consciousness without getting hung up on enlightenment?

Become the Change

In his book "On Becoming a Person", psychologist Carl Rogers wrote "The curious paradox is that when I accept myself as I am, then I can change... We cannot change, we cannot move away from what we are until we thoroughly accept what we are. Then change seems to come about unnoticed." We actually make more progress when we accept "who we are" right now, rather than resisting "who we are" and trying to change ourselves.

Change becomes possible by accepting the things that make us who we are (i.e. our thoughts, emotions and feelings), instead of judging, repressing or rejecting them. Noticing and feeling our thoughts and emotions without any agenda, judgement or resistance demonstrates our complete acceptance. The peaceful, present and aware state that accompanies this radical acceptance is the key to bringing about psychological and spiritual change.

This soul-centred state connects us with Life, and allows Life to flow through us with ease and grace, so change is inevitable. The infinite potential of Life unfolds into dynamic reality – through us. Life has a

7. Awakening, Realisation & Enlightenment

natural tendency towards harmony, integration and wholeness, so when we operate in alignment with Life, we naturally move towards harmony, integration and wholeness. Psycho-spiritual development occurs naturally, when we stop striving, fixing, resisting and interfering. But it is not a passive process; it requires an active, engaged and attuned approach to life. It means living in alignment with Life and actively going with the flow, instead of resisting it and trying to control it.

Surrender is about letting go of control and letting go of attachments to outcomes. It is about accepting our self as we are now, in this very moment. It is about accepting our life as it is right now. It is about accepting others as they are right now. It is about accepting the world as it is right now. It is about accepting everything as it is right now, rather than hoping things will get better in the future. Absolute acceptance requires a fundamental shift in our self-perception and our world-view. It is brought about by living from love instead of fear. Love allows us to accept that we are perfect as we are right now, and to accept that everything is perfect as it is right now.

Acceptance = Freedom

The more we strive to awaken, the more it eludes us. It is much the same as trying to fall asleep or trying to remember someone's name – the harder we try the more it eludes us, but as soon as we relax it happens effortlessly. We need to let go of our uptight state of ego-consciousness and allow ourselves to relax into a new state of consciousness and a new way of being.

We don't have to wait until we become enlightened to know freedom (that is just a false belief). Freedom and peace come from accepting what is (including our ego, our story and our flaws). Acceptance does not mean passively rolling over every time we encounter an obstacle in life. Life's difficulties are not obstacles on the path; they are the path – they are the challenges through which our consciousness learns and develops. There will always be ups and downs in life, but the less we resist the downs, the sooner we will be up again.

True freedom is having no concern for personal results. Whether we succeed or not on a personal level is irrelevant, because all experiences are a success on the spiritual level. We will not achieve what we truly want until we drop all personal investment in becoming awakened, enlightened, happy, fulfilled or whatever.

Our problems don't go away when we become enlightened; they just don't seem like problems any more. They were only problems because we believed they were and because resisted them. When we fully accept them they no longer seem important or worth worrying about – they are simply "what is".

Acceptance is feeling what arises within us (pleasant and unpleasant) without any resistance. When we fully feel our internal reactions to life we are able to make informed decisions about how to respond to life, appropriately and maturely, instead of automatically reacting with fear-based ego-responses. Freedom comes from being tuned into the subtle messages that Life sends us and responding consciously. If we are not tuned into Life, we will not learn from our experiences. So Life will keep sending us similar experiences again and again, until we finally learn what is required. Each subsequent lesson will be more difficult than the previous one, so we can spare ourselves a lot of unnecessary suffering by remaining consciously aware and learning from our experiences the first time around.

Discover The Truth

Whatever we are seeking in life is irrelevant – the real quest is discovering who the seeker is. Who we are is the foundation of our existence and everything in our lives, which is why discovering our true-Self is so important. If we don't even know who we are, how can we know that anything else is true?

The path to the truth involves discovering and undoing the untruths. And for many, the spiritual path itself can be an untruth. If we are trying to be spiritual, we are not being authentic, and if we are not being authentic, how can we expect to find our true-Self? Spirituality instils an image of how we think we should be and what we think we should do to in order to awaken; but how can we discover the real truth if we are searching for an image of the truth? So don't try to be spiritual – be real and authentic. This means accepting our unspiritual thoughts, emotions and behaviours, instead of trying to repress them.

7. Awakening, Realisation & Enlightenment

Life is a series of events that are designed to challenge and shake our ego structures (false beliefs, reactive emotions and conditioned behaviours) but we keep shoring them up. Life is gently encouraging us to move out of the crumbling abode of our ego and awaken to the fullness of our true nature, but we are too busy defending and rebuilding the ego to even notice. Awakening to the truth requires us to focus our attention on being our Self (i.e. who we truly are) instead of trying not to be our ego-self (i.e. who we are not).

Practice

It doesn't matter how much knowledge, inspiration or help we receive from spiritual books and teachers; it is our daily practices that expedite our journey of awakening. Meditation, self-inquiry, presence and awareness are the only things that will really help us to awaken to wholeness. These practices can seem quite difficult initially but they become easier with practise, and they gradually become our new way of being. Daily practice takes us through the four stages of learning:

1. **Unconscious Incompetence**: I have no idea how useless I am at it (Ignorant).
2. **Conscious Incompetence**: I know I make lots of mistakes (Beginner).
3. **Conscious Competence**: I can do it if I concentrate (Apprentice).
4. **Unconscious Competence**: I can do it well without even thinking about it (Master).

Being who you truly are requires no effort and no belief – simply allow it to be your living experience; right here, right now. There is nothing you need to do and nowhere you need to go in order to "be" that which you already are.

There is a common belief in spiritual circles that the mind must be brought under complete control before we can become Self-realised or attain enlightenment. Actually, the problem doesn't lie with the mind at all (which is just doing its job); the "problem" is with our soul's awareness. We do not need to train our minds to become quieter; we need to train our soul's awareness to be less affected by and less attached to the creations of our mind. We need to train our awareness to simply notice what goes on in the mind without over-emphasising its importance and feeding it with energy. The same applies to our emotions and physical impulses. Trying to repress them is almost impossible. But noticing them without attachment and allowing them to "be" prevents them from getting out of control. The personality should not be allowed to run wild, but equally its natural "spirit" should not be stifled or repressed.

Enjoy Life

Young children get a great deal of enjoyment from putting on a costume and pretending to be someone else. Our soul gets the same enjoyment from playing the part of a human being. When we truly know that we are simply playing a part, we can relax and enjoy life. But when we believe we are nothing but a human being, our negative thoughts, reactive emotions and conditioned behaviours often prevent us from enjoying life.

Taking life too seriously and trying to rush takes us out of the present moment, away from where we need to be. Maintaining present moment awareness (and inquiring/feeling into whatever arises) is the only thing we need to "do". Conscious living supplemented with periods of deeper practice (e.g. meditation and self-inquiry) is the optimal approach to life. But we must be careful not to get hung up on the results, our rate of progress or our level of development, because these are the traps of the ego.

Life provides us with all the opportunities we need to awaken, and all the clues we need to discover what is holding us back. When we are attuned to life in the present moment our repressed psychological material will start to reveal itself spontaneously and our inner work will gain a momentum of its own. We will also begin to see how the universe continually creates the life experiences that we need for our continued development. It is as if the universe exists especially for each and every one of us. This wondrous insight is not possible from the ego's perspective, because the ego sees the universe as the enemy – the unpredictable and uncontrollable nemesis that makes life so challenging. But from the soul's perspective, the universe is an amazing interactive classroom and God is our teacher.

7. Awakening, Realisation & Enlightenment

In life, there is no finish line and there is no goal; there is only the continual awakening, unfolding and evolution of consciousness. The work we do on our spiritual journey doesn't actually take us anywhere, but we need to walk the path to realise that what we have been searching for has been right here all along. In many ways the journey of awakening is more important than the actual awakening, because it is through our experiential journey that our soul evolves – so relax and enjoy life – it isn't a race.

And if you only remember one thing from this book; remember this – The only thing that needs to change for you to be who you really are is your perspective.

List of Diagrams:

Fig 1	The Self and its Field of Awareness (Soul)	Page 12
Fig 2	The Mind, Heart & Body Centres	Page 12
Fig 3	Self, Centres & Chakras	Page 13
Fig 4	The Continuum of Self	Page 19
Fig 5	The Vicious Circle of Fear	Page 21
Fig 6	Layers of an Individual Ego Structure	Page 23
Fig 7	Layers of the Entire Ego Super-Structure	Page 23
Fig 8	Freedom from the Ego	Page 29
Fig 9	The true-Self perceiving the false-self	Page 30
Fig 10	The Two-Fold Path of Awakening	Page 31
Fig 11	The Spiral Path of Transpersonal Development	Page 33
Fig 12	Egg Diagram - Practicing Presence	Page 35
Fig 13	Egg Diagram - Self-Inquiry	Page 36
Fig 14	Egg Diagram - Meditation	Page 36
Fig 15	Personal and Transpersonal Development	Page 37
Fig 16	The Composition of a Human Being	Page 39
Fig 17	The Two Sides of the Personality	Page 41
Fig 18	The ego-self's identification with the false self-image	Page 87
Fig 19	Finding Your Primary Belief	Page 128
Fig 20	The Benefits of Meditation	Page 190
Fig 21	Differences Between Regular & Enlightened People	Page 215
Fig 22	The Journey of Awakening	Page 218
Fig 23	The Development of Consciousness	Page 219
Fig 24	The Labyrinth	Page 220
Fig 25	Dualistic Perception	Page 222
Fig 26	Non-Dualistic Perception	Page 223
Fig 27	Self-Realisation	Page 224
Fig 28	Enlightenment	Page 228

List of Practices & Techniques:

Practicing Presence	Page 120
Personal Self-Inquiry	Page 121
Body Awareness	Page 132
Basic Healing and Reintegration Process	Page 136
Conscious Living	Page 141
Five Point Check-In	Page 150
Embodying an Essential Quality	Page 153
Meditating on an Essential Quality	Page 154
Feel It To Heal It	Page 159
Soul Child Reintegration	Page 161
Heal It As We Feel It	Page 161
Connect & Release Technique	Page 162
Expanded Awareness Technique	Page 163
Body Scan Technique	Page 163
Body Focus Exercise	Page 164
Dissolving Pain Exercise	Page 165
Talking To Parts Process	Page 166
Changing Chairs Technique	Page 174
Peace Talk Technique	Page 175
Mirror Technique	Page 177
Reversing Behaviours	Page 178
Reversing Negative Thoughts	Page 179
Empowered Time Travel	Page 179
Basic Meditation	Page 197
Meditating on the Centres of Consciousness	Page 198
Living Presence	Page 202
Authentic Prayer	Page 206
Discriminative Self-Inquiry	Page 208
Experiential Self-Inquiry	Page 210

Bibliography:

Psychology
J Firman & A Gila	Psychosynthesis: A Psychology of Spirit
Richard Schwartz	Internal Family Systems Therapy
Ron Kurtz	The Hakomi Method
Carl Jung	The Undiscovered Self
Carl Rogers	On Becoming a Person

Spirituality
Gangaji	The Diamond in Your Pocket
Adyashanti	The End of Your World
Andrew Cohen	Evolutionary Enlightenment
Eckhart Tolle	A New Earth
A.H. Almaas	Brilliancy
Marianne Williamson	A Return to Love

Enneagram
Beatrice Chestnut	The Complete Enneagram
Sandra Maitri	The Spiritual Dimension of the Enneagram
A.H. Almaas	Facets of Unity

Esoteric Science
Henry T Laurency	The Knowledge of Life (www.laurency.com)
Alice Bailey	Esoteric Healing
Lee Bladon	The Science of Spirituality

Index:

A.H. Almaas 122
Acceptance 76, 104, 146, 233
Addicted 57
Anxiety 68
Aura 27, 28, 197
Authentic Prayer Process 206
Autopilot 40
Avoidance 148
Avoiding 56
Awakening 147, 151, 213, 216, 217
Awakening to Wholeness .82, 92
Awareness
    Background 185
    Expanded 150
    Holistic 122
    Spreading 185
Basic Meditation 197
Be Authentic 149
Be Here Now 149

Becoming 114, 232
Becoming Self 31
Behaviours 142
Being 114, 142, 183
Being Self 31
Beingness 86
Belly Centre 11, 198
Beyond Humanity 38
Blissful States 195
Blockages 132
Body 10, 70
Body Awareness 32, 118, 147
Body Focus Exercise 164
Body Scan Technique 163
Body Sensations 150
Boredom 193
Breathing 150
Carl Jung 182
Carl Rogers 232
Catastrophising 67

Causal Body 187, 226
Causal Lotus 227
Centres of Consciousness 12, 198, 199, 227, 228
Chakras 12
Challenges 108
Change 232
Changing Chairs Technique ... 174
Childhood 72, 125
   Experiences 81
Childhood Beliefs 56
Childish 55
Civilised Stage 88, 217, 218
Compassion 152
Conception 72
Conditioned Behaviours 176
Confusion 134
Connect & Release Technique
   162
Conscious Awareness 143, 201
Conscious Expression 141
Conscious Living 32, 118, 141
Conscious Perception 141
Conscious Screening 145
Consciousness 37
   Development of 232

Focal point 210
Continuum of Self 19
Controlling 48
Core Beliefs 126, 127
Creative Power 203
Credit and Blame 52
Crisis 75
Death 81
Defensive 50
Destiny 109
Developed Stage 88, 217
Development of Consciousness
.... 232
Dialogue Techniques 166
Disclaimer 7, 158
Discomfort 194
Disease 75
Dis-Identification 130
Dissatisfied 56
Dissociation 130
Dissociative Identity Disorder . 42
Dissolving Pain 165
Distracting Thoughts 193
Distress 134
Doing 56, 142
Drive to Evolve 79

246

Index

Dualistic Perception 222
Egg Diagram 35, 36
Ego 46, 115
   Awakening from 83
   Creation of 15
   Freedom from 28
   What is? 16
   Why do we need one? 82
Ego Ideal 87
Ego Structures 22, 81, 88, 90, 136, 151
   Coping 25, 43, 151, 152
   Different types of 24
   Layers of 23
   Matrix of 69
   Protective 24, 43
Ego Super-Structure 23, 220
Ego's Path 111
Egocentric 63
Ego-Self 13, 42, 103
Embodiment 155
Emotional Body 81
Emotional Patterns 130
Emotional Signposts 67
Emotions 67, 124, 142
   Negative 68, 144

Positive 68
Repressed 69
Trapped 69
Empathic Resonance 182
Empathy 152
Empowered Time Travel 179
Emptiness 134
Energy 124
Energy Blockages 194
Energy Body 70, 81
Enjoy Life 236
Enlightened Stage 88, 217
Enlightenment 38, 151, 214, 216, 225, 228
   Beyond 231
   Re-enlightenment 216
Enneagram 10, 129
Enneatype 129
Esoteric Healing 119
Essential Qualities 19, 39, 80, 173, 214
   Developing 155
   Embodying 32, 118, 153
   Lost 151
   Meditating on 154
   Missing 89

Recovering lost	153
Evil	112
Evolution of Consciousness	37
Evolution of the Soul	90
Evolutionary Journey	217
Exiles	43, 90, 135
Expanded Awareness Technique	163
Expectations	94
Expression	71
External Validation	48
Faith	106
False Beliefs	94, 125
Discovering	127
Neutralising	129
False-Self	14, 30, 224
Creation of	13
False-Will	109
Fear	20, 134, 172, 185
Feel It To Heal It	132, 137, 159
Feeling Special	52
Field of Awareness	9, 12, 30, 193, 197
Field of Consciousness	9, 10, 16, 27, 40, 79, 119, 148, 202
Five Point Check-In	149
Freedom	233
Free-Will	109, 230
Freud	71
Frozen Consciousness	41
Frozen in Time	73
Future	105
Generational Influences	72
Gestation	72
Goal in Life	87
God	
Who or what is?	202
Grace	110, 115
Gratitude	107, 147
Guarding Programs	24
Happiness	66, 91
Authentic	94
Cultivating	97
What blocks it	96
Happy	93
Hara	10
Head Centre	11, 199
Heal It As We Feel It	161
Healer	135
Healing	25, 132
Healing & Reintegration	32, 118, 135
Process	136

Index

Heart 10
Heart Centre 11, 198
Heaven 113
Hell 112
Holding the Space 159
Holes 26, 27, 52, 89, 90, 136
   Feeling into 134
Human Being 39
   Composition of 39
Human Condition 39
Human Consciousness 9, 82
Human Doing 24
Human Potential 79
Humanistic Stage 88, 217
I Am 85
Id 70
Identification . 47, 87, 88, 90, 103
Individual Self 230
Inner Child 17, 42, 44, 167, 179, 180
Inner Critic 64, 174
Inner Work 24, 82, 136, 157
Inner World 64
Inquiry Techniques 176
Insight 124
Integral Approach 34

Internal Family Systems (IFS) 139, 167
Intuition 124
Invalidating Others 49
Jewel in the Lotus 227
Journey of Awakening ... 149, 217
Journey to Freedom 29
Judgements 95
Karma 110
Karmic Price 205
Labyrinth 113, 219
Layers 22, 140
Let Go 147
Life 104, 203
Life Path 109
Light of Awareness 185
Living Presence 34, 183, 199
Love 185
Love Life 149
Loving Presence 133, 154, 160
Meditation 34, 183, 186, 207
   Benefits of 189
   Difficulties & Distractions . 192
   Form/Object 196
   Formless/Objectless 196
   Posture 190

Two types	196
Mental Body	81
Mental Overlay	62
Mental Suffering	66
Merit (Good Karma)	110
Mind	10, 60
Mind Chatter	193
Mindfulness	122, 142, 189
Mirror Technique	176
Motivation	101
Multiple Personalities	42
Narcissism	46
Negotiating With Parts	171
New Way	113
Non-Dualistic Perception	223
Non-Duality	222, 223
Not Personal	97
Numbing	55
Objects	26, 52, 89, 185, 201, 206, 208, 222, 223
OCD	56
Open Focus	147
Pain	72, 194
And suffering	74
Pain Body	74
Parental Influences	72
Parents	14, 20, 23, 48, 49, 64, 72, 112, 125, 182, 221
Parts	41, 43, 173
Cluster of	43
Collective	43
Past	105
Past Lives	80
Peace Talk Technique	175
Perfection	104
Persona	86
Personal Development	32, 117
Personal Qualities	19
Under-Developed	152
Personality	18, 40, 225
Authentic	18, 223, 224
Ego	18, 223, 224
Two sides of	41
Physical Body	81
Physical Pain	131
Polarised	50
Positive Psychology	108
Positive Qualities	57
Power of Now	74
Practice	235
Practicing Presence	35, 120, 200
Prayer	34, 183, 202

Index

Authentic 205
Conventional 204
Presence 119, 201, 207
Presence Techniques 158
Present Moment 141
Pre-Verbal 157
Primal Drives 70
Primary Beliefs 15, 125, 127
Primary Wound 15
Primitive Stage 88, 217
Programmed 62
Projecting 53
Protector Parts 169, 173
Psychological Buffer 15
Psychological Exploration 121
Psychological Healing 135
Psychological Issues 80
Psychological Resistance 58
Psychological Wounds 29, 57, 73, 135
Psycho-Spiritual Development 79, 221, 233
Psychosynthesis 34
Pure Awareness 39, 79, 119, 133, 160, 207, 215
  Unconditioned 209
Purgatory 113

Qualitative Development 150
Quantitative Development ... 151
Reactive 53
Reincarnation 81
Reintegration 133, 160
  Stages of 140
Relationships 86
Releasing 211
Repression 24, 44, 55
Resistance 58, 102, 138, 146, 169
Restlessness 194
Reversing Behaviours 178
Reversing Negative Thoughts 179
Right Now 96
Running Commentary 63
Seeds of the Ego 80
Self 9, 27, 82
  The infinity of 184
Self's Path 111
Self-Discovery 113
Self-Help Techniques 157
Self-Image 84
Self-Importance 52
Self-Inquiry 32, 34, 184, 207

Discriminative 207	Subjective 59
Experiential 209	Sub-Personalities 41
Other types 130	Subtle Bodies 19
Personal 118, 121	Subtle Energy 69
Spiritual 206	Success 117
Self-Like Part 65	Suffering 74, 102, 111
Self-Realisation 38, 88, 207, 213, 215, 219, 221, 223, 224	Super-Conscious 34, 36, 113, 121
Sensations 143	Super-Ego 64, 174
Separation 47	Suppressing 24
Shape-Shifter 201	Sympathy 152
Skandhas 80, 81, 129, 219	Talking To Parts 166, 167
Sleepiness 194	Tan Tien 10
Soul 9, 19, 30, 226	Theosophy 11
The truth about 89	Therapeutic Relationship 181
Soul Centre 199	Thoughts 123
Soul Child 44	Identification with 61
Soul Child Reintegration 161	Spontaneous 60
Spiritual Development 183	Thoughts & Beliefs 142
Spiritual Journey 236	Trance 56
Spiritual People 114	Transformation 76
Spiritual Super-Ego 65	Transpersonal Development ... 33
Split Personalities 42	Trauma 21, 73, 112, 125, 134
Striving 98	True Nature 85
Stuckness 76	True-Self 9, 30, 115, 223, 224
Subconscious 35, 54, 121	Trust 106

Index

Truth 234
Two-Fold Path of Awakening .. 31
Unfoldment 20, 70, 98, 102, 104, 114, 117
Universal Consciousness 203, 227
Universal Will 59, 109, 115
Validation 20, 24, 48, 51
Vicious Circle 21
Victim 95
Virtual World 14
Virtual-Reality 13
Virtual-Self 85
Visualisation 159, 179
Voices 27
Void 134
Wanting 99
What Is 76, 105
Who am I? 209
Why 75
Will 9
Wonder Child 44
Yin and Yang 39

Printed in Great Britain
by Amazon